Conduct Unbecoming

Prasley

CONDUCT UNBECOMING

The Social Construction of Police Deviance and Control

MAURICE PUNCH

TAVISTOCK PUBLICATIONS

London and New York

First published in 1985 by
Tavistock Publications Ltd
11 New Fetter Lane,
London EC4P 4EE

Published in the USA by
Tavistock Publications
in association with Methuen, Inc.
29 West 35th Street,
New York NY 10001

Typeset by
Scarborough Typesetting Services
and printed in Great Britain by
Richard Clay (The Chaucer Press) Ltd
Bungay, Suffolk

British Library Cataloguing in
Publication Data

Punch, Maurice
Conduct unbecoming: The social
construction of police deviance and
control. – (Social science paperback)
1. Police corruption – Netherlands
– Amsterdam – History – 20th
century
I. Title.   II. Series
363.2'09492'3   HV8223.A4/

ISBN 0–422–79210–1

Library of Congress Cataloging in
Publication Data

Punch, Maurice.
Conduct unbecoming.
Bibliography; p.
Includes indexes.
1. Police corruption – Netherlands
– Amsterdam.   2. Crime and
criminals – Netherlands –
Amsterdam.
I. Title.
HV7936.C85P86   1985   364.1'323
85–9753

ISBN 0–422–79210–1

For Ann, Kenny, David, and Katherine

Contents

Acknowledgements

It is plainly no easy matter for organizational representatives, in the throes of a corruption scandal, to open their doors to academic research; I can only be exceedingly grateful that members of the Amsterdam police were prepared to do so and I would like to thank most sincerely all those policemen – from high to low and from unimpeachable to incorrigible – who cooperated in my research (understandably with varying degrees of enthusiasm). Perhaps I should stress here that the analysis focuses primarily on the period 1976–80 and that, while the force has since been confronted with recurring cases of serious deviance, the current Mayor and Chief Constable have taken a determined stand on the matter during the last couple of years. At various times I have also been the guest of police forces in Edinburgh, Dublin, Essex, West Midlands, Devon and Cornwall, New York, Boston, San Francisco, London (Metropolitan), and Rotterdam and wish to acknowledge the courteous and well-organized reception that I invariably received. Since moving into this area of research just over a decade ago I have been lucky in the quality of the people I have met (many of whom have helped me in ways that are vital if you work in a foreign country but have your reference-group elsewhere) and I would like to express my appreciation to Gary Marx, Mark Moore, George Kelling, Frans Jan Mulschlegel (for providing books from the library at the Police Study Centre, Warnsveld), Paul Cook, Nic van Dijk,

Patrick De Ceuster, Mary Ann Wycoff, Egon Bittner, Herman Goldstein, Aaldert van der Vlies, Geoffrey Markham, Ralph Crawshaw, Lawrence Sherman, Mike Useem, Karl Klockars, Michael Clarke, Clinton Terry III, Hans van der Horst, Scott Christianson, Dick Bennett, Paul Rock, Donald Black, David Downes, John Johnson, No Knubben, Jason Ditton, Richard Ericson, Roy Wallis, Jim Fyfe, Henk van Luijk, Simon van Steenbergen, Paul Storm, Nigel Fielding (and not forgetting Nicolas Freeling, Joseph Wambaugh, Ed McBain, Sjöwall and Wahlöö, and the cast of Hill Street).

In particular, a number of people have gone to considerable lengths to assist me over the years and I can only say that I am deeply indebted to them for their critical comments and constant encouragement. I have in mind Peter Manning, Wim Broer, Simon Holdaway, Dennis Marsden, and Michael Chatterton from whom I have learned much, and also John van Maanen who thoroughly read the final draft and commented usefully on it. In particular, Al Reiss found time from pressing commitments to read my material and his stimulating remarks helped considerably to crystallize certain key aspects of the research for me. A special word of thanks must go to Derek Phillips, not only for continuing to lose (ungraciously and raucously) at squash, but also for his constant help and encouragement.

It has proved a painful exercise to prune my text to the publisher's required length; it is difficult to have to chop juicy qualitative data that represents months of observation and hours of interviews. I hope that the cuts do not magnify any of the weaknesses in my text for which I take full responsibility. 'Conduct unbecoming' originated from military discipline codes but until recently was also widely used in police manuals (with thanks to Paul Cook and Keith Bergstrom for correspondence on this expression). And for those put off by my opening sentence I can only confess that I have not found a single reference to corrupt policewomen.

Parts of the second section of the Introduction were previously published as an article, 'When the Wheel Comes Off' in M. Clarke (ed.) (1983) *Corruption* (London: Frances Pinter). Some parts of Chapters 2 and 4 appeared in 'The Divided Organization', *Police Studies* 7 (1): Spring 1984. The second section of Chapter 6 is based closely on the chapter 'Officers and Men' in M. Punch (ed.) (1983) *Control in the Police Organisation* (Cambridge, Mass.: MIT Press), and I am grateful to the MIT Press for permission to use that material here.

The constant supply of coffee and 'krentebollen' I owe to my dear wife Corry while Julio and Maria made far fewer demands on me than I have a right to expect. My employer, Nijenrode, has provided me over the years with research and travel money that enabled me to keep in touch with the world and also financially supported an international seminar at Nijenrode Castle in 1980. I derived considerable benefit from the discussions and continue to reap reward from the contacts cemented on that occasion. At Nijenrode whenever I presented a draft chapter to the faculty's secretary, Marjon van Tol, I received it back within a matter of days. She would attack the script with demonic energy and ferociously pump it into the word-processor; I don't know what motivates her but her speed and efficiency were a great help and I am truly grateful to her, and to Monique van Rooijen, for the typing.

Finally, having spent several years delving into the seamy and sordid aspects of an institution has made me approach the police with somewhat less of my earlier enthusiasm and admiration and with more of a sad scepticism. Now when I reflect on police corruption, I sink deeper in my armchair and mutter, 'there but for fortune, and a couple of exams, go I'.

Maurice Punch,
Amstelveen, February 1985

Introduction:
The Divided Organization

Research Perspectives

This book is about policemen and their work. That work, and the institutional context in which it takes place, is shrouded in ambivalence and controversy. For example, one part of police duties, legally prescribed yet surrounded with perennial and understandable concern, consists of hunting down other people. Less typically, policemen also hunt fellow policemen. For, when a police organization is accused of abusing its mandate, this sets in train a series of repercussions and one of these may be that the organization is forced conspicuously *to police itself*. Here, a detailed sociological study of police forces labelled by society as 'corrupt' will be undertaken as an illustration of how policemen react to labelling, to the reimposition of institutional control, and to the necessity of policemen having to investigate their own kind. The essence of this study – which is an analysis of the institutionalized control of, and reactions to, police occupational and organizational deviance – is that the research material is not solely illustrative of the police world but is indicative of conflict about deviancy and control that is endemic in virtually all organizations. To a greater or lesser extent, all organizations have to cope with the dilemmas of policing themselves (Reiss 1983).

Underlying my selection of data and my interpretation of material for this study is a theoretical perspective that also colours my view of control, deviance, and organizational reality (Punch 1981a). Working within the Symbolic Interactionist 'paradigm' my approach particularly builds upon and extends those authors who adopt an interactionist perspective on the police (Holdaway 1980; Chatterton 1975; Van Maanen 1973; Rubinstein 1973; Bittner 1967; Manning 1977). People working within this paradigm emphasize the extent to which social life is fragile, negotiated and in a constant process of construction in interaction with others; men act in situations 'because they are busily assessing, evaluating, interpreting, defining, revising and, most basically, symbolizing the situation to themselves' (Brittan 1973: 23). An interpretative sociology (drawing on the work of Weber 1947; Schutz 1967; Goffman 1959; Douglas 1971; Berger and Luckman 1971) sheds light on how people differentially experience and perceive social situations. This perspective can also be employed specifically to examine organizations (Silverman 1970) and to scrutinize the situated interactions, accounts, shared understandings, face-to-face negotiations, vocabularies of motive and emergent definitions which characterize organizational reality when viewed in this manner.

POLICE WORK, CULTURE, AND ORGANIZATION

While Holdaway (1980) cogently enjoins us not to accept uncritically the notion of 'Anglo-American' policing, and while the Dutch Police are culturally and organizationally quite distinct from their British and North American counterparts (Fijnaut 1976 a and b, 1979), I nevertheless feel that it is possible to make a number of broad generalizations about the police occupational culture, police work, and the police organization derived from a scrutiny of the standard literature (Reiss 1971; Goldstein 1977; Westley 1970; Wilson 1968; Skolnick 1975; Banton 1964; Cain 1973). In brief, I have distilled from the literature the following suppositions which will inform the rest of the work. First, the police organization is not a harmonious, integrated entity with a comforting consensus but is rather characterized by a deeply divided pattern of semi-autonomous and often conflicting units. Second, the occupational culture defines the norms surrounding work in terms of 'real' police work, based on action and excitement, and of the incompatibility between legal and administrative requirements and the reality of working the streets. And, third, police work is a matter of negotiation based on context-relevant meanings where the law is used as a resource for solving practical, situational dilemmas. Techniques have to be developed to create appearances, to construct feasible accounts, and to control information reaching superiors (Chatterton 1975; Holdaway 1983; Manning 1980). And dilemmas in producing satisfactory work – owing to pressure for results, ambiguous legislation, vulnerability to legal sanctions, and precarious bargains with criminals, informants, and lawyers – can lead to short-cut methods, lies, covering-up, falsification of evidence, and intimidation of suspects. These three intertwined elements – organization, occupational culture, and work – can aid in deciphering deviance as rooted in the everyday, organizational reality of policing (Goldstein 1977: 198).

THE 'OPERATIONAL CODE' OF POLICING

The police are meant to prevent and solve crime and to preserve order. They are empowered to stop and question citizens, to search premises, to deprive people of their freedom, to interrogate suspects, to assemble evidence, and in some countries, to prosecute cases in the courts. Because of the socially and politically sensitive nature of their task they are enjoined to be impartial and to exemplify honesty and integrity; the rule of law maintains that precisely those who enforce justice should be held most accountable for conducting themselves in a just and legal manner. In practice, an array of evidence indicates that the demands made on the police are so diffuse and contradictory that the police task is unworkable and this leads to an atmosphere of 'duplicity and hypocrisy' (Goldstein 1977: 163) and of methods bordering on 'trickery and stealth' (McNee 1983: 180). Indeed, the police are something of a problem profession, experiencing frustration, anomie, depression, stress, cynicism, and disillusion (Wilson 1963; Niederhoffer 1975; Terry 1980), and being repeatedly accused of violence, racial prejudice, perjury, political bias, abuse of suspects' rights, and manipulation of the legal process. In short, police are frequently found to abuse systematically legal rights and to evade consistently their accountability.

To take just one example, a recent detailed study of the Metropolitan Police (the research was commissioned by the 'Met' and its findings were largely accepted by the police) reported opinions, observations, and allegations of racism, sexism, poor supervision, drinking on duty, bribery, and of persistent bending of legal rules in the enforcement process. This led to the conclusion that it is 'extremely disturbing to find that a substantial proportion of people who have been arrested make very specific allegations against the police involving gross misconduct in many cases'; in addition, 'survey findings strongly suggest that in a considerable minority of cases suspects are assaulted, threatened and verbally abused; and this appears to be not a few isolated incidents, but a pattern of conduct among what must be a substantial minority of police officers' (Smith 1983a: 153). Yet a retired Commissioner (McNee 1983: 228) refers to the Metropolitan Police as 'one of the most accountable organizations in society today'. Clearly there is a measure of institutional schizophrenia here which ironically Robert Mark (1978: 172), himself a former Commissioner and a champion of accountability, reveals when he displays in his biography a willingness to ignore the law (in relation to seizing the body of an IRA hunger-striker en route for burial in Ireland). He talks of two types of rule-bending, one for a share of profit in crime but also one 'for perfectly honourable reasons' in terms of combating biases in the justice system which prevent successful police prosecutions (Cox, Shirley, and Short, 1977: 214). How does one explain this apparent contradiction?

One way of explaining it is to view the policeman as an actor faced with an impossible and ambiguous job, based on a set of legal recipes derived from training that do not work in practice, and to suggest that a solution to the irreducible contradictions in his work is to fall back on a number of 'domain assumptions' shared by colleagues (personal communication, Marsden). A useful distinction is made by Reisman (1979) in examining bribery in business where he identifies on the one hand the 'myth system' which publicly bolsters institutional values, and on the other hand the 'operational code' which is covered in secrecy and which espouses how things are actually done. Bribes are deviations from the myth system, but they may be deemed appropriate under the code which constitutes a private and unacknowledged set of rules which selectively tolerates extraordinary payments as an ordinary and necessary form of doing business. At the same time he maintains that the social and personal implications of bribery may have little to do with power or economic motives; some people may derive 'a deep psychological gratification' from the act of bribery, while the moral aspects of bribing 'may be very complex, requiring exploration not only of the transaction but of the phenomenal worlds of the actors as well' (Reisman 1979: 126). I shall refer to the informal norms and practices of policing as the 'operational code' and assume that unravelling and decoding it tells us how police deviance is defined, regulated, practised, and concealed. My interest is not with political facets of police deviance which were not at issue in the three cases under consideration (c.f. Hain, *et al.* 1980; Bunyan 1977).

This study is pitched predominantly at the micro level but, as a portrait of a Dutch police force combined with a cross-national comparison of a British and an American force, it also tells us something about the nature of Dutch society. On the rare occasions that it has attracted sociological comment, Dutch society has been remarked upon for its orderliness, moderation, and sobriety (Goudsblom 1967) and among the characteritics attributed to the Dutch 'national character' are 'unemotionalism, sobriety, domesticity (a great amount of interest in family life, very little interest in public social activities), reserve, commercial spirit, bourgeois mentality, tendency to maintain a show of respectability' (Heerikhuizen 1982: 103). It has also been noted for the *absence* of corruption; an American observer wrote,

> 'Police corruption, so commonplace with us, as the recent New York City Police Department investigation underlines, is virtually unknown to them . . . [compared with the United States] the government is more scrupulous, the taxpayer more honest, and there is a relatively low level of tax evasion and fraud.'
> (Blanken 1976; 12 and 31)

Unfortunately, everyday life, casual conversations, and journalistic revelations in The Netherlands do not reflect this picture in my experience and behind the favourable image lies a more complex reality. For during the last few years it was almost impossible to open a newspaper without one's eye falling on some case of occupational misdemeanour. A Minister of Economic Affairs (currently Prime Minister) paid back 600,000 guilders to the tax authorities because he had not severed all his business connections on becoming a minister; Prince Bernhard was revealed as a 'meat-eater' eliciting bribes in the Lockheed affair; there have been stories of extensive fraud in the building industry; and court cases, press reports, or allegations have concerned corporations or institutions (some of them with previously unimpeachable reputations) such as OGEM, RSV, Slavenburgs Bank, KLM, Uniser, Frisol, Femis, Booy Clean, Tilburg Mortgage Bank, and the ABP (General Pension Fund).

Frauds, fiddles, and mismanagement have been exposed in many areas while 'black' work (paid labour, in or outside the work situation, which is not declared for tax purposes) and tax evasion are everyday topics of conversation and are allegedly universal (Punch 1981a; Heertje and Cohen 1980; de Kam and van Empel 1983; Berghuis et al. 1984); one newspaper even referred to 1978 as 'The Year of Corruption' (*De Telegraaf* 23 December, 1978). But deviance in business life tends to be shielded by the absence of investigative journalism and by academics who do not research sensitive issues, while public figures who stray are rarely severely stigmatized (*New York Times* 5 July, 1977). Also recent allegations and criminal cases are not widely reported outside of The Netherlands because few foreigners can read Dutch.

What is unforgivable, however, is to have been on the wrong side in the war (*Haagse Post* 25 November, 1978). The Dutch police were inextricably involved in enforcement with the Nazi occupiers and, in a city like Amsterdam which was a major Jewish city before the war, this has left a legacy of distrust (*Accent* 7, 14, 21 May, 1977). It was with especial glee, then, that the media mounted a sustained campaign when corrupt practices came to light among a number of Amsterdam policemen and the resulting cases were treated as a first-rate journalistic scandal. The affair, which surfaced in 1976, centred on practices such as entrapment, escorting drug deals, planting evidence on suspects, stealing from prisoners, abusing female suspects, possessing illegal firearms, and receiving gifts and/or payments from known criminals or suspected criminal figures particularly within the inner-city Chinese 'underworld'. The cases involved serious charges and, although the investigation achieved little and few heads rolled, it has left a deep, negative image (even though the affair never reached the proportions of those in London and New York – cf. Chapter One). That particular scandal comprises the central focus of this study and its genesis, development, and consequences will be related both to Dutch society's attitudes to deviance and towards dilemmas inherent in police work and the police organization.

In particular, a Dutch police agency in crisis, in the grip of a corruption scandal, provides an empirical study of an institution 'shell-shocked' by revelations of deviancy. Scandal opens up a window for us through which we can glimpse more clearly those structural features of policing that are normally shrouded in mystery and secrecy. As a foreigner in Dutch society I employ a cross-national, comparative perspective to explore some of that society's ambivalent reactions to the discovery of deviance. Furthermore, it is rare, if not unique, for a researcher to be allowed access to a police department actually in the throes of a scandal and this enabled me to follow developments from close by. This portrait of Amsterdam, with its accent on the micro-processes of institutional life, does not portray the police organization as a harmonious, integrated entity with a comforting consensus and with unbreachable defences against internal investigation and outside enquiry based on a universal code of silence. On the contrary, it reveals a deeply *divided* organization which, in endeavouring to keep itself from being labelled deviant by scapegoating and by locating deviance low down in the hierarchy, finds itself confronted with resistance from below and with counter-strategies pushing the label back up the hierarchy. By examining the dilemmas facing senior officers in terms of deviance and control this study also makes an original contribution to an understanding of the work of people in positions of responsibility within the police organization who have generally been neglected in the standard literature which has been pre-occupied with the lower ranks (Cain 1979: 146; Manning and van Maanen 1978: vii). Scandal threatens to expose the myth system and to reveal the operational code and, in response, organizational representatives energetically seek to restore and bolster up the myth system (Reisman 1979). In Amsterdam this intricate process signalled upheaval and tension within the organization because a control agency experiences immense difficulty when it is forced to *reverse* its investigative focus in order to control itself. That process reveals for us something of general significance about occupational and organizational deviance, police corruption, scandals, accountability, and our ability to exert effective control over a powerful institution in a democratic society. Above all, this is a study of what happens when a law-enforcement agency becomes itself a law-breaker. For, then, police are forced to police other policemen.

Police Deviance and Corruption

'There are three kinds of men in the department . . . I call them the birds, the grass eaters and the meat eaters. The birds just fly up high. They don't eat anything either because they are honest or because they don't have any good opportunities. The grass-eaters, well they'll accept a cup of coffee or a free meal or a television set wholesale from a merchant, but they draw a line.

The meat-eaters are different. They're out looking. They're on a pad with gamblers, they deal in junk, or they'd compromise a homicide investigation for money.'

(New York policeman, in Barker and Roebuck
1973: 35)

Many of the illicit practices found in police organizations are subsumed under the concept of 'corruption' although no satisfactory definition of this concept exists. Political scientists seem to assume that corruption can only be a footnote to Acton's dictum, that power inevitably tends to corrupt, and pessimistically assert that 'corruption is perennial and ubiquitous, to be found in any and all systems of government' (Palmier 1983: 207). There is a measure of agreement among them that it involves the use of public office for private gain (Heidenheimer 1970: 3–9). However, it is important to express wariness about the term corruption and to indicate that political scientists, economists, and sociologists tend to interpret it differently (cf. Heidenheimer 1970; Rose-Ackerman 1978; Gardiner and Olson 1974). I argue that police corruption should not be seen in isolation but should be placed in a broader perspective of general occupational and organizational deviance. And yet it has to be recognized that, while there is no reason to suppose that policemen as individuals are any less fallible than other members of society, people are often shocked and outraged when policemen are exposed violating the law. The reason is simple. Their deviance elicits a special feeling of betrayal. In a sense, they are doubly condemned; that is, not just for the infringement itself but even more for the breach of trust involved. Something extra is involved when public officials in general and policemen in particular deviate from accepted norms: 'That something more is the violation of a fiduciary *relationship*, the corruption of a public *trust*, of public *virtue*' (Reiss 1977: ix–x; emphasis in original).

If we turn to considering the nature of police corruption, then there is no unanimity on defining it and, moreover, there is a paucity of good, analytical material on the subject. The indispensable sources are Sherman (1974 and 1978), the review of the literature by Simpson (1977), the bibliographical guide of Duchaine (1979), and the typology of Barker and Roebuck (1973). These, and other works, are reviewed briefly here and insights from them inform the material presented in the rest of this book. Simpson (1977: 4–6) states that 'no functional definition of corruption has yet been agreed upon' but that 'secrecy may be a definitive characteristic of the phenomenon'. Most studies support the view that corruption is endemic, if not universal, in police departments. Comparative research, for example, is said to document it 'not as a unique pathology, but as a given feature of every police system in the world' (Sherman 1974: 13). Somewhat more parochially, Sherman (1978: xxiii) asserts that, 'Virtually every urban police department in the United States has experienced both organized corruption and a major scandal over that corruption.' The latter statement certainly does *not* hold for Great Britain and The Netherlands. Until comparatively recently in both societies there has not been a persistent history of police corruption scandals while commentators have remarked on the absence of corruption (Judge 1972; Stead 1975; Alderson 1973; Blanken 1976).

The view that corruption involves misuse of one's office for private ends is widely held and Sherman (1978: 30) adopts it when he defines police corruption as 'an illegal use of organizational power for personal gain'. The difficulty here is that legal definitions of corruption incorporating this element are generally very wide (and in practice suffer from considerable problems with evidence and proof), that personal gain tends to be seen largely in pecuniary terms, and that the word 'personal' suggests individual deviance (Clarke 1983: 15). Indeed, some virtually equate corruption with bribery involving money or material reward (Barker 1977: 356). But one crucial facet in assessing police corruption, and this is related to breach of trust and to harming the 'common interest', is that basically we do not expect policemen to favour criminals or to promote crime. It is almost as if a doctor deliberately set out to spread disease (Goldstein 1977: 180). The danger of corruption for the police, and this is also true for many public organizations, is that it may *invert* the formal goals of the organization and may lead to 'the use of organizational power to encourage and create crime rather than to deter it' (Sherman 1978: 31).

The complexity of the issues involved – what is personal gain, what are the 'real' goals, and what constitutes encouraging crime? – are reinforced if we shift the focus to the broader concept of police deviance. For then we encounter an extremely wide range of activities that may be carried out for a multiplicity of motives. What is quite clear is that widespread and systematic police deviance has been amply documented in a variety of settings and at various times. In Philadelphia, for example, police dishonesty was found to be 'continuous, pervasive and organized'

(Pennsylvania Crime Commission 1974); police burglary rings have been uncovered in Denver, Chicago, Reno, Detroit, Des Moines, Memphis, Cleveland, Birmingham, Miami, Stanford University and also in Glasgow, Bristol, Birmingham, Croydon, and Brighton; and in Albany (New York) policemen routinely stole tyres and batteries from parked cars and took burglary equipment with them when on patrol (Christianson 1973). Much of our information on these practices comes from public en-quiries and journalism, which unavoidably centre on *post facto* reconstructions and rely on biased sources, but one systematic study of patrolmen in three American cities based on observation came to the conclusion that, 'during any year a substantial minority of all police officers violate the criminal law, a majority misbehave towards citizens in an encounter, and most engage in serious violations of the rules and regulations of the department' (Reiss 1971: 169). Reiss's data reveal strikingly the extent to which rule-breaking is commonly accepted, because the police-men concerned knew that they were being observed for research purposes.

Now corruption is but one facet of police deviance, and to explain one you also have to explain the other, particularly because it is not always obvious where brutality, discrimination, and misconduct end and corruption begins. For example, a policeman shoots an unarmed suspect and then, to cover himself, plants a weapon on the body, falsifies his testimony, lies in court, and persuades several colleagues to back up his story. This is undoubtedly criminal but is it corrupt? There is no corruptor out-side the department, no bribe or material reward involved, but there is abuse of authority for personal gain, a breach of trust, and an undermining of the public interest. In order to classify a number of these issues I shall attempt a rudimentary classifi-cation of police deviance.

One widely used typology of police corruption is that of Barker and Roebuck (1973) and I wish to extend it while agreeing basi-cally with their general proposition that police corruption is best understood as not being the exclusive behaviour of individual officers, and that there is not one but many analytical types of police corruption. They elucidate eight categories of 'corruption' (corruption of authority; kickbacks; opportunistic theft; shake-downs; protection; the fix; direct criminal activities; and internal pay-offs). All of these practices are illicit, being infringements of the criminal law and/or departmental disciplinary regulations, but they cover very different types of activity (cf. Stoddard 1968;

Goldstein 1977: 194). This classification is useful but it requires amplification in two directions. First, I prefer to put more emphasis on a broader orientation to police occupational deviance and, second, I consider it necessary to examine the *intention* of corrupt practices more closely. This is because Barker and Roebuck do neglect an important category of offences, such as 'flaking' and 'padding' (planting of, or adding to, evidence – particularly in drug cases), which are sometimes designed to *enhance* the effectiveness of law enforcement. This approach is adopted in order to emphasize the spectrum from 'ordinary', 'normal', 'day-to-day', deviance – which may also involve lying, deception, and management of appearances – to the criminal activities which, not unnaturally, tend to dominate the literature.

TYPES OF GENERAL DEVIANCE IN ORGANIZATIONS

For example, it is possible to classify crudely types of deviance that one might anticipate in all organizations.

(1) *Work Avoidance and Work Manipulation:* 'cooping' (sleeping on the job), 'easing' (getting time off to attend band practice), 'cushy numbers' (easy jobs inside) (Manning 1977: 151–55; Maas 1974: 55). These forms of activity are designed to make work or working conditions more comfortable and acceptable. They are found in all organizations, at all levels, and are rarely seen as serious. In police circles, they may even be seen as partially condoned ways of avoiding the rigours of patrol work or of keeping up the personnel's morale (Cain 1973).

(2) *Employee Deviance – Against the Organization:* pilfering, sabotage, absenteeism, leaking information, neglect (Rubinstein 1973). These are ways for employees to subvert organizational ends or to hit back at the organization for various reasons. They are often confined to lower levels of the organization, but not exclusively, and are seen as negative and damaging by management.

(3) *Employee Deviance – For the Organization:* bending rules to achieve quotas, cutting administrative corners, informal deals to circumvent formal blockages. In short, these activities consist of the countless ways in which people try to get their jobs done, frequently with the intention of promoting organizational ends, but which deviate from normal rules and regulations (Dalton 1959). Often these deviations are seen as

minor and unavoidable, although they can be rarely acknowledged as such formally, but they may involve the development of an informal system that fosters neglect, inefficiency,
incompetence, conspiracy, and even crime.

(4) *Informal Rewards:* perks, fiddling, private telephone calls,
tipping, discounts, services, presents. This covers a potentially huge range of ways in which organizations provide for,
or condone, informal rewards which may increase in sophistication as one moves up the organization (where it may
extend to variations in offices, carpets, secretaries, cars,
expenses, trips, entertaining, and so on). These rewards may
be widespread but rarely acknowledged, such as informally
permitting certain levels of employee theft, and in certain
service industries may be part of the way of life (Ditton 1977;
Henry 1978; Mars 1982).

The four categories mentioned above simply acknowledge the
many practices in daily organizational life which are virtually
universal and which, in many ways, are accepted and even condoned (this is less true of (2), which one expects to find particularly in polarized or divisive organizations). If we turn more
specifically to the police and to corruption then I assume that all
four of the above categories are also to be found in police organizations but that most public concern is with relatively serious
offences.

POLICE MISCONDUCT AND CRIME: AND FOUR TYPES OF
CORRUPTION

General police deviance can include brutality, discrimination,
sexual harassment, intimidation, and illicit use of weapons.
These are disciplinary and legal infringements related to citizens,
suspects, and criminals where policemen, individually or in
groups, opportunistically or systematically, abuse their authority
in ways (not principally aimed at personal gain) which are externally considered to be illegitimate and improper. In essence, all
deviant police activities fall under this heading but I wish to
reserve it for the relatively serious abuses which are police
initiated and which are not related to organized crime or political
control (except in marginal or tenuous ways).

Corruption is one facet of police crime, but there is an ambivalence in our use and understanding of the word, for it is used to
cover both *profiting* in some way from abuse of power and the

abuse of power itself. In the former case, there is an exchange implicit or explicit, in that something is done or not done in return for some reward or promise, whereas in the second the relationship is not simply one of mutual advantage and may even be one of antagonism. The following typology takes into account the purposes of police corruption particularly in terms of inter-relationships with the policemen's environment.

I *Straightforward Corruption:* something is done or not done for some form of reward. This is most people's understanding of the word and frequently the relationship is stable, predict-able and may allow for token raids and arrests. The work-load may be low as a consequence and can lead to idleness and inefficiency (Whyte 1955: 112) and to what Marx (1981a: 227) calls 'self-interested non-enforcement'.

II *Predatory (Strategic) Corruption:* the police stimulate crime, extort money and actively organize graft (Beigel and Beigel 1977: x). In I., I am assuming a mutual accommodation between say organized crime and the police where, in essence, the former 'buy off' the latter. But when does sol-iciting a bribe move into extortion? Here the police are in the driving seat and become 'meat-eaters' who exploit legitimate and illegitimate enterprises for pursuing illicit ends (Maas 1974: 137). At certain formalized levels of organization the arrangement might be described as 'stra-tegic'.

III *Combative (Strategic) Corruption:* 'flaking', 'padding', falsify-ing testimony, 'verbals', intimidating witnesses, buying and selling drugs, 'scoring' or 'burning' informants, and paying informants with illegally obtained drugs. ('Flaking' refers to 'planting' evidence on a suspect; 'padding' means to add to drugs or evidence to strengthen a case; 'verbals' is used in Britain to indicate where words attributed to a suspect are invented by policemen to help incriminate him; 'scoring' concerns 'shakedowns' where police take money, drugs or goods from suspects or prisoners, and 'burning' means revealing the identity of an informant). Most of these prac-tices are involved in 'building a case' (Manning 1980: 85f) in which the major goal is to make arrests, obtain convictions, confiscate drugs, and get long sentences for criminals. It may involve accommodations with some criminals and certain informants but it is posited on using *illicit means for organiz-ationally and socially approved ends.* This is generally found in specialized detective units (Marx 1981a: 227). Barker and Roebuck scarcely consider this style of deviance.

IV *Corruption as Perversion of Justice:* lying under oath, intimidating witnesses, planting evidence on a suspect, etc. In I and II of my classification the relationship is one of some mutual advantage, although the power imbalance and the directional 'flow' of corruption vary, while in III the purpose is to make the law work 'effectively' or else dispense 'para-legal' law enforcement. But here the motive is to use one's power and position to ensure that justice does or does not get done for reasons that are not mercenary and not 'idealistic'. I am thinking of a policeman or group of policemen who conspire to take revenge on someone or to avoid prosecution themselves for motives other than those mentioned above. The activity is police-initiated and involves a serious breach of trust and misuse of authority. The example I gave earlier of a policeman planting a gun on an unarmed suspect whom he had shot covers the sort of case I mean (Ermann and Lundman 1978: 215). It may appear to overlap considerably with III but the *motivation* of the policemen is the distinguishing quality. It involves the perversion of justice largely in order to avoid the consequences of serious deviant behaviour. Again, Barker and Roebuck do not cover this style of deviation.

In terms of motivation – and, needless to say, motives can be mixed (a lucrative shakedown can also be seen as an informal fine) – the nature of the 'gain' involved in corruption is important. By focusing predominantly on bribery, many authors have emphasized pecuniary gain and mercenary motives whereas there are umpteen ways that people can gain advantage individually and institutionally from deviance. Also, the focus has been on corruptors offering bribes to corruptees within the police; in II and III, in contrast, the police may initiate the bribery and create extortees, though for ostensibly different reasons. Building on this I wish to adapt McMullan's (1961) definition of corruption by extending it and by amplifying the gain beyond merely pecuniary advantage. For me, then, corruption is when an official receives or is promised significant advantage or reward (personal, group, or organizational) for doing something that he is under a duty to do anyway, that he is under a duty not to do, for exercising a legitimate discretion for improper reasons, and for employing illegal means to achieve approved goals.

A major focus of my work is on a police organization's *reactions* to
the exposure of deviance. Few authors focus on what actually
occurs *inside* a police department when it is hit by a scandal and a
subsequent investigation. The exception is Sherman (1978) and in
his important book he examines four cases of 'scandal and
reform' (cf. Cohen 1970; Foster 1966; McGlennon 1977; Tifft
1970; Kornblum 1976). Furthermore, he illustrates that it is possible to reform police departments successfully, as in three of his
cases, while one, 'Central City', is classified as unsuccessful.

Sherman's starting-point is that there is almost no evidence on
the consequences of corruption scandals in urban police departments. Scandal is perceived both as a socially constructed phenomenon and as an agent of change that can lead to realignments in
the structure of power within organizations. Attention is also paid
to the nature of organizational deviance and to police departments which adopt deviant goals or means to the extent that they
are 'captured' by their external environment. In extreme cases
the 'dominant coalition' may invert the real working goals of the
organization. In Newburgh the police chief himself was involved
in systematic burglaries by policemen, while in Newburgh, Oakland, and Central City complete immunity from enforcement
could be purchased by criminals. Deviance had reached the
extent that corruption was adopted as an organizational goal. A
scandal, usually arising from internal dissatisfaction or external
criticism, may lead to crisis and internal debate about leadership,
organizational direction, and survival. Factions are likely to
crystallize and disgruntled members may look outside and even
invite external control as a weapon in the internal struggle over
power.

Generally scandals reveal that internal and external control
mechanisms have proved ineffective or have been undermined
and there follows a *reimposition* of control. The organizational
representatives react by attempting to minimize the issue, by
claiming that it is an aberration caused by a few individuals, and
they seek scapegoats among these (the 'rotten apples'), whereas
actors in the control network may try to label the deviance as
organizational (the 'rotten basket'). Successful labelling of the
department as deviant normally requires evidence of police
failures to control themselves, endorsement by high status
figures to lend credibility to the revealers and accusers, and
dramatization of the scandal by serious public figures (as in the

Knapp Commission's televised proceedings in New York). To be successful reform may require that heads will roll, that chiefs and senior personnel be removed and replaced, that new styles of control be implemented, that opportunity structures and enforcement patterns be altered, and that new norms and values be broadcast internally and externally as a reassurance that police behaviour will be changed.

There is a general pessimism about changing the police but Sherman's research does show that it is possible to reform police departments under certain circumstances. Police corruption may be 'impossible to eliminate entirely' (Sherman 1978: 242) but in Newburgh, Oakland, and New York there was significant reform. However, there is no guarantee of permanence and Sherman's message (1978: 263) is that organizations will have to learn to *control themselves.* For in essence, the lesson that scandal conveys is precisely that organizations have blatantly and conspicuously failed to control themselves. That failure is a betrayal of trust and it raises the perennial, but pivotal, question:

> 'The dominant coalition's failure to take steps to control the deviance is perhaps the most damaging kind of fact, because it raises the critical question of resources for control: *if the organization does not control the conduct of its members, who will?'*
> (Sherman 1978: 25, my emphasis)

Indeed, who will control the controllers?

Sherman's work is indispensable as a starting-point for a study of reactions to scandal but I wish to make three short comments on it. First, his concern is largely absorbed with the administrative consequences of scandal and reform and he pays little attention to the micro-processes of internal politics and reactions that are unleashed by a scandal. Second, he utilizes a rather formal model of the organization as if there is one major goal and one dominant coalition. This seems to lack subtlety in that the dominant coalition may be opposed to corruption (or may be shielded from knowledge about it – Kennedy School of Government 1977c: 7), whereas influential members of sub-units may foster it and protect it in their own squads. Third, and this is related to my second point, Sherman's views are based solely on North American experience. Compared to most of western Europe, the United States provides extreme examples of flagrant corruption where the police department is a tool of the political machine or the 'cabal', or where the department seems to spend more time promoting crime than fighting it (Chambliss 1971; Maas 1974: 137).

Many European police forces have not normally been exposed to this comprehensive form of 'capture' by a political or criminal environment. This makes it difficult for an *entire* department to adopt a deviant goal, although sub-units may well do so. It is part of understanding the ironies, ambivalences, and paradoxes of institutional life that a police department may be conducting a wide range of police activity, including good police work, at the same time that parts of it are engaged in corruption.

Deviance in Organizations

All organizations contain within them the seeds of conflict. Weber (1947), in his lapidary analysis, saw modern bureaucracy as rescuing us from capriciousness and venality; in practice, empirical studies of bureaucracies reveal that conflict and dilemmas constantly arise from the differential interpretation of rules, from accommodating to the culture and personalities of officials and clients, and from the perennial need for the bureaucrat to balance impersonal, rigid, rule-bound conduct with flexibility, understanding, and humanity (Blau 1955; Crozier 1964). This last dilemma is examined here in terms of the working world of the policeman, a bureaucrat with a peculiar, if not 'impossible' (Goldstein 1977: 10), mission. For it is his job to enter polluted and dangerous segments of society, there to mingle in the 'underworld' with criminals and informants in order to apprehend some of them. But his position as enforcer of the law makes him not only a target for manipulation and corruption but also an actor uniquely protected by the law should he deviate from it. The central focus of this book is the predicament of the policeman, engaging in 'dirty work' (Hughes 1963), and assailed by contradictory pressures including encouragement from within the organization, and inducements from outside it, to break the law. 'Why do policemen who are meant to enforce the law end up breaking the law?'; and 'How does the police organization cope with this apparently paradoxical deviance?', are the two questions that I explore throughout this book.

The sociological rationale for studying 'bent' policemen is based on the ability of this material to tell us something of general significance about the complex interplay between deviance, control, identity, and forms of social organization. All organizations have to construct mechanisms of control, to specify tolerance limits for deviance, to impose sanctions, and to regulate relationships with other organizations. Normal social processes may be characterized as devious and deceptive (Goffman 1961; 1972), while the game of poker, for example, legitimately encourages distrust, cunning, and concealment of the players' strengths and weaknesses (Carr 1968). But the size and complexity of modern organizations create dilemmas, cultures, and opportunities which promote deviance and practices that may be camouflaged in sophisticated and intricate ways and that may elicit deception and deceit from those involved. Practically every organizational study ever undertaken documents deviance from formal rules and espoused goals (be it in prisons, schools, unions, universities, offices, factories, or hospitals) while recently, a number of studies have pushed enquiry on 'policing' into relatively new areas such as crime and deviance in business organizations and government agencies (Reiss 1983; Vaughan 1983; Hawkins 1984; Carson 1982; Ermann and Lundman 1982b; Clinard and Yeager 1980).

This book is not primarily a theoretical study. The research was also not designed as a policy-relevant project, although it may contain implications for policy. It grew out of an ethnography of patrol-work which placed me conveniently close to a police force where I was fortunate to gain access when a corruption scandal developed. As such, this is a modest empirical study based on the descriptive analysis of the nature and creation of deviance, order, and control in a pivotal institution for modern society, the police organization. Furthermore, it highlights the constant interaction between policemen's perception of, and involvement in, deviance and conformity as related to their work, occupational culture, and organization. In particular, attention will be focused on internal and external reactions to the exposure of deviance in three police forces – New York, London, and Amsterdam – and the data, gained from observation, interviews, and documents, will be employed to illustrate how deviance is socially constructed by key actors, through social processes, and in specific situations. Corruption scandals do not just happen; they have to be made.

I take as granted that in organized social life, deviance and social order are problematic and are continually being redefined and recreated (Rock 1979). From this perspective I wish to make the fundamental point that it raises dilemmas related to deviance and control which arise in *all* organizations. To illustrate this position I shall briefly summarize a number of points from studies in this area. First, accidents, scandals, public enquiries and research have graphically revealed 'corruption' in a wide range of governmental and business organizations and the evidence indicates that certain deviant practices are not simply incidental and scattered but, rather, they are pervasive, flagrant, and highly articulated (Boulton 1978; Cornwell 1983; Bernstein and Woodward 1975). Deviance exists 'alongside legitimate organizational activities and frequently serves to advance important organizational goals' (Ermann and Lundman 1982a: 91). Second, deviance and corruption are concepts that readily conjure up exotic, conspiratorial imagery (some accounts are byzantine and 'read like fiction': Kanter and Stein 1979: 313). Yet many authors are at pains to point out that most revelations concern relatively routine practices that were perceived as 'normal' and even mundane by those concerned (Gross 1980; Geis 1967). But, third, it is also plain that certain reports of deviance and corruption do excite great interest and may elicit feelings of outrage, betrayal, and moral condemnation (President's Commission 1967: 104). In some countries, corruption can become a symbol of near universal decay, of pathology, and of profound social anomie and moral reaction to it may sponsor change and even social revolution (Kicinski 1982; Whitehead 1983). Fourth, this helps to explain why some 'scandals', seen as media-generated events, take-off and others fail: the time needs to be ripe and the media need the will, the resources, and the lucky breaks to capitalize on information. 'Investigative' journalism is expensive, time-consuming and risky, while powerful deviants may be able to manipulate the production of news (Murphy 1983; Doig 1983) and may successfully resist labelling and sanctioning (Ermann and Lundman 1982a: 235). Fifth, and last, many scholars observe that, although 'organizational deviance' is virtually endemic in contemporary society and is severely damaging in many ways, enforcement is highly selective, sanctions are often feeble, and there is a reluctance to prosecute (Geis and Stotland 1980; Johnson and Douglas 1978). This indicates a general problem in contemporary society, and one that is not simply confined to the police: namely that those in power fail to allocate adequate resources to the external control of organizations (Pearce 1976; Krisberg 1975).

Finally, the social construction of police deviance and control explored in the rest of this book is meant to illustrate and illuminate the contention that deviance is endemic in organizations and that control is continually problematic. As Durkheim (1964: 67) elegantly expressed it, in a 'society of saints' even an apparently trivial infraction may cause considerable upheaval and, in turning to police deviance, we are dealing with an occupational group that attracts many epithets, though 'saintly' is rarely one of them.

1
Scandal in New York and London

In the 1970s, three metropolitan police forces in cosmopolitan cities – in New York, London, and Amsterdam – were rocked by corruption scandals. These three examples are useful in bringing a comparative emphasis to this study particularly as many people remain fundamentally ignorant about how police elsewhere in the world function (Bayley 1983: 34). This is particularly true of police deviance where there is a paucity of cross-national analysis, as most comparative research is concerned with political or official corruption (Heidenheimer 1970; Scott 1972). This book is not, alas, based on extensive comparative field-work. Brief visits and off-the-record interviews were possible in New York and London (where I met ordinary policemen as well as those involved in investigating deviance, including officers of the Organized Crime Control Unit in the NYPD and of A10 at Scotland Yard), and the American and British experience is utilized as a cross-national backcloth to highlight and contrast the Amsterdam affair which is dealt with in greater detail later.

All the cities are 'capital' cities; London and Amsterdam are real capitals, although Amsterdam is not the centre of government, whereas I take New York to be the uncrowned capital of the United States. This does mean that the three examples are not representative of policing in the three countries concerned. All three cases represent highly publicized scandals that are well documented and this makes the departments partially accessible to the scrutiny of outsiders. A major reason why there were scandals at all in these three cities is related to the fact that they are centres of the national media (particularly printed journalism which is best suited to intensive corruption investigations). These are usually more independent than the provincial media which may be closely tied to the local power structure (Doig, 1983). For the presence of police, organized crime, and a critical media spells scandal. The three cases will be examined in terms of the origins, nature and extent of corruption and the societal and institutional reactions to its exposure.

New York: City of Sharks

'. . . then before you know it, you're up to your ears. I can't even remember where the money was coming from. You know, taking money is like getting laid. You remember the first time with a broad; after that it's a blur'.

(police witness before Knapp Commission: Shecter and
Phillips 1973: 87–8)

In the United States there exists a long history of police corruption particularly in relation to city politics and organized crime (Steffens 1957; Richardson 1974; Cook 1966; Lexow Commission 1895). The police department was important to the political machine for funds and for jobs so that it became an arena for patronage and favours. Prospective policemen literally bought their jobs and officers paid for their promotion (Sherman 1974: 48–50). The police did not seek to suppress vice or to eradicate crime, rather they licensed the one and regulated the other. Typically the major sources of 'graft' were liquor, prostitution, gambling, and local ordinances related to traffic, health, building and Sunday closing (Ward, 1975). If this suggests benign 'grass-eaters' accepting with philosophic resignation 'clean money' from a public determined and willing to pay for breaking the law and for avoiding prosecution, then there was also a disturbing and distressing list of predatory, police-initiated crime and extortion of victims that included armed robbery, looting, stealing cars, advising robbers on likely targets in exchange for a share of the loot, stealing from the city treasurer's office, and being members of the Ku Klux Klan (all of these in Chicago: Beigel and Beigel 1977: 150).

Despite successive reform efforts corruption flourished, as a series of post-war scandals have revealed (Fogelson 1977: 149).

American politics continued to be plagued by corruption (Gardiner and Olson 1974; Royko 1971). Indeed in 1973 the city of Philadelphia refused to cooperate in an investigation of police corruption (Birch 1983: 84) and in 1979 the federal prosecutor, in an unprecedented step, indicted the *entire* police force for its dubious methods (*Time*, 27 August, 1979). In Chicago an investigation lasting six years led to over sixty prison sentences and uncovered in the nineteen-seventies a thriving, 'traditional' relationship between the police, organized crime and city government involving bribery, extortion, conspiracy, and perjury (Beigel and Beigel 1977). And, when the Police Foundation began to collect press clippings on corruption in 1973 it received within two months reports of deviance from all types of department and from some thirty states (Goldstein 1977: 220). This background, so unlike that of most of Europe (i.e. since, but of course not *before*, municipal and bureaucratic reform), helps to explain the resilience of corruption in American police departments.

SERPICO AND THE KNAPP COMMISSION

New York, for instance, has had no less than five major scandals concerning its police department within a century. (The NYPD now has 24,000 sworn officers, although it used to have 32,000 officers, to police around eight million inhabitants.) The last one attracted national and international press coverage, largely due to the impact of the Knapp Commission's televised hearings and the ordeal of the 'honest cop', Serpico, who fruitlessly endeavoured to report corruption to his superiors. The Knapp Commission (Knapp 1972) found corruption to be widespread and in some areas it was highly organized with 'the pad', 'the nut', and 'bagmen'. The 'pad' meant the organized system of graft and those who were on it; the 'nut' was what an individual policeman could expect to earn from the pad; the money was collected regularly by policemen or ex-policemen, usually in unmarked cars, who were known as 'bagmen'; and officers transferred to less lucrative assignments could expect a form of 'severance pay' (Barker and Roebuck 1973: 33). A great deal of the information revealed traditional 'straight-forward' corruption that was seen as clean, easy money that led to a pleasant life-style and an undemanding work situation. Serpico (Maas 1974: 133) described this 'cushy' style in one particular unit where the plainclothesmen would sign in for work then hang around drinking coffee, go to the movies, or return home for a dip in the pool or a game of cards with their colleagues; 'As Serpico soon observed, the main function of the division plainclothesmen was to protect the entire pad while servicing their racketeer clients.' In Serpico's account the usual range of deviant practices are exposed – free meals, cooping, carrying illegal weapons, trading arrests for favours between policemen, and also highly regularized and extremely lucrative graft – but his story is important for two reasons.

First he conveys a deep disillusion about law enforcement among policemen. Second, and this is crucial, he describes the unenviable position of the straight policeman in a corrupt environment. His attempts to warn senior officers and politicians fell on deaf ears, he faced ostracism and threats from colleagues, and may even have been set up in a shooting incident because he broke the rule of silence in taking his story to the *New York Times* and by testifying openly before the Knapp Commission (Maas 1974: 21).

A major revelation of the commission was the extent to which narcotics had become a key activity associated with corruption and how the distinction between 'clean' and 'dirty' money had become diluted in practice. A senior officer testified before the commission that,

'Police officers have been involved in activities such as extortion of money and/or narcotics from narcotics violators in order to avoid arrest; they have accepted bribes; they have sold narcotics. They have known of narcotics violations and have failed to take proper enforcement action. They have entered into personal associations with narcotics criminals and in some cases have used narcotics. They have given false testimony in court in order to obtain dismissal of the charges against a defendant.'

(Sherman 1974: 129)

In a few cases the following was reported: determining the purity and strength of unfamiliar drugs detectives had seized by giving small quantities to addict–informants to test on themselves; introducing potential customers to narcotics pushers; revealing the identity of a government informant to narcotics criminals; kidnapping critical witnesses at the time of trial to prevent them testifying; providing armed protection for deals; and offering to obtain 'hit' men to kill potential witnesses (Sherman 1974).

LEUCI AND THE SPECIAL INVESTIGATION UNIT

With this sort of behaviour it is clear that some policemen were engaged in strategic corruption, both 'predatory' and 'combative', and also in corruption of justice. This emerges graphically in the account of Bob Leuci who, in return for immunity against prosecution, was used as an undercover agent to gather incriminating evidence against his fellow detectives. Narcotics changes the setting because dealers are often more dangerous and competitive than say organized gamblers, because the sums of money involved are huge (and may be present along with the drugs at the time of arrest, allowing the police 'to score' dealers and/or buyers) and because arrests for large deals are glamorous and elicit high status (Moore 1977). Leuci's colleagues in the elite Special Investigation Unit (SIU) were suave, slick 'stars' (not unlike their prisoners), who were highly motivated and whose cases were mounted with considerable skill and panache. But their methods were patently illegal and their motives were dubiously ambivalent. Like the plainclothesmen that Serpico described, they were virtually unsupervised and rarely went to the office; but, in contrast, these SIU men were 'hunters' and could expertly tap phones, plant bugging devices, pick locks, and commit burglaries. Their cases were typically 'imaginative, efficient, illegal' (Daley 1979: 70). Perjury was said to be routine 'in the interest of putting bad people in jail', while 'scoring' of wealthy South American dealers was perceived as doing what the justice system was incapable of doing, fining them and deporting them. And yet, the methods were clearly criminal, they took money for themselves, and they put heroin back into circulation because it was the medium of exchange with informants. Leuci maintains rather speciously that only on two occasions, one of them involving the disappearance of the 'French Connection' drugs from the Property Clerk's Office (involving 185 pounds of heroin and 31 pounds of cocaine), were drugs sold back to the streets. Yet this made the NYPD one of the major suppliers of 'dope' in the city (Murphy and Plate 1977: 244).

Leuci's disturbing account shows us a criminal justice system that was rampantly corrupt. Lawyers, district attorneys, even judges were corrupt, and seemingly everyone and everything (even a murder charge) was up for sale, cases had a price (with bribes being offered actually in the court room), and it was 'never too late to do business' (Maas 1974: 135). In this corruptive environment policemen learned to bend or break rules for personal advantage, for obtaining convictions, and for informally 'punishing' criminals, and this meant lies, perjury, and falsifying and fabricating evidence. Leuci had 'lied so much he could hardly think straight anymore' (Daley 1979: 165). Indeed, part of Serpico's and Leuci's motivation was to expose the wider corruption in the legal system as part of police corruption. Leuci accused Scoppetta (a former District Attorney (DA) working with Knapp) of using the police as scapegoats:

> 'It's absolutely incredible. Cops are looking at you and saying: You bastards. It's you guys, the assistant district attorneys, lawyers, judges who run the system, *and the whole fucking thing from top to bottom is corrupt.* We know how you become a judge. You pay $50,000 and you become a judge. You want to lay on us the responsibility of fucking up the system.'
>
> (Daley 1979: 29)

This sceptical view must have been reinforced when the Queens County DA was indicted for corruption and when a member of the Knapp Commission was later convicted on corruption charges (Sherman 1978: xxvii). A number of New York policemen told me that whenever there is a scandal the focus is on police, 'because cops give you headlines'; but then, mysteriously, the funding for commissions and special investigations always seems to run out just when the investigation starts to shift towards DAs, lawyers, judges, and politicians.

This style of work in the SIU was based on close, almost familial ties with colleagues while partners built up especially deep relationships. The tragic and bitter element is that, when the edifice of lies and fabrication begins to crumble, betrayal of close friends becomes the price of survival. In New York, 'a city of sharks' as Murphy called it, it seemed as if everyone preyed on everyone else, and it became difficult to know whose side you were on and who you could trust. The personal side of the scandal involved guilt, remorse, betrayal, shame, mental illness, suicides, and a range of sanctions ranging from dismissal from the force to ten years in prison. For the Commissioner (who himself encountered hostility, loneliness, threats of walk-outs by personnel, and who was booed by policemen's wives at a ceremony) the SIU represented 'the most corrupt single unit in the history of American law enforcement' (Murphy and Plate 1977: 242). In Leuci's eyes, in contrast, they were eager, effective policemen who had simply slipped up along the way:

> 'S.I.U. detectives, Leuci insisted, arrested more pushers, seized more narcotics than any other agency by far. The S.I.U. guys

were great detectives who committed corrupt acts once in a
while. It was just something that happened. It was just there
one day, and then it grew.'

(Daley 1979: 311)

The revelations of deviance over a number of years labelled the
New York Police Department as corrupt. People were shocked
by the scope and magnitude of the deviance and particularly by
the blatant failure of internal institutional attempts to deal with it
(Meyer 1976; Kennedy School of Government 1977a). In response
the mayor appointed a commission of enquiry, rapidly replaced it
with the more acceptable 'Knapp' Commission, and attracted Pat
Murphy back to New York to become Chief of Police. Murphy
was a scathing critic of American police leadership – he derided it
as 'Keystone Cops' management – and was determined to reform,
ruthlessly if necessary, the department. Murphy admits that he
needed the Commission, and the publicity it consciously bathed
in (Kennedy School of Government 1977c: 2), in order to im-
plement change in a department enmeshed in a highly complex
political environment (Daley 1971: 37–46). Knapp, for instance,
concluded that loyalty, born of a suspicion and hostility to outsiders and an intense desire to be proud of the department, had
led to a stubborn refusal at all levels to recognize that a serious
problem existed – 'we talked about corruption with all the
enthusiasm of a group of little old ladies talking about venereal
disease' was how one policeman put it (Knapp 1972: 5).

Murphy set out to make corruption the focus for fundamentally
altering the whole department. He instituted a new policy of
accountability and decentralization, informing 180 commanders
'I hold each of you personally responsible for any misconduct
within the ranks at any level of command' (Murphy and Plate
1977: 167). There were massive transfers of senior officers,
rotation of policemen in sensitive areas, and the autonomy of the
detective branch was severely reduced. He reinvigorated the
internal investigatory system – which seemed 'deliberately
designed not to work' – and sponsored 'proactive' internal affairs
work with integrity tests and 'field associates' (Sherman
1978: 157). (Integrity tests involved handing wallets to policemen
to see if they would be handed in to lost property; as part of
'proactive' anti-corruption enforcement field-associates were
new recruits who were asked to report secretly on deviancy in

the units to which they were attached; unit commanders did not know who these 'spies' were and at one stage they numbered roughly one in ten members of certain units – Murphy and Plate 1977: 237.) And he endeavoured to alter the opportunity structure by exercising wide discretion in virtually not enforcing the laws on gambling and the Sabbath, by providing policemen with sufficient funds to pay informants, and by starting a campaign to arrest those offering bribes (Murphy and Plate 1977; Kennedy School 1977, a–d).

With political, legal, and press support, Murphy tried to do what many said was impossible – 'you can't change the job' – and, as a result, Sherman (1978: xxxix) contends that, 'From all indicators, the most recent episode of scandal and reform in the New York City Police Department has reduced police corruption to a very minimal level'.

Certainly, in a number of informal interviews with members of the NYPD conducted in 1980 and 1981 I was told with some conviction that this was the case; and now some men speak of a 'revolution' ('But as a widespread and organized thing, as something that was once accepted, that's gone. The whole climate of the department has been reversed since Knapp' – *New York Times*, 29 November, 1982). But we should perhaps be sceptical because in a city-wide 'corruption profile' compiled by the Intelligence Section of the Internal Affairs Department in 1973, it was reported that, while some traditional sources of graft such as gambling had diminished, other forms of deviance seemed on the increase in certain precincts, such as theft from suspects and impounded cars while 'a major growing problem [in one precinct] is the use of prostitutes' services under threat of arrest'. Thus only a year after Knapp certain forms of corruption were still being reported (Command Corruption Profile NYPD, 1973). And, more recently in 1983 there have been familiar accusations of police accepting bribes to protect nightclubs. Nevertheless, Commissioner McGuire remarked that 'there is in the whole country no other police force of this size that is so free of corruption as this one, and that spends so much effort on the issue of integrity' (*Vrij Nederland* 21 January, 1984: 4).

London: Firm Within a Firm

'For Williamson the problem could be summed up in three short, sharp verdicts on the only three sorts of detective believed to exist in the Met: those who were themselves corrupt, those who knew that others were corrupt but did nothing about it, and those who were too stupid to notice what was going on around them.'

(Cox, Shirley, and Short 1977: 69)

Many of the gross forms of corruption encountered in the United States, and particularly the close ties between corrupt local government and the police, have not been typical of British policing (and probably also not of much of Northern European policing) since the formation of the 'new police' in the early and mid-nineteenth century (Critchley 1978; Tobias 1972). Before that, of course, law enforcement and the judicial system were a tawdry shambles but this was little more than a reflection of widespread venality in public life where official positions, commissions in the army, and seats in parliament were up for sale. Thanks to a line of reformers, notably Peel, Rowan and Mayne, the members of the Metropolitan Police (hereafter 'Met') established themselves slowly as a legitimate uniformed presence on the streets of London and set an example for courteous, low-key policing (Miller 1977; Gillers 1977: 118). This image even went so far as to paint the detective branch of the Met (colloquially known as 'Scotland Yard') as incorruptible and as comprising the most competent policemen in the world.

But there have certainly been periodic scandals relating to police deviance and corruption. In the post-war period, for example, there has been a series of incidents involving Chief Constables in Cardiganshire, Worcester, Brighton, Nottingham, Southend, and, more recently, Lancashire which have led to resignations, dismissals, and even prison sentences. Earlier there was a major outcry surrounding the 'Turf Frauds' case of 1877 in which Inspector Meiklejohn of the Met, along with three colleagues, was tried and convicted for obstructing the course of justice. In effect, this led to the formation of a separate detective department (The Criminal Investigation Department, CID) within the Met which was to be of immense significance later. The autonomy and protection that this afforded probably cloaked some quite devious practices which were only occasionally glimpsed, as in the Goddard case of 1928. This sergeant was alleged to have organized protection on a grand scale for the flourishing vice establishments of the West End and was fortunate to have been leniently sentenced to eighteen months for conspiring to pervert the course of justice (Sherman 1974: 98). In retrospect, this is seen as a missed opportunity for a more general appraisal of detective methods as there were implications of perjury, ill-treatment, and corruption, while the level of organization and, for the time, large sums of money involved suggested a wider level of involvement than this one sergeant. The historian of the Met, Ascoli (1979: 198), argues that by the early twenties the CID had become 'a thoroughly venal private army' but that successive commissioners drew back from grasping the thorny nettle of reforming it.

Growing general dissatisfaction with the police, particularly in the area of handling complaints, had helped bring about a Royal Commission (1962) and, particularly from the mid-1960s, there has been almost unrelenting critical comment on the police in relation to public order, racism, interrogations, violence in arrest situations, prisoners in custody, drugs, pornography, and civil rights (Whitaker 1964; Hain, Humphry, and Rose-Smith 1979; Hain et al. 1980; Bowes 1968). (In the post-war period the Met was consistently around 20 per cent under establishment, which is about 25,000 officers, and it is responsible for an area covering 787 square miles and containing almost eight million inhabitants – Commissioner of Police 1976.)

THE TIMES INVESTIGATION

By the end of the 1960s it was widely alleged that in London policemen planted evidence, committed perjury, and 'verballed' suspects (Laurie 1972: 260–72). Nevertheless, the bombshell of *The Times* revelations of corruption which were printed in November 1969 had a tremendous impact. Not only had a major paper of high repute entered an area usually reserved for the yellow press but it could back up its story with tape-recordings and photographs. It is no exaggeration to say that *The Times* sparked off a chain reaction which was to alter fundamentally the positive image of London policing, was to hasten the outside pressure for fundamental change, and was to subject Scotland Yard to one of the most painful and lengthy sets of enquiries that almost any institution has ever had to endure. In the process, a great deal was revealed about the nature of corruption among the capital's detective force.

Only in the barest detail can I touch on these highly complex developments which raise in acute form dilemmas related to controlling the controllers. Here I shall touch on the four series of investigations, on Commissioner Robert Mark's reforms, and on the tenacity of corruption in sections of the Met. Crucial in all this is the growth of sophisticated criminal gangs (and also a number of unscrupulous lawyers), whose routine tactics were to counterattack the police in and out of court with accusations of 'lying, bribery, fabricating and planting evidence, perjury, theft, threatening witnesses, assault and drunkenness' (Ball, Chester, and Perrott 1979: 159). In this world of lies, bragging, and mutual disclaimers, *The Times* suddenly came out with detailed accusations of policemen planting evidence, committing perjury to obtain a false conviction, taking money from criminals in return for showing favours, urging a criminal to act as an *agent provocateur*, and selling 'licences' to commit crime without fear of arrest (Cox, Shirley, and Short 1977). This was predatory strategic corruption in which vulnerable criminals were exploited: they could be 'set-up', then recruited either as an informant and/or as a payee for services rendered, and, if they did not stick to the rules, then they would be prosecuted. One criminal, facing years in prison on framed evidence (fingerprints left on gelignite when shaking hands with a detective), was introduced to *The Times* and the reporters there had stumbled by accident on police corruption.

But the police were not simply predatory as *The Times* tapes revealed; one friendly local detective told a criminal,

> 'Don't forget always to let me know straight away if you need anything, because I know people everywhere. Because I'm in a little firm in a firm. Don't matter where, anywhere in London I can get on to the phone to someone I know I can trust, that talks the same as me. And if he's not the right person who can do it, he'll know the person that can. All right? If you are nicked anywhere in London . . . I can get on to the blower to someone in my firm who will know someone who can get something done.'
> (Cox, Shirley, and Short 1977: 15–16)

The 'firm within a firm' motif (in police–underworld slang 'firm' means a criminal gang) highlighted the existence of systematic police deviance covering the whole of the London area. Senior officers were devastated that this could be said of the 'world's greatest police force' and responded with stubborn disbelief while attacking bitterly the integrity of *The Times* reporters (Cox, Shirley, and Short 1977: 28). Their inadequate response signalled a protracted and acrimonious battle between internal factions, notably the CID and the rest of the force, and externally with the press, politicians, the Home Office, and other agencies of control, but particularly the provincial police. Provincial distrust of the

Met is widespread (McClure 1980: 129; Parker 1981: 15) and a senior provincial officer told me in 1980, 'Nobody trusts the Met. In twenty-one years of service I've encountered nothing but total mistrust of the Met. I'll coordinate readily with a provincial force but not with the Met and I speak from bitter experience. I could tell you horror stories about them but, really, I wouldn't give them the time of day.'

For provincial forces are open to outside investigation whereas the Met falls uniquely under the responsibility of the Home Secretary rather than a police authority. Further, since the administrative reform of 1877 in the wake of the Meiklejohn affair, the CID was responsible for investigating *all* allegations against policemen both uniformed and detective. It was said that the CID had developed the 'special loyalties and codes of a closed and introverted society' (Cox, Shirley, and Short 1977: 37) and now it was being asked to investigate itself. The result was a predictable and blatant failure. One investigating officer was taken off the case and was replaced by Chief Superintendent Moody (who was later to be convicted himself). And Frank Williamson, a member of Her Majesty's Inspectorate and the first outsider ever to be brought in to investigate the Met, became so disgusted at running his head against a brick wall that he resigned prematurely from the service (*New Statesman* 20 May, 1977). He remarked 'I was very conscious of one fact. . . . You musn't talk about misbehaviour because half the officers would be foaming at the mouth' (*Sunday Times Magazine* 3 November, 1977). At the trial arising from *The Times'* allegations, two detectives were sentenced to six and seven years imprisonment for a number of offences involving bribes, blackmail and conspiracy.

THE DRUG SQUAD

In the following two sets of cases there was a neat contrast in styles exemplifying the distinction between combative and strategic corruption and concerning the Drug Squad and the 'Porn' Squad (officially the Obscene Publications Squad or OPS) respectively. The Drug Squad, under Detective Chief Inspector Kelaher had begun to employ somewhat unorthodox methods, having enthusiastically imported them from the United States. This brought them into conflict with some powerful people including liberal opinion makers, the Home Office, the Foreign Office, provincial forces, and, above all, Her Majesty's Customs. There were accusations of planting drugs, of granting immunity to a group of dealers in return for 'bodies' and rewarding them with part of the haul, and of actively instigating deals in the American style, sometimes with the help of the BNDD (Bureau for Narcotics and Dangerous Drugs, later the Drug Enforcement Agency, DEA). Kelaher even defended a dealer openly in court as being one of his informants. The Squad's activities brought it into conflict with Customs and there developed a 'total animosity' between the two agencies. When Kelaher's intervention for the defence in the case of a major dealer (who claimed to be working as Kelaher's informant) proved unsuccessful, and the dealer was sentenced to seven years, this destroyed his credibility and raised earnest questions about his Squad's style of work. In fact, this was a turning-point in relationships between the Yard and the outside world because, for the first time, a full external enquiry was mounted and this was manned by provincial officers from Lancashire. And another outsider, Robert Mark – the provincial policeman with a largely uniformed administrative career outside of the CID (so that many refused to accept him as a 'real' policeman, as also happened with Murphy) – was appointed Commissioner. It was said that this appointment saved the Met from demands for a full-scale, parliamentary enquiry or even a Royal Commission (Cox, Shirley, and Short 1977: 121; Mark 1978: 120).

But it seems that the Squad was primarily motivated to make arrests and did not seek profit for itself (Honeycombe 1974). Its unorthodox style, which was plainly called 'illegal' by the Home Office (Cox, Shirley, and Short 1977: 100), but which developed under conditions of near autonomy, was a good example of combative strategic corruption conducted to enhance law enforcement and to make major 'busts'. The demise of the Squad, however, was but one element in a whole series of interlocked events. The excellent chroniclers of those events, on whom I rely considerably here, spotlight three features arising from these events (ibid.: 129–30):

'First, London's detective force had by the late 1960's clearly been corrupted by almost absolute power. They had become a law unto themselves. . . . Secondly, the Drug Squad's basic reliance on a very close relationship with criminal informants lead to a dangerous system of law enforcement. London's drug dealers were effectively divided into two classes: those who operated with the blessing of the Drug Squad, and those who did not. . . . The arrogance of the Yard displayed in the Drug Squad affair did not pay off, because it forced the Government to take action against the old regime.'

One of those events was the appearance of a photograph in *The Sunday People* which showed Commander Drury, one of London's top detectives, enjoying a holiday on Cyprus with the Soho pornographer James Humphreys. The unglamorous 'Porn Squad' or OPS functioned in ideal conditions for straightforward corruption. Soho was the small red-light district of West London where the industry was concentrated, the law was a shambles, and it was easy to 'license' some premises and shut their competitors, which also provided the Squad with arrests. The arrangements were business-like; pornographers prudently took precautions against the hazards of their trade by investing in 'bent' police officers and Chief Superintendent Moody 'liked things to be done systematically. It was Moody's intention to bring a measure of organization into the corruption of Scotland Yard's Obscene Publications Squad, to put it on a business footing as it were' (*Sunday Times* 15 May, 1977).

While it was practical for both parties to regulate the trade in this way it also opened up the possibility of predatory strategic corruption employed against those not included in the arrangements. For there can be no doubt that the members of the Porn Squad were 'meat-eaters' who helped to initiate the system; large sums of money were involved, there were regular payments, and graft was graded according to rank; one pornography dealer wearing a CID tie was allowed into the basement of Holborn Police Station to view confiscated material which was then 'recycled'; and new members were initiated into the Squad with money thrust into their pockets and assurances that 'it's the easiest money you will ever get. It's safe money. You have nothing to worry about' (*Sunday Times* 21 November, 1976). Moody, the man who had moved at a critical stage into the internal enquiry following *The Times* exposé, set about refining the system of corruption with 'almost evangelical fervour' (*Sunday Times* 6 March, 1977). About this time the newspaper *The Sunday People* had put unlimited funds and time into a project on pornography and had come up, unexpectedly, with evidence of police corruption.

Mark set up a Special Squad, separate even from the new investigatory A10 branch, to investigate OPS, while he called in the

Serious Crimes Squad from outside the West End of London to raid the porn empires of Soho. With the heat on, Humphreys fled to Holland, was arrested and deported, and began to talk aided by his impeccably kept diaries. As a result, fifteen policemen including two who held the rank of commander (i.e. two of the top sixty men in the force) were tried and thirteen of them went to prison for a total of ninety-six years. At the trial the judge spoke of an 'evil conspiracy which turned the Obscene Publications Squad into a vast protection racket'. In court a pornographer said, 'I was not corrupted: I was blackmailed,' while Humphreys said that one policeman had paid his own trip to meet him in Ibiza, and added revealingly, 'He was the only policeman who ever took me out to lunch and paid the bill' (Cox, Shirley, and Short 1977: 209).

MARK'S REFORMS

Robert Mark, Commissioner from 1972 to 1977, and sometimes referred to as the 'Lone Ranger from Leicester' (Leicester being his previous appointment), set out to tackle corruption, to break the power of the CID and to establish the supremacy of the uniformed branch. To a certain extent his reforms parallel those of Murphy in New York but Mark did not have the advantage of a Knapp Commission, a Special Prosecutor, and the overt backing of a political figure like Mayor Lindsay. There can be no doubt that Mark had political backing at a distance but the reforms are largely attributable to his own implacable, determined, and even ruthless approach. He had been helped by the series of press exposures which enabled him to push on against hostility to his appointment and despite bitter feuds within the organization. In brief, Mark established a new department (A10, with eighty men on a twenty-four-hour roster with supra-departmental authority) to investigate *all* complaints against policemen, placed a uniformed man in charge of CID at the Yard, placed all divisional detectives under control of their uniformed superiors, moved a number of detectives back into uniform, rotated personnel in sensitive areas, and instituted a new policy of openness with the press (Mark 1977: 126–29).

Mark conveyed his abrasive views to representatives of the CID:

'I told them simply that they represented what had long been the most routinely corrupt organization in London, that nothing and no-one would prevent me from putting an end to it and that if necessary I would put the whole of the C.I.D. back into uniform and make a fresh start. . . . I left them in no doubt that I thought bent detectives were a cancer in society, worse even than the criminals and some of the lawyers with whom we have to deal.'

(Mark 1978: 130)

During his five years as Commissioner, almost 500 policemen left the force, many of them voluntarily in anticipation of procedures against them, and a key plank in Mark's strategy was to back up painstaking and time-consuming criminal enquiries with a determined application of the force's internal disciplinary regulations. By showing the outside world that the police could handle corruption themselves he preserved the autonomy of the police in general and Chief Constables in particular (Laurie 1973). In a sense, he *needed* the corruption cases and success in them as a catalyst for change (in the same way that Murphy did) and as a shield against outsiders' attempts to intervene in police affairs (Mark 1978).

COUNTRYMAN

But some indication of the depths and resilience of police corruption in London came with the realization that Mark's scalpel had not removed all the 'cancer'. In May 1978 a gang held up a delivery of money to the *Daily Mirror* newspaper and a security guard who intervened was shot dead: 'He was cold-bloodedly murdered as a result of a carefully organized and ruthlessly executed crime – and the accusation is that an equally organized group of policemen were involved in the circumstances surrounding his killing' (*New Statesman* 18 January, 1980: 80). The allegations which now emerged were shocking and revealed both predatory strategic corruption – as one robber complained, 'at the finish all you was doing was working for the police to give them a lion's share of what you were getting' (*The Economist* 7 August, 1982: 19–20) – and pure criminal involvement not in the fairly predictable areas, such as vice and drugs, but in violent, organized, armed robbery. The seventies had witnessed the emergence of a number of 'supergrasses' (informants on a grand scale) who 'shopped' large numbers of their colleagues in serious crime (Ball, Chester and Perrott 1979): but their accusations cut both ways in that they also implicated policemen as being involved in robberies.

As a result, 'Operation Countryman' (the bucolic name was deliberately provocative) was set up under the leadership of the

Dorset Police, and, with a staff of eighty provincial policemen working out of a building in Surrey to avoid contamination by the Met, it commenced a four-year enquiry which investigated over two hundred policemen including senior officers. The allegations involved not only Met detectives from elite groups, such as the Robbery and the Flying Squads, but also detectives from the City of London force (catering for the financial quarter of the city); and accusations arose of police helping to set up robberies, deflecting police attention away during raids, helping criminals (but framing and verballing others), and receiving pay-offs that ran 'into hundreds of thousands of pounds' (*New Statesman* 18 January, 1980: 83). It was said that a City of London detective had masterminded the *Daily Mirror* raid: 'he helped pinpoint the target: recruited an underworld "draughtsman" or detailed planner: and later sub-contracted the job out to a gang of armed robbers with whom he was already corruptly involved' (*Sunday Times* 2 December, 1979). Yet four years later Countryman had come up with only two convictions and this lead to suspicions of a cover-up within the Met (*The Observer* 4 April, 1982).

From the beginning there were rumours that Countryman was obstructed and, in a most unusual step, the ex-Chief Constable of Dorset, Hambleton, claimed on television that the investigation had been sabotaged and his team had been prevented from combing out the Yard. There were also smear campaigns against 'Countryman', its men were nicknamed 'Swedey' ('Swede' being a Met term of contempt for country coppers), and rumours circulated that one senior investigating officer was himself corrupt and his marriage was breaking down (*New Statesman* 18 January, 1980: 84). One of the detectives on Countryman complained of leaks to 'villains' from the Met, of being checked by Met officers when they were engaged in surveillance, or of a Met patrol car turning up in situations which immediately warned suspects that they were being watched (*Sunday Times* 16 September, 1979). In return, there were comments on the quality of the Countryman Enquiry, that it became swamped in unrelated information which it could not handle, and that it engaged in unprofessional conduct (McNee 1983). The then Commissioner, McNee, argues strongly that there was no general obstruction, that Hambleton involved himself in an extraordinary private war with the Director of Public Prosecutions and the Attorney General, that a higher proportion of accused Met officers were criminally convicted during his tenure than during Mark's, and that the Met would have achieved far more if they had conducted the investigation internally (McNee 1983).

McNee may be right but that is not the point. The public has to believe in the impartially of enquiries and this had become difficult in relation to the Met. In Britain it is most unusual for senior police officers to criticize one another in public and the skirmishes surrounding the relationships between Countryman, the Met, the DPP, and the Attorney General inevitably raised suspicions of cover-up and obstruction at the highest levels. Indeed, the suggestion was that the price for Countryman's continuance was to collude in covering up the friction; for example, Hambleton went to a meeting at the Yard to complain about obstruction in the Met and lack of support from the DPP but

> 'during it, he was reluctantly persuaded that the only way to keep the Countryman investigation in progress was to agree to make a joint statement with Scotland Yard denying his own earlier allegations of obstruction. Scotland Yard promptly denied any obstruction, attacked the conduct of the Countryman team and questioned the credibility of Mr. Hambleton.'
> (*The Economist* 7 August, 1982).

Yet one Chief Constable stated that corruption in the Met had become 'more institutionalized than it was' and had for some officers become 'a way of life' (*The Economist* 7 August, 1982). The incidents referred to above covered a period of thirty years (accounts of corrupt practices went back to the early fifties: Parker 1981: Read 1979: 169). And for thirteen years the Metropolitan Police was subjected to a seemingly unceasing series of investigations. Despite Mark's reforms and McNee's assurances that corruption has been substantially reduced, there is continuing concern that perhaps the 'cancer', particularly in the CID, has not been completely eradicated. But it is not possible to root out corruption in the CID, according to Cain (1984: 89), 'without tackling the fundamentally closed, self-sustaining and routinely illegal structure of everyday policing'.

Conclusion

At the beginning of this chapter I argued for a comparative and historical approach to aid in understanding police deviance. Two police scandals were selected to provide material that can be compared and contrasted with the Amsterdam experience. The lessons of New York and London provide us with illustrations of the patterns and resilience of police corruption, the circumstances under which external forces are provoked into questioning the legitimacy of police methods and into exerting pressure for change, and of the efforts of two reforming chiefs to tackle deep-rooted deviance within their organizations and to change fundamentally the way in which police work is structured.

A number of common themes emerge from the analysis of the two forces. The press played a vital role; chiefs were brought in from outside; the new men were determined, even ruthlessly so, to change their departments and enjoyed political support; they both instituted considerable organizational reforms focusing on decentralization, accountability, new measures to investigate deviance, and a diminution of autonomy for the detective branch; deviance was widespread but the most serious forms were found in detective units dealing with 'victimless' crimes and particularly in specialized squads coping with drugs; and the scandals acquired powerful external agencies pushing for stringent investigation (in London the provincial forces, the Home Office, and the Customs, and in New York the Knapp Commission and Special Prosecutor's Office). Scandals depend not only on the friends you have and the victims you make, but also on the enemies you provoke.

One might ask to what extent the determination to push the reforms was personal to Murphy and Mark, how long-lasting were the institutional changes and to what extent the deviant practices were eliminated. London suggests that thirteen years of investigation has not rid the Met of corruption, which may in fact have taken more devious and dangerous forms, while New York fits into a pattern of recurring corruption spreading over a century. In both scandals there can be no question of corruption arising solely from cosy arrangements in the victimless crimes area. Plainly, police deviance can be related to extortion, blackmail, intimidation, and violence (including murder), while it creates victims not only among criminals but also among ordinary people in no way involved in crime. And, one might add, it also creates victims among policemen.

In this chapter I have tried to portray the internal upheavals of two departments engaged in prolonged, bitter, and factionalized struggles surrounding what I take to be genuine attempts to reform the operational code of policing. The police in The Netherlands have also been subjected to considerable scrutiny since the middle-1960s and whether or not the patterns documented in New York and London were replicated during the scandal in Amsterdam will be explored in the rest of this book.

2
Amsterdam – The Wheel Comes Off

The City and its Police: 'Anything Goes'

Amsterdam is one of those cosmopolitan cities that are tolerant of a wide-range of life-styles and of forms of deviance that would be frowned upon, if not sanctioned, elsewhere. As such it is quite unlike other Dutch cities, and has to be compared with New York, San Francisco, Paris, London, and West Berlin. For generally, Dutch society has been remarked upon for its orderliness and sobriety (Goudsblom 1967; De Baena 1967) whereas Amsterdam has traditionally been the free-thinking, avant-garde, politically restless heart of The Netherlands. Compared to many other capitals it is small, with just over 700,000 inhabitants, and retains its intimacy despite being the largest city in the country. In the late sixties, it became a magnet for the beat generation who embraced it as 'the swinging city' (ten Have 1972). Indeed, in The Netherlands there was considerable cultural change at this time which ushered in progressive norms and practices in many areas of social and public life (Middendorp 1978). The crucial period for our analysis is that between the mid-sixties and mid-seventies when social life in Amsterdam was typified by the saying 'alles mag' – anything goes.

At the beginning of the sixties the Amsterdam Police was old-fashioned, poorly equipped, and decentralized. Dutch police forces tend to be small – at the time of writing there are over 140 city forces and many of these have less than one hundred men and women (Perrick 1982) – and Amsterdam, with around 3000 personnel, is by far the largest. In The Netherlands, the mayor is the civil head of the city police and he is responsible to the Ministry of Home Affairs, while the Attorney General is the judicial head of the police and is responsible for setting policy on criminal investigations and he, in turn, is answerable to the Ministry of Justice. This dual structure of control, where the police chief has two external 'bosses' and power is divided between several ministries, is typical of many European forces (Fijnaut 1979).

For the Amsterdam police, the watershed in its contemporary development undoubtedly came in 1966. Then riots in the city, surrounding the marriage of Princess Beatrix, were badly handled and the police use of violence led to intense negative press coverage (Bianchi 1975: 55). A Commission of Enquiry published a highly critical report which led to the resignations of the Chief Constable and of the Mayor (*Commissie Enschedé* 1967; van Hall, 1976). This was a trauma for the department and as a consequence there developed somewhat defensive views which are instrumental in shedding light on the corruption scandal a decade later. The senior officers became both wary of negative publicity and closely attuned to the political demands of the mayor. In practice, this meant a series of lenient policies related to prostitution, pornography, drugs, youth movements, demonstrations, squatting, and aliens. The lower ranks reacted to what they saw as opportunism and careerism from above – as evidenced, they claimed, by a chronic failure to back them up – with a nonchalant, casual style that was sometimes perceived as cheeky, indifferent, or rude by the public. During the same period there was a growing consciousness that patterns of crime were changing and the Amsterdam Department responded with centralization and specialization, bringing more power to headquarters and setting up new squads.

During this period many young people were attracted from abroad to this 'oasis of tolerance'. Other factors, moreover, including ease of travel, loosening of border control, the increasing mobility and internationalization of criminals, meant that imperceptibly criminal elements were also attracted to Amsterdam where they congregated in the inner-city. Amsterdam had allegedly become a 'sick city', the old city centre was seen as a 'square mile of misery', and the town was being called 'the Chicago of Europe' (*Elseviers Magazine* 19 February, 1977;

De Volkskrant 9 and 16 July, 1977). In terms of law enforcement, for instance, selective leniency from the authorities (i.e. following negotiations between the mayor and town council, the public prosecutor and police chief) in relation to gambling, prostitution, drugs, homosexuality, and pornography has virtually recreated the 'rookeries' of nineteenth-century London where criminals found refuge, where the police were reluctant to enter, and where a gentleman went at his own risk (personal communication A. J. Reiss, Jr., and cf. Greenwood 1876; Beames 1850).

By the mid-seventies the authorities had inadvertently created in the inner-city of Amsterdam a flourishing criminal subculture, an area of 'tolerance' for deviants, a paradigm of selective enforcement, and, in retrospect, an excellent opportunity structure for police corruption. One staple element in this complex development, and the element that has received the most media attention over the past decade, has been that of drugs and, in particular, heroin.

Fishing with Live Bait: The Changing Nature of Police Work in Amsterdam

'I'm convinced that no policeman who works with drugs is "clean". This applies to the youngest cop as well as to his highest boss. My Amsterdam period would have turned me into a junkie if I hadn't left in time.'
(Policeman writing to me after leaving Amsterdam)

Amsterdam enjoyed a flourishing 'soft' drug culture in the late 1960s, but it is the dramatic arrival of heroin in 1972 that is perceived by many as the turning-point in the criminalization of the city centre (*Vrij Nederland* 10 January, 1981). The elevation of Amsterdam to a world-centre for Chinese-controlled trafficking in 'hard' drugs evinced, not surprisingly, a profound impact on police work at all levels. First, the Amsterdam police was confronted with international, syndicated crime for the first time and found itself ill-equipped and legally hamstrung in coping with it. Second, the drug trade spawned a rash of petty crimes by addicts who needed saleable items for cash and who also presented easy arrests and easily manipulable suspects and informants. And, third, the police were exposed to the classical conditions for corruption, namely a highly lucrative illegal market supported by inelastic demand and surrounded by moral and legal ambivalence ('for sellers in illicit markets, their focal points for effective control of their market must be enforcement agents' – Manning and Redlinger 1977: 285).

Generally detective work involves a working reliance on informants and an intimate relationship with criminal subcultures (Simpson 1977: 96). The former is true everywhere – 'a detective is only as good as his snitches' holds almost universally – but in Holland the detective was traditionally more restrained and bureaucratic than his racy, hard-drinking, 'flashy' counterparts in Britain and America. Close contacts with criminals were normally frowned upon, undercover work was practically unknown, and when heroin arrived in Amsterdam the members of the Drug Squad simply *did not know what it was*. Burgeoning street-crime at one end, and violent Chinese gang-warfare at the other, provided a new spectrum of problems for the police that revealed a creaking legal machinery, an undermanned, administrative apparatus clogged with cases, and a loosely coordinated response where ill-prepared policemen developed innovative styles of work to cope with the challenge. Some of those men became 'corrupt' and their cases almost invariably revolved around illegal Chinese immigrants and the Chinese-run drug trade in the inner-city.

The heroin trade developed swiftly and the Chinese ran it although Surinamers, and occasionally Europeans, were the street dealers. Its rise can be crudely gauged by the amount confiscated – 50 grammes in 1971, 2.5 kilos in 1972, 25 kilos in 1973, 30 kilos in 1974 and 60 kilos in 1975 (and most of it was taken in Amsterdam: Erkelens and Janssen, 1979). Within a year Chinese criminals transformed Amsterdam into the major European distribution centre for the hard-drugs trade. Estimates of the numbers 'bitten by the great elephant', i.e. addicted, ranged from 7–10,000, three-quarters of whom were foreigners, and in 1976 there were 1,625 arrests (compared to 615 in 1970) for drug offences of which the vast majority involved heroin (van Straten 1977; Annual Crime Statistics, Amsterdam City Police 1977).

Here I can only give a flavour of how the Chinese presence coloured life in the inner-city. There have been Chinese in Amsterdam for over fifty years (Van Heek 1934) but their numbers increased considerably in the sixties when Dutch prosperity, lenient sentencing, and ease of access attracted them from Hong Kong, Singapore, and Taiwan. There are over 400 Chinese restaurants in Amsterdam, a community of around 20,000 Chinese, and in the middle-seventies there were an estimated 8–10,000 illegal Chinese immigrants (*De Volkskrant* 26 February, 1983; Verwey 1983). They sometimes sought the 'typical pleasures of lonely men', namely prostitutes, stupefaction (smoking opium), and gambling (Lyman 1971: 22). By agreement with the Public Prosecutor a number of illegal Chinese gambling dens were permitted to operate in the inner-city on the grounds that gambling was inseparable from Chinese culture and that concentrating the practice made it easier to supervise. These casinos became the front for the triads and for distributing drugs.

For, within the 'China-town' of the Zeedijk and the Binnenbantammerstraat, there developed a highly efficient drugs industry in the hands of secret societies which were almost impenetrable, and quite ruthless (van Straten, 1976). The modern criminal 'triads' are tightly organized with 'a strongly ritualised system of initiation ceremonies, blood promises, pass words, secret signs and poems and a strongly enforced military hierarchy of officers and other ranks' (Bresler 1981: 40; Morgan 1960; Fong 1981; Davies and Goodstadt 1975). Rivalry between Hong Kong and Singapore groups lead to violence in Amsterdam. In April 1975, Chung Mon (real name), the so-called 'godfather' of the Chinese community, was murdered by assassins from a rival group. There were gang shoot-outs, beatings, and sixteen murders around this period in connection with gang rivalry and the drug trade. Policemen became aware that the triads were controlling the drug business not only in the Far East but also in Amsterdam. Yen Muk Chang (real name, nicknamed 'Mao'), who was murdered in April 1976, was a leading member of the '14K' triad (he had the rank of a '486' or 'Sjan Tsjoe' – Bresler 1981: 160) and it was said that he had robbed a rival group of two and a half million guilders' worth of heroin.

Clearly, the Chinese criminals were quite unlike the relatively unorganized and largely non-violent native criminals to whom most policemen were accustomed. For Dutch policemen the Chinese community was hermetically sealed because of language and ethnic identity, the Chinese criminals were highly organized, and some of the leaders in the Chinese community were powerful personalities who were dispensers of munificent hospitality and patronage, and commanded considerable allegiance (when Chung Mon was buried, over sixty cars took part in the cortege). All of this was new and the police had to adapt to this new situation. They had to do so with inadequate resources, with no conspiracy laws, with entrapment expressly forbidden, with no tradition of undercover work, with no Chinese ethnics among their personnel, and with no pattern of 'substantial buying' as routinely practised by the DEA elsewhere (*Time Magazine* 29 November, 1976).

More so than in other areas of crime, these factors made police reliance on informants almost total. Of the work of the detective in this area Manning (1980: 3) wrote, 'he is reduced to operating in microarenas of interaction characterized by duplicity, lying, fraud, misrepresentation and extortion.' In addition, Marx (1974: 422) notes generally that police are warned to be careful, 'Because the informant may lie, exaggerate, misperceive, improperly evaluate, misunderstand his relationship with police, entrap, or be a double agent'.

At Scotland Yard it was said that informants were treated with more consideration than some policemen's wives (Honeycombe 1974: 102) yet, while the ability to develop informants is a 'vital investigatory skill', it is clear that not all policemen are equally astute at this craft (Wilson 1978: 35). There may be wide divergences between detectives in their acumen at recruiting and running informants.

The deception and duplicity inherent in criminality and certain areas of police work (Schoeman 1981; Marx 1981b) are magnified in these curious relationships between policemen and informers that run the gamut of exploitation, dependency, mutual advantage, paternalism, and even friendship. In some cases the real coin of reciprocation is immunity from prosecution, freedom to continue in crime, and protection from other police personnel (Ericson 1981: 125; while Leuci assures his 'stool' – 'I'll even get you off a homicide': Daley 1979: 244). And, predictably, in the world of narcotics the medium of exchange is drugs. Both elements, guaranteeing immunity and providing drugs, are illegal for policemen yet most 'narcs' would see them as essential and justified mechanisms for achieving results (Skolnick 1975; Manning 1980).

Another technique for achieving this aim is infiltration and undercover work. But this style of operation was not normally employed in The Netherlands while entrapment is specifically forbidden. However, a significant feature of the drug business is that it is international and efforts to cope with it have to be international. The Americans appreciated this early on and the DEA was to be found all over the world in the seventies and not least in Europe. It brought to Holland undercover methods and substantial buying. The process by which this was accomplished is surrounded in mystery but apparently DEA agents would set up deals 'with a suitcase full of dollars', inform the police, and then disappear at the time of the bust. Police reports would be innocuously cast in terms of 'acting on anonymous information' and 'in the confusion the purchasers made good their escape' while the

Justice Department would neglect to follow up on who got away. A policeman respondent confirmed this and told me 'I know because I've been there when it happened. I've put it down on paper for the bosses. I've seen it all.' Eventually the Amsterdam police also became involved in deals – a senior officer explained that there was a standing arrangement that allowed him to withdraw up to half a million guilders (then c. £100,000 or $200,000) at a certain bank to use as 'bait' in transactions. Normally this would have to be conducted in cooperation with the Justice Department and under Dutch law the police cannot initiate the arrangements (i.e., they must pose as buyers not sellers and must buy into a deal which has first been set rolling by criminals). A detective in the Drugs Squad was said to have had 'sleepless nights and sweaty palms' about the 'dicey' reports he had to write to cover certain operations and was relieved when he was transferred because in Dutch law the DEA men were as guilty as anyone else involved in a deal (*Haagse Post, Heroin Special* 14 May, 1977). A number of cases were thrown out of court at this time because of police secrecy on their methods which left the suggestion of entrapment, *agents provocateurs*, and informants dealing on behalf of the police (*Vrij Nederland* 3 February, 1977; *De Volkskrant* 4 November, 1978, 24 January, 1979, 3 February, 1979, 22 February, 1979; *De Telegraaf* 17 March, 1979). However, the High Court in Amsterdam did eventually accept DEA agents working as middlemen in deals and posing as buyers. The cloudy evidence on this development suggests that native police methods were altered by the intervention of the DEA, that in the mid-seventies there were some extremely curious games being played within the drug scene in which foreign agents were involved, and that this meant substantially bending and testing Dutch legal rules. It also introduced a further element of cloak-and-dagger mystique into the Amsterdam situation.

Yet, apart from the occasional spectacular bust, most detectives at all levels were engaged in the mundane, routine processing of low-level dealers and users. Generally detective work has high status among policemen (Sorrentino 1980: 47) but most accounts of actual detective work emphasize paperwork, tedium, long hours, high case loads, and that it is not so much exciting as 'downright boring' (Goldstein 1977: 55). The secrecy surrounding the highly personal control of information, jealousy, rivalry, envy, and fear of 'poaching' (having a case taken off one by another detective and losing the kudos for it) contrast with the more solidaristic world of the patrol group (Wycoff 1981). This mode of operation is well illustrated in Manning's (1980: 18) analysis of narcotics detectives where the reality 'is mostly boring, unsystematic, catch as catch can, and focused on obtaining immediate rewards of arrest and charge and hassling low-level users of non-narcotic drugs, primarily marijuana'.

The nature of drugs enforcement seems to accentuate some of the classic features of detective work and it fundamentally altered police work in New York, London, and Amsterdam. In Amsterdam by the middle seventies there was a booming Chinese-run drug trade, thousands of users, a great deal of drug-related street crime, and increasing concern in the wider society about the drugs problem ('Amsterdam is becoming a mad-house for Europe' said one social worker: *De Volkskrant*, 3 August 1974; Cohen 1976). The police considered themselves undermanned, ill-equipped, legally hamstrung, and inundated with work. One detective told me that The Netherlands was 'fifty years behind the times' in terms of drug enforcement (Punch 1976: 66). The Chinese triads, the drug business, and the DEA all assisted in changing the nature and style of police work in Amsterdam. Some illegal Chinese immigrants and dealers were well-off, carried large sums of money and/or drugs on them, and were determined to avoid incarceration (although it was extremely rare for them to be violent towards the police). In retrospect, it is easy to see a corruptive environment developing as Chinese criminals adopted tactics that had proved successful with officials elsewhere (Lee 1977). Probably some Chinese criminals set out deliberately to compromise policemen. This brings us to a world replete with lies, doublethink, duplicity, and deception that is far from easy to unravel. What is clear is that at the same time some Amsterdam policemen were beginning the risky habit of fishing with live bait by which I mean using a low-level suspect to help ensare a bigger 'fish': 'sometimes', a senior detective told me, 'you have to let out a sprat to catch a cod'.

The Unfolding of the Amsterdam Scandal

'You can really trust the Amsterdam Police. For instance, if you buy your horse from Constable "Kroes", then you can be sure that it's good stuff and the right weight.'
(Underworld figure, *Haagse Post*, 4 November, 1978)

When the corruption cases within the Amsterdam Police became public knowledge they excited intense press coverage. This sort of police corruption was unprecedented in The Netherlands; my respondents could only recall a case in the 1940s when several policemen were involved in the black market, while in the early 1960s three men in the Licensing Department were disciplined for accepting money. Now for four years corruption was scarcely ever out of the headlines. The scandal unfolded relatively slowly and the issues were only partially apparent to many people as successive revelations peeled away yet another layer of the affair. In retrospect, it is relatively easy for us to see what happens when the 'wheel comes off' (or as Americans would put it more colourfully, 'when the shit hits the fan') but one should bear in mind that the situation was often far from clear to people at the time as facts and issues emerged piecemeal. Initially, the matter was brought to a head in 1976 when an internal investigation into dubious practices by plainclothesmen (hereafter the PCS or Plain Clothes Squad) in the Warmoesstraat Station was launched by two active young officers acting on complaints from underworld figures in the inner city. It is highly likely that, without the determined action of these men, the cases would have been swept under the carpet.

Only *after* this enquiry (Enquiry 1) had been transferred to Police Headquarters did news of it leak out, so that, unlike London and New York, the press could not claim credit for actually sparking off the enquiry. In terms of public presentation via the media the affair developed in four main phases. These phases reflected segments of the investigation which evolved into five separate component parts. Enquiry 1 began as an informal, district-level examination and looked at incidents in the inner city involving a number of low-level, but strategically placed, policemen; when this was transferred to Headquarters it became a formal investigation into possible corruption (Enquiry 2). This failed to produce significant convictions and led to an internal disciplinary case against the men involved in Enquiry 2 (Enquiry 3); lines of enquiry led subsequently to scrutinizing the workings of the Drug Squad at Headquarters (Enquiry 4) and a spin-off of this was that suspicion was raised concerning a certain senior officer (Enquiry 5, which was at first informal and secret but was later formalized with external assistance). By dividing the scandal into four phases, with in effect five separate but related investigations, I am imposing some order on events which, in practice, tended to run into each other and at the time were not always clear as components to the participants. The investigative procedures followed in Amsterdam are dealt with below in Chapter Five.

ORIGINS: SUMMER 1976 TO EARLY 1977

An internal disciplinary investigation in the Warmoesstraat Station focused on close contacts between members of the PCS and certain bars with hostesses in the red-light district (Enquiry 1). A number of men were put back into uniform or transferred out of the area. The enquiries also led to the arrest of two policemen from the district's Licensing Department in relation to payments from people involved in vice. One of these men died of an heart-attack following interrogation by State Detectives (centrally appointed detectives who investigate crimes by officials), although it was widely rumoured to have been a case of suicide. When it became clear that the offences might be criminal the officers in the Warmoesstraat were formally obliged to tell Headquarters, and this in turn led to the Chief Constable informing the Mayor and, as in most serious cases involving policemen, to the calling in of the State Detectives to carry out an external investigation (Enquiry 2). An article 'Is the Amsterdam Police Corrupt?' in the weekly magazine *Haagse Post* (9 October, 1976) raised the issue of corruption for the first time but did not arouse much attention.

What really caught the limelight in a sensational fashion, and brought the affair to a wide public, was the interview with an ex-policeman, 'Jac. Zijlstra', in the weekly magazine *Nieuwe Revue* ('Police Succumb to Money', 28 January, 1977). 'Zijlstra' had been something of an *enfant terrible* in the Warmoesstraat, truculent towards sergeants and aggressive towards suspects, and had built up close connections with certain dubious elements in the Chinese community. This invited the disapproval of his superiors and he was moved to another district. In disgust he resigned and in order to finance a move abroad sold his story to the press. Described as the 'Serpico of the Low Countries' (*sic*) he decided to blow the whistle on his former colleagues. For really the first time, illicit practices linking policemen and criminals were explicitly spelled out and were given seemingly irrefutable authenticity by the ex-policeman's words. Zijlstra went on to make the following accusations against his former colleagues. Two men from the PCS visited a club in the Rembrandtsplein where they used the services of two prostitutes who had each been paid 300 guilders by the owner of a Chinese gambling-house. Heroin was used to pay informants, money was stolen from suspects and from drunks, goods were stolen at the scene of burglaries on the understanding that the insurance would pay for it anyway, and Chinese criminals were warned about forthcoming raids. He mentioned that a colleague arrested a dealer with a 'bag' on him (an ounce or 28 grammes of heroin), that this was not reported in the station-diary, and that the heroin was sold to an informant. It was also alleged that Chung Mon had sent copious fruit-baskets, containing warm turkey and envelopes with 2000–3000 guilders in them, to several policemen and also to a number of Public Prosecutors. In essence, these accusations were to be reiterated time and again throughout the affair and formed the core of the cases. *Nieuwe Revue* had dramatically put corruption in the public eye. This article generated an enormous amount of copy about corruption which culminated in the Spring of 1977 with the publicity surrounding the arrest of eight policemen (Enquiry 2).

ARRESTS: SPRING 1977

In the second phase, virtually every daily paper and weekly magazine turned their attention to the issue of corruption within the Amsterdam Police. The *Haagse Post* had the advantage that the journalist Ton van Dijk had moved from *Nieuwe Revue* to them and had brought his tapes of the interview with Zijlstra along with him (30 April, 1977). He particularly tried to show that the publicized cases were only the tip of an iceberg. Van Dijk claimed that an anonymous policeman had told him that Zijlstra had only mentioned the small fry and had failed to name crucial figures in the 'factory' (i.e. police headquarters). Then, in a rather insinuating style, he tried to implicate members of the Vice Squad, the head of the Uniformed Branch, and the head of the Central Detective Branch in a range of dubious practices. He detailed allegations of policemen dealing in drugs, of planting drugs on suspects, of possessing drugs and illegal weapons, and of a detective who borrowed the Mercedes of a Chinese criminal for a trip to Antwerp which was said to have been used for a heroin transaction.

In April 1977 eight policemen were arrested – two detectives concerned with Chinese criminals, two detectives from the Aliens Police concerned with controlling illegal immigrants in the Chinese community, and four plainclothesmen involved in the red-light area where street-dealing and Chinese gambling dens were concentrated. None of them were senior officers (all were in the rank of constable or detective constable). Widespread negative publicity against the Amsterdam police led to a massive national demonstration of policemen in support of their colleagues in Amsterdam. Following a critical television programme on police deviance, patrolmen in the Warmoesstraat Station in the centre of Amsterdam refused to go out on patrol. Following the arrests a good deal of inside information was leaked to the press. Some policemen under suspicion clearly felt that they were being set up as scapegoats and consciously used the press as a means of keeping the department's role in the public eye. The internal struggle between investigators and investigated was thus played out in the papers and helps to explain why journalists were so well informed. Because members of the central detective branches often have good contacts with reporters from *De Telegraaf* (a conservative daily paper), there was a special degree of sympathy from that paper for the two detectives known as the 'Chinese experts' whom, it was claimed, the Chinese wanted out of the way ('Policemen Nobbled by Opposition', 30 April, 1977). The arrests took place in April 1977. Clearly this was big news ('Scandal Within Amsterdam Police Grows: Most Important Chinese Experts Arrested', 26 April, 1977) and within days the grounds of the arrests were being bandied about, ('Revealing Facts in Corruption Scandal: Policemen Were On Chinese "Payroll"', 26 April, 1977). The arrest of this many policemen on such serious charges was without precedent in The Netherlands. The police investigation proved to be a long drawn-out affair and the suspects were soon released after their arrests pending trial, while later the criminal cases against the two 'Chinese experts' were dropped for lack of evidence.

PRE-TRIAL AND THE TRIAL: SPRING 1977 – SUMMER 1978

The third phase was characterized by an initial falling off of interest following the spectacular news of the arrests. Some of the suspects, hoping to influence their cases, began to give extensive interviews and to leak documents (rules of *sub judice* effectively do not exist in The Netherlands). So much was leaked that the trial came almost as an anti-climax although, inevitably, it was widely covered. When the cases came to court in May 1978, roughly one year after the arrests, two weeklies had managed to get their hands on the investigation's 350-page dossier (leaked via a defence lawyer and sold by one of the suspects to a journalist), which named around thirty policemen and contained statements of witnesses, and they published extensive extracts from these. Although these were more vivid and authentic than previous leaks they did not in essence add much more to the pre-trial revelations (*Haagse Post* and *Vrij Nederland* 13 May, 1978).

Some of the key elements of the cases – Chinese pay-days, lucky money, fruit-baskets, and a cash-book recording payments to the police – emerged in this phase and entered Amsterdam folk-lore. 'Freddy' Li Hun Fat of the 'Wah Yong' gambling house on the Geldersekade emerged as a crucial character in the affair. He had been a disciple of Chung Mon and, after his death, took up on his own account. Freddy was on good terms with the police; he had bought his red Mercedes with the assistance of a detective; the cash-book in Chinese of his 'Club Number One' recorded payments of 400–600 guilders a time to the police; he sent bulging fruit-baskets to policemen at New Year; he paid sums of 100–200 guilders to policemen on the 2nd and 16th of the month which were 'pay-days' for share holders in his gambling house; Chinese who won at the gambling-table distributed 'lucky-money' to people in the vicinity and some policemen used this money to gamble; one of the police suspects (known to the Chinese as 'Lo So Tsai' or 'Little Mouse') was said to have regularly taken lucky-money worth 25–50 guilders from Freddy, which he then placed on the gambling-table, and he had often left with over 200 guilders in winnings.

The Public Prosecutor launched a strong plea for stiff sentences at the trial ('No Pardon for "Corrupt" Policemen', *De Telegraaf* 1 June, 1978) which would have meant the automatic sacking of all six policemen from the department. But the judges were lenient, imposed mild sentences, and suggested that an internal disciplinary investigation be mounted as soon as possible (*De Volkskrant* 15 June, 1978). Of the six men who appeared on trial one was set free and five were fined on the grounds of accepting gifts and small amounts of money. For many years the informal rule was that if judges did not pass a prison sentence then a policeman who had been fined or given a mild suspended prison sentence could expect not to be sacked from his department (*De Telegraaf* 28 February, 1984; interview with defence lawyer who had represented policemen for some thirty years). In effect the court forced the Chief Constable to mount an internal enquiry in terms of departmental discipline (Enquiry 3). Suddenly, the attention switched away from fruit-baskets, lucky money, and the ritual of the court-room towards the internal functioning of the Amsterdam Police.

ENQUIRY SPREADS TO HEADQUARTERS: AUTUMN 1970–1980

In anticipation of this one article endeavoured to sum up the lessons. This was from the conservative weekly, *Elseviers Magazine,* which generally likes to paint a sombre picture of decaying Amsterdam. It commented critically on the vacillating judicial policies in relation to the gambling-houses, on superiors who let subordinates sink or swim, and on the faulty policy of the city council. The theme, which came to dominate the fourth phase, of looking for scapegoats and of distributing blame (if possible, high up the hierarchy) was clearly spelt out ('The Lessons of the Amsterdam "Police Corruption Case"', *Elseviers Magazine* 27 May, 1978):

> 'It is obvious that in the so-called Amsterdam "police corruption scandal" it hasn't been the highest trees which have been ruffled by the wind. Rather it was the small bushes. They were left in the lurch by their superiors, were suffocated in a mass of work, and continually had to reach compromises without the benefit of an elementary handbook or even of simple instructions.'

If the first three phases tended to be dominated by the errant members of the PCS in the Warmoesstraat, and their contacts with suspects, dealers, and Chinese underworld figures, then the fourth phase saw a shift in emphasis to headquarters, to internal rivalries and personal tensions, and particularly to the functioning of the Drug Squad (Enquiry 4). Rather than detailing with relish the deviant antics of a number of low-level policemen, the press now turned its attention full square on the internal functioning of the department, and especially on the methods used by the Drug Squad in combating crime. The revelations surrounding this investigation brought an even more acrimonious level to the affair and raised the possibility of sophisticated, 'strategic', corruption involving senior officers.

POSTSCRIPT: THE LABELLING OF THE AMSTERDAM POLICE

In early 1979 the Chief Constable shuffled his senior officers with a series of transfers and some of the moves were interpreted as sanctions against those on whom suspicion had fallen (either of involvement in dubious practices, or of failure to do anything energetically about the practices, or of too close associations with the discredited Litjen's faction). One officer, for example, who was moved died of a heart-attack (but it was rumoured that he shot himself with his service-pistol). One of the top detectives, Commissioner Litjens, was moved to a district station, which was, in effect, a severe demotion. The two detectives (the 'Chinese experts') who were suspended for two years and who awaited the result of a disciplinary enquiry gave extensive interviews to the press suggesting that their bosses were puppets of the DEA (the American 'Drug Enforcement Agency') and that the bosses themselves routinely employed questionable practices. The Mayor, as official head of the police, refused to sack the two men and they were reinstated in administrative functions (March 1979). Earlier in 1978 a number of serious accusations had been levelled at the Drug Squad by a dealer-informant in a court case (Enquiry 4) and a secret internal enquiry was started which paid attention to Commissioner Litjens (Enquiry 5). A clique of young middle-ranking officers helped to push the Chief Constable in this direction. Of the remaining six suspects two were declared medically unfit for duty and retired on health grounds, and four were reinstated and returned to work (two on uniform duty and two in low-level administrative positions but with a suspended dismissal hanging over their heads for three years). The daily newspaper *De Telegraaf* claimed a crisis of confidence in the leadership of the Chief Constable and he appeared on television to deny this. Some left-wing councillors demanded a debate on police corruption in the Amsterdam city council but this did not materialize. Public interest in the cases began to fade. In 1980 the Chief Constable retired and was replaced by a managerially oriented man from outside the Amsterdam force. It was finally announced that no further action would be taken against Commissioner Litjens who was said to have been guilty merely of 'errors of judgement' rather than of any criminal offence. The scandal was to all intents and purposes dead.

Although the press had not originated the affair they managed to keep it bubbling over a period of four years. Indeed, police corruption had become a household word. Although there was no 'investigative' journalism of the sort that might have brought new evidence to light or generated new cases the media did pull out all the stops to keep interest in the cases active and one technique of doing this was to swoop on any morsel representing police deviance. The media presentation was dominated by printed journalism with the conservative press (the daily paper *De Telegraaf* and the weekly *Elseviers Magazine*) and the rather sensationalist 'glossy' weeklies (*Nieuwe Revue, Accent* and *Extra*, which were sometimes equalled by the normally more reputable *Haagse Post*) in the vanguard; the press campaign managed to combine an attack on authority, for being too weak, with demands for bolstering it (Reisman 1979: 103) and was itself part of a rising groundswell of criticism surrounding the 'laxity' of law enforcement in Amsterdam and The Netherlands.

Thus throughout the period of the corruption investigation, and ever since, the Amsterdam Police continued to attract criticism which served to reinforce the force's negative image. For example a constable sexually molested a Surinamese prostitute, another policeman fraudently obtained a confiscated car, a patrolman was convicted and dismissed the force for stealing from a suspect during a search inside the station, and it was revealed that the 'godfather' of the Amsterdam underworld, 'Black Henkie Boersma', was sponsoring the police auto rally (*De Telegraaf* 16 April, 1977). A 'lonely' young constable was sentenced for forcing over thirty prostitutes to have sexual relationships with him as an alternative to prosecution (*De Volkskrant* 24 May, 1978). A particularly serious case emerged in District South when two detectives were arrested and subsequently jailed because they had advised criminals on suitable houses to break into and then shared in the proceeds including reward money from insurance companies for the recovery of stolen property. They were also accused of supplying a firearm to a criminal and of manipulating evidence. This was undeniably corrupt and was reflected in the relatively serious sentences of two years for one and six months for the other man (*De Volkskrant* 22 January, 1980). Since then there have been cases involving the theft of confiscated clothing (leading to the sacking of five detectives), the stripping of parts from confiscated cars, the disappearance of 150,000 guilders from the safe in headquarters, a policeman who helped to burgle a flat, and articles detailing how policemen 'cadge' (*dalven*, equivalent to the American terms 'mooching' and 'chiselling' and the British 'mumping') particularly by inviting businesses to contribute to their Christmas parcels and bingo (*De Telegraaf* 28 February, 1984). Indeed, the publicity surrounding deviant behaviour (in Dutch, *norm afwijkend gedrag*, or *n.a.g.*) has led to the neologism in police circles of *naggen* (a verb usually meaning using one's police position for material advantage). And, as we shall see later, Commissioner Litjens continued to attract publicity.

The unfolding of the corruption scandal, and the attendant press campaign which has continued to the present, confirmed the deviant label attributed to the Amsterdam Police since the late 1960s. Finally, in the period under consideration serious questions had been raised about the quality of police work in Amsterdam, about the laxity of control over the lower ranks, and about weaknesses in the senior leadership of the department.

Conclusion: Change and the Amsterdam Police

During the decade 1965–75 the Amsterdam Police was exposed to change unprecedented in peace-time. The corruption scandal heightened demands for change, demands that coincidentally found strong support in the widely read and influential government-sponsored report 'A Changing Police' (POS 1977; Broer and van der Vijver 1982), which etched a progressive blueprint for the future development of the Dutch Police, and accelerated the introduction of an ambitious organizational change programme *Kreapol* (that for a number of reasons achieved little – Punch 1981b). A new Chief Constable was appointed in 1980 and has strongly emphasized integrity programmes, organizational change, and the tackling of deviant behaviour (*De Volkskrant* 3 January, 1984). In the early part of this period Amsterdam was characterized by a culture of tolerance, both socially and in terms of law-enforcement, while the department faced a rising workload, a continued manpower shortage, a rapid turnover of personnel (with considerable loss of experienced police to smaller towns), falling clear-up rates for crimes, and changes in the nature of crime and the style of criminals. Criticism, defensiveness, and constant proposals for change have been the hallmarks of the Amsterdam Police since the mid-1960s and this has induced frustration and disillusion among some policemen ('Police See Task as Hopeless', *Elseviers Magazine* 18 July, 1981).

From the middle 1970s there was a moral panic surrounding the consequences of the drugs–aliens–crime connection which has continued unabated to the present and which initially accentuated the futility of the battle, the hopeless weakness of the police, and the laxity of legal provision. There is an enormous press output on this subject, some of it deliberately generated by the police as a lobby for more resources (Angenent and Steensma 1977; van der Wolk 1977; *De Volkskrant*, 23 April 1982). The message even reached abroad, 'Amsterdam has long been a mecca for addicts and dealers because of The Netherlands wrist-tapping drug laws. But the mounting flow of "horse" though the city has become a narc's nightmare.' The chief of Amsterdam's criminal investigations division commented, 'It's raining heroin in The Netherlands' (*Time Magazine* 29 November, 1976). Two significant measures grew out of this press campaign. First, in November 1976 the penalties contained in the Drug Law were stiffened, with the maximum sentence for possession of hard drugs increasing from four years to twelve years in prison, while in Autumn 1976 the Amsterdam Police received reinforcements from the Marechaussee (military police responsible for border control) in order to commence stricter enforcement of the regulations controlling entry and residence of aliens. Both developments were aimed principally, but not exclusively, at the Chinese criminal community in the centre of Amsterdam (and, in turn, had consequences for the corruption investigation).

Between 1976–80 press interest in the Amsterdam Police was dominated by a corruption scandal which initially raised serious charges against a number of policemen but which failed to produce either convictions for corruption or significant institutional change. Most forms of police deviance were at issue but some evidence pointed to straightforward, predatory, and combative types of corruption as well as perversion of justice. The chief was not replaced but retired as planned, there were no major organizational changes in terms of how police work was conducted and how investigating deviance was carried out; the investigation ran into problems in gaining evidence, confessions, and convictions; no heads rolled, no one was sacked, and no senior officers were prosecuted; and despite a prolonged press campaign there was no really sustained political pressure in the form of a parliamentary (or even town council) debate, an external commission of enquiry, intervention by the Ministers of Justice or Home Affairs, or a moral crusader determined personally and dramatically to scourge the department. There emerged no sustained groundswell of moral indignation with the impact to impose reforms to the extent that occurred in New York and London. In effect, Amsterdam represents a failed scandal although the legacy of 1976–80 has undoubtedly assisted the new chief in his ambitious plans for change.

The consequences of the rapid succession of changes in the social and criminal environment of the Amsterdam Police was highlighted by the corruption scandal which revealed that the style of police work had changed considerably. A wide discrepancy had developed between formal legal provision and enforcement on the street. Such periods of change represent heightened anxiety for traditionalists but they also open up considerable opportunities for those prepared to adjust and to innovate (Reisman 1979: 36). In terms of coping with the new subculture of drugs, it became essential for success that policemen looked the part, talked the argot, recruited good informants, and adopted the style of the streets (Wilson 1978: 48). But not everyone was equally equipped to adjust to the changes that had fundamentally altered the nature and style of practical policing in the inner city.

3
Perspectives of Lower and Senior Ranks

To the outsider the police organization conveys the image of a disciplined bureaucracy infused with the paraphernalia and practices of military institutions. Ostensibly rules abound, leaders are visible, control is explicit, and discipline is potentially harsh. Yet a great deal of evidence exists that policemen can evade control, create autonomy, and undermine supervision (Rubinstein 1973). This should not surprise us in that many studies of organizational life document disharmony, conflicts between groups in the hierarchy, and employee attempts to create initiative in the face of subordination (Watson 1980). However, there may be features of policing that accentuate these characteristics. For example, police employ secret, covert, and deceptive forms of behaviour in order to combat criminal organizations but these patterns may also serve to frustrate internal control (Reiss 1983). Furthermore, one can perceive organizations as arenas where some groups try to impose control while others accept, resist, or deflect it (Salaman 1979). In Amsterdam, for instance, the research station was characterized by a fluid situation where leadership was lax, supervision was weak, control was almost non-existent, and rivalry was rampant. An attempt to reimpose control led to media exposure, scandal, investigation, resistance from below, and considerable internal upheaval. This analysis illustrates the difficulty for senior officers in regaining and exerting control and the acute internal problems that a scandal may foster. For, what began as an attempt to reassert control and to affix blame, erupted into a long and bitter conflict of the sort that afflicts the relationships between bosses and workers in other types of work organization (Gouldner 1965) and which revolve around varying and conflicting interpretations on the legitimacy of authority and control. In the parlance of the Warmoesstraat, 'upstairs' (the officers) decided to get a grip on 'downstairs' (the lower ranks) and the result was four years of turmoil.

Gold, Shit, and Fruit-Baskets: Detective Work and the Rival Groups

'You approach every incident with the view that the person present has a bag of gold in one hand and a bucket of shit in the other. The good copper is the man who can get the gold without landing himself in the shit.'

(Chatterton 1975: 394)

THE INDULGENCY PATTERN

Many Dutch policemen that I have spoken to over the years from outside the city hold a strong negative stereotype of the Amsterdam Police and consider the police there to be slack, ill-disciplined, and even delinquent. Certainly, when I arrived in 1974 to commence my research I was struck by the casual, relaxed, uncoordinated way in which work was carried out. Here I was, inside the entrails of the state apparatus, and, instead of a slickly oiled repressive machine peopled by keenly motivated enforcers, I was confronted by a world of languid coffee-breaks, laborious two-fingered typing, incessant card-playing, sloppy discipline, and an off-hand approach to much of the work. Long-haired constables would arrive in civilian clothes, would go out late and come back early on patrol, would eat and drink behind the counter in view of the public, while a sergeant might be watching football on a portable TV in between attending to 'customers' at the front desk. There was no roll-call and little evidence of overt discipline. Indeed, the predominant style of control at the time of the research could be typified as exemplifying a pronounced indulgency pattern (Gouldner 1954); the catchphrase was 'sort it out for yourself'. I encountered a situation where the senior officers generally worked office-hours on weekdays only and were largely desk-bound. Daily patrol work was organized and run by the sergeants who also rarely ventured out on the streets. (One informant assured me that with the help of a friendly prostitute he was able to put a chair on a table and peep through a skylight at a sergeant in the next room embracing a prostitute; if true, one assumes this was not likely to promote discipline in the station.) The adjutants, in effect the senior NCOs (i.e. noncommissioned officers), had been reduced to filling in duty and vacation rosters and had lost their supervisory function. Because of the enormous pressure of work the detectives were virtually chained to their typewriters and rarely got out in the area (one of them bemoaned his predicament, 'It's becoming pretty well impossible to stay in touch with your patch and with your informants. You just sit here like a sort of computer – you stick the paper in at one end and it comes out at the other end').

There was a laissez-faire style of leadership in the district which led to 'hobbyism' where individuals or groups developed their own specialisms to the detriment of the general police task. Some policemen's lives were dominated by controlling lorries, others were obsessed with stopping motorbikes, while others were oriented only to youth gangs. In particular 'heroin fever', as one sergeant called it, had hit the station and many arrests were on suspicion of possessing drugs. Some uniformed policemen were fixated on junkies and black dealers, the PCS was almost exclusively concerned with drug offences and tried to keep the uniformed men out of certain clubs and youth hostels, the Drug Squad (which operated out of Headquarters) was only interested in large deals and tried to keep the PCS out of the Chinese gambling houses, and seemingly everyone was dependent on the two detectives who specialized in Chinese affairs. (These detectives worked for the central CID, i.e. the Criminal *Intelligence* Department, but were used exclusively for Chinese cases.) What this meant, in effect, was that at one and the same time law enforcement in the inner-city was being conducted by a number of virtually autonomous groups who more often than not did not cooperate with each other and each of which had its own private information system (cf. Bittner 1970: 64). Uniformed policemen and detectives from the Warmoesstraat, the PCS, the Aliens Police, the Vice Squad, the Licensing Officials, the two 'Chinese experts', and different factions of the central detective squads were all cultivating their own informants and chasing a 'good pinch'. This picture is important because it reveals a disjointed and largely uncontrolled situation where the relationships with criminals could easily flourish without adequate supervision.

And, furthermore, it indicates that here the police organization just did not function like a classical bureaucracy with a high degree of coordination (Clark and Sykes 1974: 414). Rather the organizational reality for the members was that their world was more like a series of semi-autonomous fiefs, run either by spiritual (if not physical) absentees or else by feudal potentates, who often used nepotism to promote their favourites, where people might conceal information rather than share it, and where policemen were more likely to compete rather than cooperate with one another (Kanter 1977: 181; Crozier 1973: 57). There had also developed a detective and, to a lesser extent, a patrolman style which consisted of a 'Starsky and Hutch' or 'cowboy' syndrome, composed of flashing one's gun (shoulder and ankle holsters were particularly in fashion while pistols were conspicuously clipped on the belt while in the office), of involvement in overtly masculine sports (rally driving, parachute jumping, and, in particular, martial arts), and of chewing a tooth-pick ruminatively as if engaged on the case of the century.

The emergence of the indulgency pattern is an indication that not only was the task structure of police work changing but also the style in which it was conducted had altered. This was frequently contrasted with the strict discipline of the 'good old days' (cf. Skolnick 1975: 265; Ball, Chester, and Perrott 1979: 68). The pattern was manifested in several ways such as casual dress, carrying unauthorized weapons, joking relationships with supervisors, drinking before and after duty (and for detectives while on duty), relationships with prostitutes, flouting of rules and regulations, deals with informants, and an anti-officer feeling. During the investigation it emerged that since the early 1970s a number of incidents had indicated that dubious patterns were developing particularly in terms of involvement with the criminal subculture (such as a warning in 1973 about policemen on duty driving out to Zandvoort on the coast with prostitutes) and that several of the later suspects were implicated and even warned but that no effective action was taken.

There were different adjustments to work, however, and rather than seeing behaviour as the fixed quality of individuals I prefer the position that people had different priorities at different times and in different contexts (Daniel 1973). Not everyone displayed the culture of the cowboys but few condemned it partly because groups may accept a degree of slacking and incompetence (Goode 1967) but partly because policemen tended to admire the deviants. The almost universal model of the good detective is, stereotypically, someone who is witty, good at banter and repartee, a ladies' man, someone who can hold his drink, and an almost impudent bender of rules. Some groups reduce roles to a dichotomy between mugs and manipulators (in Sicily there is approval for the *furbi* or cunning ones preying on the *fessi* or mugs – Smart 1983: 129), and the manipulator is legitimately expected to be something of a bluffer, a showman, and a conman (e.g. the view of Peron as a folk hero precisely because he was a *chanta* or confidence trickster of genius, admired for his blatant but dramatic effrontery – Cox 1983: 19). Policemen have also been noted for this reductionism (Harris 1973) and a result of this stereotyping can be that the deviant policeman, in flouting authority while revelling in the stigmata of dirty work, becomes something of a hero surrounded by myth. There was, however, an element of risk for the proponents of the new style as they were conspicuous and there was the possibility that they would go too far, making control unavoidable; or as one respondent colourfully put it, 'Well, what do they expect? I mean if you're lying naked between the legs of a tart, with a free packet of fags in one hand, with a buckshee bowl of fried rice in the other, and with your warrant card sticking out of your arse, then you're asking for trouble, aren't you?'

In Roy's (1960: 156) seminal work on how men structure their work situation to create amusement and to break up the monotony of time he spoke of workers in a factory 'clinging to the remnants of joy in work'. In contrast, I had the feeling in Amsterdam that some of the policemen were not just clinging to joy: they were having the time of their lives. The members of the repressive state apparatus were all doing their own thing.

THE PLAIN CLOTHES SQUAD (PCS)

In order to enter the everyday reality of the policemen concerned it is vital to appreciate how police work was actually carried out in the inner city. I shall look at the dilemmas faced by four sets of people in policing a deviant community. Their situation and the meanings they attached to their activities are constructed on the basis of observation, interviews, media revelations, and the official corruption dossier; all such sources are biased in certain ways and as the accounts were recorded after the events they have to be evaluated in the light of special pleading or retrospective justification. The four groups are the PCS (in the Warmoesstraat), the Aliens Department, the CID (in effect, the two 'Chinese experts') and a number of the centralized detective

squads (in particular, the Drug Squad), all of which were intimately involved in the drugs–Chinese–inner-city connection and
all of which came under suspicion. There is no way that I can
present an accurate, objective picture of what precisely went on
among large numbers of people who were engaged over a long
period of time in intricate, shifting and devious relationships.
However, it is worth bearing in mind that the inner-city can be
viewed as a corruptive environment where, rather like certain
departments of Sociology where marriages are guaranteed to
dissolve within a given period, any 'normal' person might be
sorely tempted, if not foredoomed, to stray from the path of
virtue (in New York policemen usually became corrupt within
two months of assignment to gambling enforcement: Simpson
1977: 51). One could argue the strong case, then, that in Amsterdam the authorities had structured corruption for themselves.

In the inner-city area the various groups of patrolmen, plainclothesmen, district detectives, and specialized detectives, all
had distinctive ways of approaching work and lived in real or
jocular rivalry with other units. Rivalry, competition, non-
cooperation, concealment of information, active dislike and
distrust, 'poaching' of cases, and denial of facilities were as
common, if not more so, than cooperation (Sanders 1977: 30;
Chatterton 1975: 261). In the Met a senior officer stated, 'It is not
being disloyal or hypocritical when one admits that within the
police, and within the CID itself, rivalry sometimes reached the
heights of idiocy' (Ball, Chester, and Perrott 1979: 26).

My respondents in the Warmoesstraat regaled me with complaints, often expressed in bitter terms, of detectives trying to
'poach' good cases from them or refusing to assist them; one said
'If you phoned the Drug Squad with information then they'd say,
"oh, we already knew that a long time ago", when they didn't
know it at all or you'd see a photo of a suspect at HQ and say "yes,
that's him" and then with your information they'd go out and
nick him. And they never even thanked you'. 'Zijlstra' complained that he approached the Drug Squad at Headquarters with
a tip abut a heroin shipment but they refused to help and tried to
get his informant off him: 'The team-spirit is worthless. They'd
rather cut each other's throats before they're prepared to help
each other. The Drug Squad wants to keep everything for itself
and they won't share the prestige with an ordinary copper'
(*Nieuwe Revue* 28 January, 1977). Interaction patterns with other
policemen were based on specific institutional loyalties which
were frequently in terms of the smallest group to which one

belonged – the patrol group, the specialized detective unit, or even where two detectives formed a tightly knit partnership. At close inspection the daily organization reality was that of an intricate patchwork quilt of personal antagonisms, collusion, manipulation, obligations and favours, power struggles, and competition for status. In addition, units or pairs of policemen endeavoured to create autonomy for themselves and jealously guarded their own territory and private information.

The PCS was a group of eight policemen and a sergeant, formally belonging to the uniformed branch and with no detective training (or any special training), who operated in plain clothes primarily to enhance the apprehension of street criminals and also to control various premises and street prostitution. This group had, in practice, no set hours of work, almost never came on duty together as a group, defined its own roster and priorities, worked different hours from the supervising sergeant (who had permanent day-duty), built up a private set of informants, and independently changed its task to take in the drugs–Chinese–alien connection in the area. One of its members later said,

> 'There was just no leadership, no coordination, no control, there was nothing. Nobody ever said anything, like "What time are you going home?" or "When are you coming back?" Nobody asked you anything. You just messed around as much as you wanted. We used to be frightened of the bosses, but now you don't give a shit for them.'

A junior officer explained that the unit was meant to work in coordination with the uniformed branch, but 'You could never find them; they were always messing about somewhere. They were like grains of drift-sand.'

The PCS had originally been set up in the early 1960s with the subsidiary function of providing *temporary* relief from patrol work for the uniformed man. Yet some members managed to become almost permanent fixtures in the unit and, instead of constant circulation of personnel, several people had spent as much as fourteen years in the PCS and perhaps more than twenty years in the same station. What began as a relaxed, non-competitive unit – designed 'to help restore the psychological balance of the uniformed man' – gradually evolved in the 1960s as an intelligence-gathering unit in the face of the Provo disturbances. To a certain extent the PCS became the ears and legs for headquarters and was even sought after for information by the BVD (the Dutch Secret Service). The original general task was neglected and this development was swiftly accelerated by the arrival of drugs, as a member of the PCS told me. 'We were the first to come across heroin and we started bringing it in. This was at the time that [Commissioner] Litjens was saying ''We don't have heroin in Amsterdam'' and yet wherever I went I could find some. He didn't see that it was coming.' A degree of self-induced pressure for results emerged which was partly fanned by encouragement from some senior officers.

One pair of men became known as a 'golden twosome' (the Amsterdam expression for a highly successful partnership) because of their ability to bring in cases (cf. Daley 1979: 180, on partners). Simply by being in the right place at the right time they became involved in a world of drugs, informants, and Chinese criminals that was not meant to be part of their work. They were an incongruous looking couple, with the one smallish and the other rotund (they were referred to as 'Biggie Nosso' and 'Biggie Bear' in the area), and did not fit the conventional stereotype of the detective. If you met them you would almost certainly under-estimate them because of their appearance and language whereas in fact they were shrewd, resourceful, a mine of information, and, above all, thoroughly at home in the criminal milieu of the inner-city. In particular, the one known as 'The Nose' (because of his large nose which also caused him to be nicknamed 'Pinochio') was gifted at striking up relationships with underworld charac-ters because he could slip into their language and create confi-dence that he was at home in their milieu. From interviews with them and others I shall endeavour to reconstruct their working style (which I also observed in the station and on the streets during my research with patrolmen while very occasionally I went out with members of the PCS).

'Bert' told me he would come into the station and read the telex messages on arrests, releases from prison, and on people wanted by the police. He would make notes on these and, as he also had an excellent memory for faces, would go out looking for suspects aided by his partner 'Jan' who, having worked in the area since the late 1940s, knew it like the back of his hand. They would stroll around chatting to prostitutes and bar-owners hoping to pick up tips, although at first they had no real informants. But with thirty or more arrests per month for felonies their reputation grew and clearly they had hit it off together as a partnership. They began to make arrests for possession of LSD and opium, for firearms, and for wanted persons, and received commendations for their work from the Chief Constables of Amsterdam, Assen, and Den Haag. Around 1972 they began to gain access to the Chinese community, where traditionally small amounts of opium for smoking were sold, and could enter freely the two opium dens and the gambling dens where they were welcomed with a cognac and a cigar. (It was rather disconcerting to walk down a busy Dutch street, accompanied by a plainclothesman, to open a door, and to enter a warm, grubby room with Chinese men lying around on low beds and rush mats smoking opium from bamboo pipes as if it was a scene from the Far East. And if you went into a gambling-house, where vast sums of money changed hands rapidly on apparently infantile games of 'fan-tan' and 'pai-kau' – a casino might need one million guilders in the bank on a busy weekend – then the manager would rush up, press an expensive cigar into your hand, and ask if you wanted tea, fruit, or cognac.) Following the influx of heroin they became more involved with drug arrests: 'We would raid people's rooms, search people on the street, and we were taking hundreds of grammes out on the street.' They became accepted by the Chinese because they over-looked the habitual opium-smoking in the Chinese community whereas some overkeen uniformed constable might arrest an elderly Chinese for possession of a tiny amount of opium only to have the case thrown out later by the Drug Squad as trivial – 'We never nicked grandpa so we were good and the word got around until everyone knew us.' This acceptance also meant that Chinese acquaintances would bring official forms in Dutch to them and Bert and Jan would help to fill them in and then 'they'd be all smiles and say "you really sorted that out well for us".'

They almost never saw their supervising sergeant and might tell the station-sergeant they were going out but 'no one ever asked "Where are you going?" or "What are you going to do?"' They focused on clubs and bars for students, 'hippies' and Surinamers, where drugs might be in circulation. Jan told me when they started working together it clicked immediately and they fitted together perfectly: 'We didn't need to say anything to each other, we'd just walk out on the street, and we wouldn't say "Shall we go right or shall we go left"? We just did it.' In one year they had over 400 arrests, which is spectacular by any standards, and a mythology developed around them (with almost magical powers of detection being attributed to 'The Nose'). They might pass on a tip to HQ but the Drug Squad was apparently fastidious about searching in dirty places: 'Not Bert, though, he'd look *anywhere*. Whenever we went into a place I'd stay by the door, keep an eye on everyone, let no one in or out, and Bert would go searching for it and he'd find it. He *always* found it.' On their rounds they would drink a beer here and there, would usually drink in their favourite bar after duty, and get a bite to eat more often than not in a Chinese restaurant. Eating out in Chinese restaurants became the established pattern until Maartens and van Thiel (Chief Inspectors) arrived at the station. Drinking on duty was also informally condoned for the PCS because of their special task in the area which brought them into bars (but they could not declare drinks as expenses and also could not offer money for information).

Bert and Jan got into heroin arrests through their contact with an informant–dealer, 'Johnny Fynaut'. But there was too encouragement from above for 'in 1974 and 1975 the message was that everything had to be done to bring in heroin and no stone was to be left unturned in order to bring in the stuff.' Clearly, the PCS was ideally placed to move into the vacuum caused by the absorption of the district detectives in routine cases and the involvement of the specialist detectives in large cases. The PCS started to do the leg work for the Drug Squad and, eventually, even to rival it. Some members threw themselves into the drug culture with a vengeance and began to get involved in cases outside of their district and technically above their competence and authority. This led to an uneasy relationship of alternating rivalry and cooperation with headquarters and, in particular, the Drug Squad (with which on several occasions 'peace councils' had to be arranged to defuse matters). The members of the PCS were apparently encouraged to some extent and there seems to have been a degree of pride on the part of the district and the uniformed branch that they could compete with the 'super-detectives' at HQ. This is exemplified in the almost childishly gleeful remark of a senior officer which, according to one informant, was used to taunt detectives. 'Commissioner Hagen [Head of Uniformed Branch], said to the detectives at HQ, "Where's the Drug Squad?" And when they said, "In room 102 [in headquarters] of course" he replied, "No it isn't, the real Drug Squad is in the Warmoesstraat, and you lot don't bring anything in!" ' The PCS was not only a pawn in inter-departmental rivalry but was particularly disliked by the specialized detectives at headquarters who looked down on them as 'a bunch of wankers' who were not qualified to do detective work. At all levels, interviews revealed bickering, distrust, friction, poaching, and envy.

'Success is important to a detective and the Drug Squad wants their cases to be as spectacular as possible. And the real reason why [Commissioner] Litjens was telling the press at first that there was no heroin in Amsterdam was because *his* men weren't capturing any. But we already had it and had taken kilos but he didn't want to have to admit that ordinary cops, not even detectives, were on to it and not his squad. We used to bitch like mad because we'd arrest someone for HQ but we'd never be mentioned in the press report. Then Chief Inspector Geels [in the Warmoesstraat] would phone Litjens and say, "Mister Litjens, you can simply tell the papers that District Two was responsible for arresting the suspect, and not your people, because your men never lifted a finger to help".'

(Interview, constable PCS)

The involvement of Bert and Jan in drugs was enhanced when they cultivated the informant Fynaut. Headquarters wanted to get hold of Fynaut as informant but he refused, saying 'I'm an informant for Bert and Jan and I can always find them in the Warmoesstraat, on my patch.' Fynaut would phone them at home or in the station with a tip and they would move in and make the bust. One of the two men assured me that he never saw heroin at Fynaut's place while the other said that only much later was he warned by the Drug Squad that Fynaut was a dealer: 'Apparently he'd let us arrest the small buyers but he'd keep the big customers for himself; he just used us.' The two men claimed that when they passed on tips from Fynaut to headquarters that the detectives virtually sabotaged the case in order to claim the PCS men had useless information;

'they said we didn't really want to cooperate with them. But it's impossible to cooperate with anyone in this force. The Drug Squad only phones you up about shit cases and tries to sell you a line when they only really want to use you for their useless cases. Once we passed on a good tip about a deal in Central Station [the main railway terminus for Amsterdam] and they said, "you can come on it as well". They put everything into it, cars, lookouts, the Shadow Squad [for undercover surveillance], the works. Everyone except us. Because "we couldn't get in touch with you". How on earth can you cooperate with people like that?'

The significance of this rivalry was that, when the PCS became embroiled in the drugs–Chinese–informants set up and began to indulge in suspect practices, various rumours and suspicions were smothered by departmental loyalty and the backing of senior officers. At a later stage a senior officer at Headquarters raised a number of critical questions about this process (claiming that when he took over the Drug Squad he sent back crime reports to the PCS on the grounds that they were 'more or less lies and we often made people rewrite them saying "you just can't get away with this"'). 'It's incredible that no-one said anything, when it was clear that things were going wrong. Some of the previous bosses must have known that not everything was kosher, such as the arrangement with the informer Fynaut. But too many people just stayed comfortably sitting in their chairs.' But the early symptoms were not taken seriously and were brushed aside. I was told of mutual accusations that were not investigated because they were seen as part of personal vendettas and because people did not want to take sides and spark off a war between the rival groups. People were told to keep quiet. One former member of the PCS, with a somewhat jaundiced view of the affair, told me: 'No one wanted any bother. But the chance was missed. That was the first symptom of bribery and the bosses were too scared to come to grips with it. They didn't have the guts to face up to it then, otherwise it would never have got so far.' For example, there were apparently accusations by detectives at Headquarters against members of the PCS pointing in the direction of corruption but in the interests of harmony and not starting counter-accusations the accusers and accused were encouraged by senior officers to work together. The respondent continued, 'Now they [certain members of the PCS and the CID at HQ] were colleagues out of necessity. Bert must have thought to himself, "So you want to get me, do you? Well, I've nobbled you!"'

An important reason for this shelving of internal complaints was that senior officers were prepared to back their own men against criticism. Litjens tried to tell the PCS 'Stop messing about in our business' but Chief Inspector Geels (then head of the Warmoesstraat) replied, 'But my men bring in more drugs than yours do; the PCS is bringing in more suspects and heroin in a week than HQ does in a whole year!' My jaundiced respondent went on to claim that members of the PCS were put on a pedestal, their bosses were proud of them, and consequently they began to feel secure in their methods whereas in fact they were getting dangerously involved with informants, were letting people go after arrest, were not arresting certain suspects, and were keeping back heroin. The patronage and protection was revealed by an incident that occurred long before there was much attention paid to the grey area of drug enforcement and the dubious role of informants in affecting arrests ('A Heroin Deal, The Police, and an Informant', *Haagse Post* 16 November, 1973).

In January 1973 a deal took place involving two foreign buyers. One of the sellers was the dealer, Fynaut, who was well-known to two members of the PCS. Apparently the buyers tried to rob the sellers at gun-point but Fynaut managed to escape, shouting 'they're going to shoot me, they've already got Orlando'. Outside three policemen, of whom two were later suspects in the corruption cases, were waiting and, one of them (Kramer), drew his pistol and, wounded one of the buyers. In court, there was a suspicion of entrapment but this seems to have been quickly brushed aside even though one of the policemen, Toxopeus, admitted that they had often visited the dealer Fynaut two or three times a week. The article suggested Fynaut had been arrested *the day after* the first court sitting because his role as informant had been blown and he had to be protected against reprisals. It also asked if it was necessary for Kramer to exchange a broad wink in court with Fynaut and to pose for the press brandishing his pistol. The head of the Drugs Squad at that time, Inspector Haan, was not happy about the incident, about which he was not forwarned, but apparently it was backed by the head of the uniformed branch, Commissioner Hagen, to which the policemen formally belonged. Haan was tight-lipped about the use made of informants but claimed that informers who also dealt were *never* used and were *never* given any freedom from prosecution. It is important to appreciate that this misty incident, clouded in uncertainties, took place four years before the corruption arrests, that the circumstances of the shooting remain obscure, that one of the sellers was not traced, that the heroin was never recovered, that a close connection between the policemen and a dealer-informant was established, that the policemen were operating outside of their district, and that two of the three policemen were clearly identified in newspaper photos.

Yet this dubious incident only served to *increase* the prestige of those involved and did not lead to any serious questioning of their methods. Indeed, the participants found spokesmen for them both at headquarters and the district level as one of them explained.

'There was that business of the shoot-out in the First Jan Steen-straat. We had to go to Headquarters because we were outside our district and were working with an informant. Chief Inspector Haan [then head of Drug Squad] was really mad and blew his top, and wanted to throw us in the cell straightaway! Fortunately

Commissioner Litjens came down on our side and said that there was really nothing the matter. When we got back to the Warmoesstraat we told the governor, and he shouted "what the hell does he think he's up to?" and phoned Haan at HQ and really told him where to get off.'

This material on the PCS is important both because the corruption cases started initially with the PCS and because it reveals graphically how police work was being carried out in the inner-city. An appreciation of that environment is essential to understanding both the cases and the later justifications of the suspects. In brief, an experienced detective saw the men of the PCS both as intoxicated with success and as the victims of lack of leadership.

'A degree of rivalry grew up among the members as to see who could get the most arrests and out of that zeal came a degree of corruption. But to what extent were they encouraged by bosses and by policies to bring in as much as possible? The starting-point was positive and they did it for the job. Unacceptable behaviour grew out of zeal, out of the sweet smell of success, until they became less vigilant.'

THE CID, THE ALIENS SQUAD, AND THE CHINESE COMMUNITY

Two key figures in the corruption case were the so-called 'Chinese experts' who were widely admired folk-heroes within the Amsterdam Police and who, because of their many successes, also enjoyed the mystique of being known as a 'golden twosome'. Initially, they had played a vital role in the rapid developments in the inner city. As detectives in the Warmoesstraat they had specialized in the affairs of the Chinese community (one had learned elementary Chinese, collected Chinese stamps, and studied Chinese culture and tradition) and were instrumental in solving a number of important cases in that world. Hoogland (known as 'Kau Foe' or 'Godfather' to the Chinese and also as 'Baldy' or 'Egg-Roll') had begun to focus on the Chinese community in the inner city from 1969 and had been joined in 1973 by Lighthart (known as 'Tai Loo', or 'Big Brother', and more colloquially as 'Tom Jones'). Because of their special knowledge they were moved, under Litjen's patronage, to headquarters, where they were members of the CID (an elite detective unit for gathering information from the underworld). In particular they always displayed no interest in drugs and claimed that their area was solving crimes of violence. They appear to have had *carte blanche*

to continue their intimate involvement in the Chinese underworld and built up an archive with photos of every Chinese
person they were concerned with which was reputed to be the
best source of information in The Netherlands on Chinese
criminals.

If the work of the CID could be considered 'real' detective
work then the work of the Aliens Squad (in Amsterdam the regis-
tration of aliens is a police matter) was generally perceived to be
routine, dull, and administrative. The Aliens Squad was a central
detective unit, housed in a building separate from Headquarters,
but of relatively low status. The head of the Squad told me that
the Central Detective Branch at Headquarters became involved
in the spectacular cases and attracted publicity whereas his unit
had low status and was even used for detectives with slight
infirmities: 'That creates a certain amount of jealousy as we are
not great detectives and the big boys at HQ more or less say,
"We're the real detectives and you lot are only all right for the
small cases."' Two men, Lucas and Drucker, had worked
together for some ten years and they became closely involved in
the Chinese world as part of their work. During that decade, The
Netherlands had experienced a considerable growth in legal and
illegal immigration and certain members of ethnic groups began
to play a conspicuous role in crime.

Before moving on to the fourth group of actors in our story,
namely the specialized detectives at headquarters, it is worth
reflecting on the crucial significance of the Chinese element and
how this influenced the style of work. The Chinese people in
Amsterdam are important because at one level they provided a
reservoir of visible, vulnerable suspects for the police, and
because at another level their leaders were men of influence who
engaged in largesse and hospitality. Furthermore, some of them
were experienced criminals adept at corrupting officials. Chung
Mon, for instance, would hold the passports and papers of people
under his sway and the men from the Aliens Squad were obliged
to come to Chung Mon for assistance whenever they wanted to
extradite an illegal Chinese immigrant. This process was essential
to keep the machinery of the Aliens Squad functioning because it
was increasingly swamped with work and this method short-
circuited a search that would be handicapped by the language
barrier, the confusing commonality of Chinese surnames, and
the, to western eyes, difficulty of discerning individual
differences in Chinese facial features. Information on drugs and
aliens came through Chinese contacts and a measure of tolerance

grew between the police and the Chinese community until the moral panic on drugs and crime led to the crackdown on illegal Chinese immigrants in November 1976 (leading to the expulsion of 1,200 Chinese within two years – Bresler 1981: 153).

The Chief of the Aliens Squad recognized that the work with Chinese and aliens implied the risk of corruption. Chinese, he said, will always try to give you something, a cigar or a snack, or even a fruit-basket delivered to your home, and will insist, 'You must accept it, otherwise it is impolite, and we will be offended.' According to another senior officer the Chinese employed deliberate tactics to trap policemen: 'Slowly but surely they enmeshed people. It was first a cigar, then a beer, then a meal, and then a fruit-basket.' An experienced detective said how difficult it was to refuse food and drink from insistent Chinese: 'I ask for tea but he says "I've only got cognac" and he offers me food and it's very tasty; you see food and drink is sacramental and draws people together but if I find a hundred guilders under my plate then that's where I draw the line and then I can feel free of obligations.' Members of the PCS told me they were constantly offered tea, cigars, cognac, fried prawns, bottles of spirits at Christmas, and when Chinese would win at the gambling-table they would give everyone a present and say 'it's not for you but for the wife and kids'. They were also offered substantial bribes to overlook offences including one bribe of 45,000 guilders (then abut £10,000 or $20,000). One man, who was nicknamed 'the Devil' by the Chinese because of his strictness and incorruptibility ('they even wanted to shoot me and in a Hong Kong newspaper it said I was the only Amsterdam policeman you couldn't buy'), was once asked to name his price for letting a Chinese suspect go and he wrote down 'for a joke' on a piece of paper 'three million guilders'.

THE DRUG SQUAD AND CENTRAL DETECTIVE UNITS

If this world of gambling houses and Chinese hospitality was one side of the coin, then drugs represented the other side. And both elements were central to the accusations in the corruption case. In particular, a number of specialized units (the Drug Squad, CID, and Shadow Squad for tracking criminals) became more important than before as a result of these developments and informally the detectives in them considered themselves superior to the ordinary detectives in the districts and less favoured departments, while new styles emerged in the detective subculture, emphasizing success in spectacular cases and close involvement with the criminal culture. The rise of the drugs trade in Amsterdam stimulated this because of the large amounts of heroin involved, the attendant publicity, and the necessity of gaining information from within the drug world itself. Initially the Drug Squad was small and ignorant of heroin and triads while it scampered along after events until gradually it became the kingpin department at headquarters, attracting manpower, resources, international contacts, and high informal status within the detective subculture. Senior officers attended FBI and DEA courses, travelled to the Far East, and attracted considerable publicity. (The office was decorated with opium pipes, a British police helmet, emblems from American departments and an Interpol badge from Tokyo, and a diploma from the FBI Academy, while once when I was there a KLM plane schedule lay on the desk while a phone call in English came in from Bangkok.) Everyone – senior officers, detectives, and press – became mesmerized by drugs and the man responsible for the Squad in the early 1970s, Litjens, was not shy at grasping publicity (the Squad fell under his command as Head of Special Investigations while his successes there paved the way to his becoming chief of all the central detective units at headquarters). Later, the Squad was run by van Rossum, who also did not shy away from publicity (he was photographed with one eye grotesquely enlarged behind a magnifying-glass), but he was more cerebral and managerially oriented than Litjens. Litjens was more the 'kick-down-the-door' type and once when I interviewed him he rubbed his hands together vigorously and said with infectious enthusiasm,

> 'I go to work everyday like this because I've got the greatest job in Holland. What with the Caransa case [kidnapping] and this RAF-business [German terrorists] I've been putting in a hundred hours overtime a month and I'm on the go Saturdays and Sundays and I tell my men to call me out at any time of the night or day, whether I'm at home or at a party.'

What is clear is that the Drug Squad went rapidly from being a rather haphazard, backward element in detective enforcement to being a major unit with close links with foreign enforcement agencies and with methods that, in some cases, stretched Dutch legal practice to its limits (a senior officer admitted that 'It was a bit of a wild-west scene with regard to deals and crime reports amounted to a sham because "anonymous information" from neighbours who happened to see things was mentioned except the "neighbours" never actually existed'). It may well be that this new found 'flexibility' also encouraged somewhat dubious practices at lower levels. These developments opened up a whole world of informal arrangements, secret deals, and bargains with criminals which was never satisfactorily aired later although much was hinted at. They do, however, reveal the precarious predicament of the detective as someone endeavouring to achieve results without landing himself in the shit.

Piggy in the Middle: The Senior Officers

'But, if when a boss comes in . . . you say, "Oh Christ, sir, I'm glad yer here! I'm going fokkin' mad!" – then he's off, gone, doesn't want to know!.'

(McClure 1980: 254)

The senior officer is the neglected man of police research. In many studies the lower ranks often appear as almost fully autonomous beings, unhindered by supervision and remote from anything resembling an organization (Bittner 1967); and, where the relationship between supervisors and patrolmen is examined, it is normally conducted in terms of front-line supervision by the sergeant or inspector (Rubinstein 1973; Chatterton 1975; Muir 1977; van Maanen 1983). But there are almost no studies that directly highlight the culture, values, and behaviour of senior ranking officers, apart from memoires and historical works. Often they are referred to as obscure figures in the background – 'seen from afar and infrequently' (Muir 1977: 235) – whose functions and role are imprecise (Sanders 1977; 45), and who only rarely see their men at work (Smith 1983: 127–29). And yet a number of people have pointed to the undercurrent of tension in police organizations in terms of controlling the lower ranks. For the structure of the work means that the 'manager' is largely ignorant of what his 'workers' are getting up to because of his weakness in obtaining reliable information about their activities whereas he remains potentially responsible for their mistakes (Chatterton 1975: 40; Manning 1979: 35). The dilemma of leaders who find that they have responsibility but little power has been noted in many organizations, while relationships of dominance and subordination can be highly complex (Kanter and Stein 1979: 8). But in the police organization the normal state of affairs is reversed in that people with relatively low status and low autonomy endeavour to control others who enjoy high status and considerable autonomy (Manning 1978: 75).

In the situation under consideration, however, the officers played a crucial role in defining deviance, exercising control, initiating the investigation, handling environmental pressures, pushing for (or resisting) change, and in attracting hostility from 'below' as well as attempts from outside to label *them* deviant. Importantly, the picture was not merely an unambiguous one of the lower orders shaped as a 'combat team at war with the management' (Roy 1955: 257) because alongside the battle between the two major factions of higher and lower ranks, there developed a complex, shifting reality of cliques, coalitions, private deals, secret meetings, hidden investigations, and office politics involving several layers of the organization. Here I shall look at the culture of senior officers in Amsterdam, the attitudes of the men towards them, the role the officers played in trying to sponsor organizational change and to reimpose control, and their uncovering of occupational deviance. In particular, this section will examine the predicament of the middle-ranking officers, sandwiched between the lower ranks and the force elite, who sparked off the whole scandal and who found themselves caught in some venomous cross-fire.

THE CULTURE OF SENIOR OFFICERS

In turning to the world of senior officers it is important to bear in mind that in The Netherlands, unlike the United States and the United Kingdom, there is 'lateral entry' for officers. Officers enter a force following a four-year course at The Netherlands Police Academy which selects young people, often straight from school, with university entrance qualifications (Goodendorp 1978). Other ranks have almost no chance of ever reaching senior rank. A constable may climb via examinations to the supervisory rank of 'adjutant' but that is usually the limit. In short, it is like the military system of officers and men where young officers often lead older men and outrank vastly more experienced NCOs. A graduate from the Academy enters a police force directly as an inspector (perhaps at the age of 22) and, apart from experience with units during training, he will not normally work closely on the streets with patrolmen or detectives but will immediately assume a supervisory function. From then on promotion is automatic, with no more studying, no more compulsory courses, and all officers can expect to reach the rank of 'expensive' chief inspector (the second rung on the chief inspector scale and the final position before commissioner). After that, promotion to commissioner is by crown appointment although, again, no more study or courses are required. Not only is there guaranteed promotion, but most forces operate a rigid system of seniority whereby posts are distributed to the next in line in terms of years of service.

What this meant, in effect, was that senior ranks were more or less encouraged to be passive, non-competitive, and even perhaps lazy. To be considered ambitious was to be disapproved of as everyone knew that you would get there in the end anyhow, providing you did not make any big mistakes. Generally in the Dutch system, then, it was not done to take risks. Furthermore, most of the top officers in Amsterdam had witnessed the turbulent 1960s where the political backlash of the riots had sent heads rolling. That was a clear lesson not to be rash and not to tread on sensitive political corns. The young guard of junior officers, on the other hand, were recruited about, or after, the riots and have never known the tranquillity of the pre-Provo period. Through structural change (the retirement of the generation recruited just after the war), however, a new guard of officers moved swiftly up the ladder to relatively high rank at a young age in positions which previously would have been held by much older men. They have known nothing but the relaxed, nonchalant style of policing in the late 1960s and 1970s in Amsterdam together with the spiralling consciousness of criminal and social problems in the capital. A number of the 'middle management', then, was restless, pushy, critical, eager to exert influence, and conscious of the defects in the police organization in general and the force leadership in particular.

THE PRINCIPAL ACTORS

The *Chief Constable*, 'Adema', reacted rather ineptly to the crisis sparked off by the scandal and proved to be somewhat emotional and unpredictable. As the figurehead of the department he proved unable to establish harmony internally and did not inspire confidence externally. He supported the internal investigation and took side with a faction of middle-ranking officers determined to push the cases even if this meant that other senior officers would come under suspicion. He was also a strong advocate of change and was instrumental in bringing in the 'Kreapol' campaign.

The Department Top. Beneath the Chief were the four heads of the major branches – Traffic, Detective, Uniform and Staff (in the rank of Commissioner). Generally, these men were uninspiring bureaucrats, awaiting retirement, who reacted defensively and ineffectively to developments.

The Sub-Top comprised the heads of specialized units at headquarters (usually Commissioner or Chief Inspector 'expensive') and they enjoyed high status and considerable autonomy. They tended to defend their 'turf' vociferously and to demand priority for their specific needs. The six district chiefs were rather weak institutionally, partly because they were physically removed from the power-centres at headquarters.

Middle management was composed of officers in staff functions at headquarters or in charge of units within a district. A district has a head of district, a head of the uniform branch, and a head of the detective branch who are generally chief inspectors. The most powerful and coherent call for responsibility and reform came from this group. They were concerned with developing a more effective organization at the cutting-edge, i.e. on the streets, but faced resistance from below and inflexibility from above.

Junior management meant the young inspectors at headquarters and in the districts who move annually in order to gain experience in various branches within their first few years before being given a more or less settled post. There is considerable rotation at this level and the men rarely exercise much power or influence because of their temporary postings and because their lack of experience lands them uncomfortably between more powerful superiors and more experienced subordinates.

Considerable conflict took place between the shifting coalitions of these groups. A constant theme later in internal and external criticism was that the force leadership was either naive, hypocritical, or incompetent. An experienced constable assured me that the 'top' knew what was going on 'but they washed their hands of the affair'. Yet, crucially, this view was not confined to disgruntled members of the lower ranks and a chief inspector with a staff function expressed sympathy with the counteraccusations of one of the suspects:

> 'In a way, in my heart, I agree with Kramer. There should also have been bosses standing alongside him in the dock. Too few questions were asked and bosses neglected to set clear guidelines. The end justified the means. Only the result was important and that is still the golden rule for most governors.'

Indeed, the Chief Constable himself admitted the shortcomings of the leadership and even his own failure, while also conveying the feeling of the force hierarchy being somewhat out of their depth.

'I feel that I have failed to a certain extent and that other top officers have failed. From the beginning I couldn't see it. I had enormous confidence, almost a blind faith, in my men. But now it seems that things existed about which the leadership remained blind. . . . You have to appreciate that the police organization is an after-the-incident, reacting, reactive operating concern. We only do something when things get out of hand. We've been completely swamped by this whole business. This whole heroin affair hit us like a tidal wave.'

THE LOWER RANKS' VIEW OF OFFICERS

In Amsterdam the attitude of lower ranks towards bosses was highly ambivalent because, under the indulgency pattern, the men rejoiced when the officers were absent, for then they were free to pursue their own ends in their own manner without irksome supervision, yet they resented it when things went wrong and they did not have a superior officer to back them up. Holdaway (1980: 130) notes that senior ranks may deliberately avoid trouble while 'supervisory officers were constantly criticized by their subordinates for their failure to back and support their decisions.' In the research station and elsewhere there was generally a strong negative stereotype of bosses who were seen as variously incompetent, careerist, mercenary, slippery, cowardly, and lazy. Yet, while complaining about absentee and ineffective bosses, I believe that many policemen revelled in this absence of control and, in interviews, many gave it as an important reason for their work satisfaction (Punch 1976). Of course, negative stereotypes of bosses abound in many work organizations, as do deflating stories of the incompetence of people guided by theoretical knowledge rather than practical experience (Watson 1980; Roy 1955), and the police organization is no exception. I was inundated with colourful stories of officers who were said to be incompetent, alcoholic, senile, or who had been caught driving through red lights or driving under the influence (Holdaway 1980: 283). For example, one senior detective was derided because he had turned up to a murder scene under the influence of drink and proceeded to step into a pool of blood while he also managed to kick a couple of cartridges into a canal. An additional feature among policemen, however, is that they have a nostalgic view of the 'good old days' and the 'old-time coppers' (Reuss-Ianni 1983). This positive view of the past was strongly present in Amsterdam and was employed to portray the dilution of 'real' police work and the lack of 'real' leadership.

Previously, in the nostalgic view, the policeman was the 'boss' on the streets, could use rough justice without fear of getting complaints, and could rely on automatic backing from the 'governors' against civilians. Now, in contrast, the force leadership as well as other officers were seen as at fault and as weak by some respondents. This view may, of course, simply be the sort of institutionalized griping which one gets in any hierarchical organization and in an 'officers–men' caste system, as operates in The Netherlands, it may be a protective mechanism to transpose blame and guilt on to those 'above'. But it also appears related to the loss of authority that the policeman experienced in the late 1970s which made him more vulnerable to external criticism, at the same time that protection from above became less automatic. My jaundiced respondent from the PCS was a vocal exponent of the anti-bosses theme and told me how in the 1960s riots the 'governors were as frightened as weasels'. He continued, 'Twenty years ago you had real governors who stood firm among you and who didn't shy away from responsibility. Now the bosses dare not, and cannot, show leadership and the police force is going to the dogs because we've got absolutely no leadership.' He also went on to assert that a number of senior officers and officials from Customs and the Justice Department had enjoyed the hospitality of the Chinese leaders, that this had been observed, and had been adopted as acceptable practice by the lower ranks: 'Of course the men thought, "If they can do it so can we."'

'MIDDLE MANAGEMENT' ATTEMPTS TO REIMPOSE CONTROL

In explaining how and why the wheel came off in a certain place at a particular time, it is perhaps the most ironical aspect of this whole affair that it was two young officers, who wanted to be *real* and not token bosses, who sparked off the entire scandal. Two senior members in middle-management positions were appointed to the Warmeosstraat and they were not frightened to make decisions and to take responsibility. And the result was four years of unprecedented institutional upheaval. This is comparable to Gouldner's (1954) study of a gypsum company, which indicated that, once the indulgency pattern has become institutionalized, it is damned difficult to reimpose control and to return to a 'punishment-centred' style of authority. The arrival of the new manager, Peele, led to a cycle of bureaucratization and wilful deviance that eventually exploded in a wild-cat strike (Gouldner 1965). In Amsterdam internal organizational change, external pressure for change, rapid mobility through the hierarchy, and a consequent generation gap between middle and top officers, all contributed to a situation where some senior men were no longer content merely to perpetuate the status quo.

Yet even these interlocking and accumulating pressures might not have been enough to generate a crisis without the accident that the leadership in the Warmoesstraat comprised one weak superior and two strong subordinates. The former exemplified the traditional, somewhat passive, laissez-faire style of leadership which informal norms valued and rewarded. Some men called him 'the politician' and one constable described him as 'a weak figure who's never taken a firm decision in his whole career. That way you never make a mistake and you can go a long way in this force.' Had he been a strong personality, he might have been able to keep the lid on the can of worms when his colleagues tried to prise it open. But he found himself with two strong subordinates in charge of the detective and uniform branches who were young 'expensive' chief inspectors in their early 30s who were determined to leave their mark on the organization. Their aim was to cooperate together in order to have more effective enforcement and to gain a larger measure of control over the lower ranks. But in endeavouring to get to grips with the productivity of the lower ranks, the new-found trio stumbled on working methods which they considered highly questionable. The head of the district, for example, saw the issue as largely something that he had inherited. Previous 'governors' had apparently 'swept it all under the carpet' while some of them had 'skated on thin ice' by spending a lot of time themselves in the area. He blamed his predecessors for not taking any measures as 'the same practices that we found were present then but they did nothing about it'.

In contrast, the head of the detective branch in the district, van Thiel, was active, enthusiastic, and well-organized but his motivation to get to grips with the flourishing criminality in his area brought him into conflict both with headquarters and with his own personnel. He began to set priorities for serious crimes and cooperated fully with the Aliens Department in the crack-down

on the Chinese community. A certain commissioner had said,
' "The Chinese are mine, and they should all be together to help
us combat the heroin trade." But there's no way he can sell that to
us here in the district because this is our patch.' He set about
mounting well-organized actions and raids in which detectives
and the PCS approached the problem collectively with the uniformed branch for the first time. Although this was designed to
give the men confidence that at last they were tackling the problems in the area seriously he was, nevertheless, regarded with
suspicion by the men. 'When I first came the detectives looked at
me as the new young man, who was going to get stuck in with a
new broom. When these corruption cases began I had a head-on
collision with them and they could have happily slit my throat.'

The head of the district's uniformed branch, Chief Inspector
Maartens, was serious, thoughtful, and articulate on how his
personal viewpoint brought him into confrontation with mal-
practice. He had not come consciously to 'clean up the place' but
he was determined to exercise influence as a boss over the men in
his district.

> 'Look, I can play Santa Claus. I can allow people to pull the wool
> over my eyes and just simply cover up for everything that goes
> on. But I refuse to do it. And that means you inevitably set up
> tensions and these incidents led to tremendous conflict and to
> the border of a real crisis of confidence here in the station. . . .
> I'm concerned with how the police organization ticks and I'm
> determined to see that everyone functions as the boss wants
> him to. If you're not careful then the whole concern is messing
> around and no one knows exactly where they're going. That
> was the sort of situation which developed slowly over the years
> here and that's what we found. No one concerned himself with
> efficient leadership. Then, when we tried to get things moving,
> everything we did was seen as repressive.'

Two men did know where they were going and the time was
ripe. And it was precisely the attempt by two young officers,
backed up hesitantly by an older chief, to reshape the police organization at the district level that led to a clash when long-established
patterns of deviance were uncovered. This brought to the surface
two separate conflicts. One was between the senior supervisory
personnel and the lower ranks in the Warmoesstraat and the other
was between middle management and the force top. In all this
Maartens and van Thiel played a key role and the arrival of two
strong personalities at the same time in the Warmoesstraat is

fundamental to understanding how and why the corruption came to light at this particular juncture (although a number of structural changes contributed considerably to their impact).

UNCOVERING OCCUPATIONAL DEVIANCE IN THE WARMOESSTRAAT

The 'new brooms' in the Warmoesstraat did not set out to expose deviance but were primarily concerned with running an efficient and responsible organization. Maartens, however, explained how their efforts to get a grip on the work of the lower ranks led to the gradual uncovering of suspect practices. For instance, when he planned raids they came to nothing because of leaks (cf. on leaks Laurie 1972: 285; Honeycombe 1974: 172; Murphy and Plate 1977: 209; Beigel and Beigel 1977: 142). Then there were stories circulating about 'policemen, whores, drinks, and money', which in the past had been ignored on the grounds that there were always rumours to discredit policemen, but he decided to look into them. 'Suddenly we had someone in the station who said straight out, "That person gives money to the police."' The new senior officers followed up the matter and discovered that two policemen had taken money during their controls on premises (bars and brothels). This accusation was put to them and they admitted it: 'We had a case and the ball was rolling; we put it down on paper and it's dated 21st April 1976.'

Earlier, in January 1976, the new man had set about reorganizing the PCS in order to make it more effective. This reduced its autonomy by coordinating its activities with the uniformed and detective branches, by requiring that the men function to a set roster and as a team, and by preventing them from mounting raids on their own initiative. This move brought both resentment from the old guard and also brought to light a number of informal practices such as hanging around with 'hostesses' in bars and drinking at the expense of Chinese people. As a result of the incidents related to the PCS four men were either moved elsewhere or else put back into uniform. This in turn led to suspicions about detectives and the decision was taken to investigate these.

'So we went out on our own and played detective. The three of us started watching the movements of colleagues through binoculars. People latched on to this and now we were seen as potentially dangerous people. The situation was full of tension. The detectives in our own district set up an investigation against us, and they looked into *our* methods to see if we'd used blackmail and if we'd got unreliable statements from witnesses. This all brought the men against us and there's been incredible suspicion of us. When we came into the canteen all the conversations stopped. The behaviour of some men descended to below zero. But we're convinced that we're engaged in an honest struggle. Our position is, we intend to investigate these cases seriously.'

The enquiries of the senior officers raised the possibility of more serious offences and of detective involvement in them which, in turn, meant the matter had become too large for the district to handle. But they had to start the investigation themselves before handing it over to Headquarters, while they also cooperated with the State Detectives. 'Our behaviour was a demonstration of the police organization's ability to take responsibility itself for such matters. In effect, if we wanted to, *we could sabotage virtually every investigation from outside*' (my emphasis).

The dilemma for the senior officers in the Warmoesstraat was that the cases started as rumours but that, once they had taken those rumours seriously, they then had to set out to substantiate them themselves and this involved 'spying' on their own personnel. But, once the cases got under way, they had a tendency to escalate as more witnesses came forward. For example, a young inspector in the Warmoesstraat became closely involved in investigating the cases and he explained to me that once the investigation got under way it had a 'snowball effect'. For instance, there were stories of people confiscating heroin, keeping it to themselves, and then selling it. To investigate these allegations the senior officers decided to play detectives themselves. Photographs of policemen borrowed from the Personnel Department were shown to witnesses in order to identify police suspects ('But the photos never went outside this building; we used them in this room and nowhere else'). On the 'pay-days' for share-holders in the Chinese gambling-houses, the 2nd and 16th of the month, the officers would lie in the gutters up on the roofs of buildings watching with binoculars until two in the morning to see if police suspects entered – 'We saw all the familiar names on the list going in there including __ [policeman suspect], even when he was not in the PCS anymore but was working in another district.'

The affair began to escalate. Early on there was the death of Wouters (from the Licensing Department in the station and following his interrogation); 'That brought about a flood of unrest and we had our hands full trying to cope with it; during the group discussions with the men we talked and talked in order to stop things exploding.' And, then, he recalled that:

'the really big blow was the arrest of Jan and Bert and then followed the other six. During that whole period I was stared at incredibly. Some of the men didn't talk to me anymore and if I went down to the canteen they would look the other way. I tried to act normally but the business dragged on for such a long time. We were seen as the bogeymen just at the moment that we wanted to build up confidence in us. We were putting in 80–90 hours' overtime per month to put the cases together and at the same time there were all the stories about us going around showing photos of our own men in the area. So it was a very tough load for us to bear.'

The initial rumours had triggered off an investigation of the men in Licensing, which led to suspicions about the PCS, which, in turn, pointed to questionable practices among detectives. About two months after his arrival rumours began to reach van Thiel from some detectives about other policemen, including one detective who had made a trip to Antwerp in a Mercedes borrowed from a Chinese criminal. He looked into this and questioned witnesses about the ownership of the car. 'But the other detectives took it badly, that I'd begun an investigation of one of them and I met enormous resistance. The detective himself knew I was watching him, and he was watching me, so it was an incredibly difficult situation. They saw me as a bloodhound who was out to nobble one of them.' The old way was not to 'hang your dirty washing out in public', and to deal with such matters entirely inside the district. But he insisted that the issue be taken to HQ. If he was expecting applause for his efforts then he certainly did not receive any.

'But what we've done is considered the most stupid thing that anyone could do – destroy the force by attracting negative publicity in the press. Now there's a curse on us and maybe over five or ten years the top will get their own back. Now some people say, "You're dragging the reputation of the force through the mud." That couldn't interest us less. We're not going to cover up things. But probably older people would never have started this investigation.'

The coincidence that two strong personalities arrived at the same time in the Warmoesstraat, and that both were determined to leave their mark on the organization, is instrumental in explaining why the cases came to light at the time they did. In trying to gain more control over the lower ranks they encountered first hostility, resistance, and lack of communication and then, second, they stumbled on malpractices. Their predicament was that conventionally such unwholesome issues were handled discreetly and privately but never with exposure. But they were convinced that such serious suspicions had to be investigated thoroughly and through formal channels. In so doing they initiated enormous unrest, heated personal emotions, powerful informal sanctions, and helped bring the station to a crisis of confidence and to the verge of mutiny. Many policemen did not perceive the cases as involving 'corruption', displayed a strong identification with their suspect colleagues, and claimed that what they did was 'normal', unavoidable, and part of their work. But perhaps the strongest objection was to the fact that policemen hunted other policemen and this was quite unacceptable in terms of occupational solidarity. A detective explained,

'A boss shouldn't be laughing and joking with a colleague during the day and then go around in the evening in the area flashing a photo of the man around. It doesn't actually make for a relationship of trust and so the atmosphere was just bloody miserable with all sorts of sly cracks being made. Amongst ourselves though there was a very strong bond, in opposition to it all, and a boss was seen as something evil.'

Members of the lower ranks began to see the cases as a smoke-screen designed to cover-up for senior officers. One ex-member of the PCS saw it as an investigation that got out of hand and started to point in the wrong direction (i.e. upwards). The men accused in the Licensing Department pointed at the PCS who then implicated the district detectives and, in turn, fingers were pointed at Headquarters and at Litjens. The two 'Chinese experts' saw what was going on and said

' '' now you've got to stop otherwise they'll get to the governors and you'll put Litjens inside''. So it was talked out of the window. And Jan [in PCS] has seen the fruit-baskets from the Chinese bosses standing there at New Year with the addresses on them. They've all had them [he points upstairs in the Warmoesstraat to the rooms of the officers – MP], Litjens as well. There were baskets full of fruit, with bottles of champagne and turkeys, and envelopes with 500 guilders in them.'

Ironically, the lower ranks strongly resented the young clique of officers – who stood for change, accountability, and managerial responsibility in the organization – who began the investigation yet without their revolt against the top the cases would have almost certainly led to a ritual cleansing with the minimum of publicity. Stimulated by the press, encouraged by a couple of rebel officers, and desperate to save themselves, several suspects decided to talk and named names and darkened reputations. In the following chapter we shall see that what no-one succeeded in doing, however, was to secure the arrest of an officer or go so far as to bring an officer to trial. As one of the suspects said, 'In the thirty-five years I've been in the Amsterdam police an officer has never done anything wrong. That's unthinkable. And it holds for higher-ups too, like Public Prosecutors, who just can do no wrong.'

Conclusion

The material presented in this chapter has endeavoured to crystallize a complex, shifting situation into a condensed description of how a changing environment (socially, politically, and in patterns of crime) lead to significant alterations in the task structure, organization, and style of police work in the inner city of Amsterdam. Success went to those who adapted by taking on the style of the streets or by building up confidential relationships with key Chinese characters. In particular, the principal sets of actors – the PCS, the CID, the Aliens Squad, and centralized detectives at headquarters – became involved, under circumstances of considerable autonomy, with close contacts in the Chinese world, with informants, and with drug-related criminality. Within this convoluted and continually evolving network of deals, lies, deception, rivalry, and manipulation it was possible for all sorts of dubious relationships and practices to flourish and, later, for various types of *post facto* rationalizations to emerge. A persistent theme subsequently revolved around the absence of control and the lack of leadership, which left a great deal of initiative for discretionary enforcement to policemen low in the hierarchy. When two new senior officers attempted to reimpose control on this apparently chaotic and slippery situation they set off a chain reaction of events which uncovered deviance, sponsored an investigation into corruption, led to considerable inter-rank hostility within the station, and pointed to seamy and dubious practices in central detective units at headquarters and among highly placed officers. For some people the events sparked off four years or more of misery.

I wish here to accentuate two possible interpretations of this material. First, in terms of the 'implicit bargain' (Baldamus 1961) between bosses and workers I would argue that in the police organization the senior officers are aware that they do not have effective control of the work process and implicitly delegate responsibility to the lower orders on the understanding that deviance will be kept in bounds and they will not be embarrassed or compromised by excesses (Holdaway 1980: 121). When deviance does get out of hand and the higher ranks feel forced to intervene then the 'implicit contract' switches from a diffuse one based on discretion and trust to a restricted position of low trust, close supervision, and direct control (Fox 1974). Uncovering deviance exposes the lack of control at the top *forcing* officers to reimpose conspicuously their hold on the lower ranks who resent this illegitimate interference with their traditional 'rights' to autonomy (Gouldner 1954). In Amsterdam, the lapse into a largely uncontrolled and even chaotic indulgency pattern meant that almost any significant move to control or to change the situation was likely to be disruptive and the corruption issue was merely the most significant catalyst in a larger dialectic of control and adaptations to control.

Second, the two new officers in the Warmoesstraat can be seen as 'the good guys' virtuously and courageously setting out to erase deviance. From another perspective, they can be viewed as naive or even as fools, as not being 'house-trained' or as 'plastic policemen' trying to go by the book, and as not understanding the 'real' rules of the game (Reisman 1979: 18). They let the worms out of the can instead of putting the lid back on. Perhaps I can illustrate this by referring to my third project when I returned to the station in 1979 and observed closely the officers and the detectives. The former assured me that they now had the confidence of their men and that the old-style deviance was abolished. Certainly the detectives were young, motivated, and ostensibly 'clean'. But I do not believe that they genuinely gave their full confidence to the officers, while in some respects deviance continued as usual (particularly in terms of 'work manipulation' and 'perks'). There was drinking on duty, 'police prices' in restaurants, inflated bills for meals were declared, fictitious declarations for meals in the names of detectives who had gone home to eat were made, officers' signatures were forged on blank search-warrants, key decisions were taken without reference to senior officers, and arrests and searches were conducted by detectives on their own initiative causing their boss once to shake his head and murmur, 'I don't feel well when I hear all this.' Now none of this may be particularly shocking but it indicates not only that even under a tough 'governor' certain forms of deviance continued to flourish but also that to a certain extent he condoned, and even colluded, in them. For instance, I noticed him blindly signing declarations for overtime which everyone knew were fabricated as a means of increasing the detective's salary. When I mentioned this to him he replied, 'I do it because I know that if it's Sunday afternoon and there's a panic on then I can call on my men and they will all come in to work willingly.'

It is precisely such forms of implicitly agreed reciprocal obligations which are built into the work situation that make certain forms of deviance so resilient and their erasure such an intractable issue (Dalton 1959). In the last resort, the two 'new brooms' not only failed to tackle the milder forms of deviance that had started the whole affair initially but also succumbed to other forms of deviance built into mutual understandings about the work situation. Far more attention needs to be paid to the predicament of such middle-ranking officers, standing for accountability and change, who find themselves stymied by defensiveness from above and resistance from below. Kanter (1982) argues generally that middle management is neglected in studies of organizations and that the middle '*is* the quintessential organization' (Kanter and Stein 1979: 81). Here we can graphically witness the unenviable position of middle management in a conservative bureaucracy caught between top and bottom making them truly 'piggies in the middle'.

4

The Investigation and the Allegations

Introduction: Dilemmas of Investigating Police Deviance

For members of a police organization the investigation of internal deviance is a painful if not a bitter experience. Crucially, it does not involve a clinical, mechanical, and somehow automatic chain of self-sustaining events; rather it is a political process that needs to be initiated, guided, stimulated, defended, and pushed by strategically placed groups against factions inside (and/or outside) the organization calling for cover-up, scapegoating, and avoidance of publicity. When policemen set out to hunt other policemen this provokes tensions of a quite different order to, say, an external control agency entering a corporation to pursue 'white-collar' deviants where 'white-collar crimes make documentary work for white-collar professionals – accountants and lawyers' (Katz 1979: 435). Here 'blue-coat' crime makes investigative work for fellow 'blue-coat' colleagues and the sanctions and techniques used against the criminal class and suspect-citizens are suddenly reversed to be employed *against* precisely those professionals who monopolize them in their daily work. The investigation of police deviance not surprisingly, then, leads to bitterness, banishment, hostility, and hatred (Beigel and Beigel 1977: xi).

Normally, internal mechanisms for dealing with deviance are reactive, following the style of conventional police work, but under exceptional circumstances, as in London and New York, proactive and even aggressive styles of control may be employed while considerable internal and external resources may be mobilized to combat and investigate deviance (Sherman 1974: 175). Internal 'enforcement entrepreneurs' (Marx 1974: 433) may emerge who make combating corruption their implacable mission. Murphy said that reducing corruption was more important than convicting organized crime figures 'even the overlords – the dons', viewed the SIU as 'being the most corrupt single unit in the history of American law enforcement', and when he rewarded six officers for their anti-corruption efforts he remarked pointedly that 'this was the largest group of officers ever rewarded for catching criminals who were cops' (Murphy and Plate 1977: 213, 240, 252). Mark admitted that he was more interested in capturing bent detectives than criminals, told the CID they represented 'what had long been the most routinely corrupt organization in London', and lauded the special Anti-Corruption Squad's (separate even from A10) breaking of the 'Dirty Squad's' corruption network in the pornography world 'as probably the greatest ever single piece of detective work' (Mark 1978: 130; Cox, Shirley, and Short 1977: 142). Also, when the work of Internal Affairs (for internal investigations of police deviance) is seen to be taken seriously it may be viewed as a path to promotion and there can develop a 'thirst to come up with bodies' (Sorrentino 1980: 7). This was the case in New York, apparently, where, 'as Murphy describes it, bright young captains soon got his central message: "ooh, new ball game! I advance my career by proving to these characters Murphy has around him that I'm really a corruption fighter. Watch me go. And boy, they did go"' (Kennedy School of Government 1977c: 12). External control agents, who have long been suspicious of deviant policemen, or who have had running battles with them as rivals or watchdogs, may wish to settle old scores and some externally mounted investigations can be bitter and acrimonious. When the Customs Authorities came into conflict with the Met Drug Squad in London a senior Customs official said, 'even Sands [the dealer] isn't important: I want Kelaher [head of the Met Drug Squad]' (Honeycombe 1974: 144). Ambitious prosecutors, moreover, may be highly motivated to push a notorious case as in the 'French Connection ripoff' (of drugs from NYPD property office): nine separate prosecutors were conducting cases on the 'most celebrated crime any of these men might ever hope to solve' (Daley 1979: 274).

Policemen are, in fact, exposed to a paradoxical situation in that they enjoy considerable autonomy in the work situation but are

subject to the quasi-military discipline of a bureaucratic organization (Reiner 1978: 187). Force orders tend to be a long series of
'negative precepts', the NYPD has 'thousands of standing
orders', and the Met has a 10,000-paragraph 'General Order'
representing '140 years of fuck ups. You can't go eight hours on
the job without breaking the disciplinary code' (Goldstein
1977: 192; Murphy and Plate 1977: 177; Manning 1977: 165).
Workers in many settings resent overt control (Dalton 1959: 100),
but policemen seem to be particularly abrasive about internal
discipline (Alex 1976: 59). The irritation and antagonism are
especially aroused by three features of internal discipline; the
lack of legal safeguards in disciplinary enquiries; the feeling of
being exposed to 'double jeopardy', whereby someone acquitted
in court may later be found guilty in a departmental trial and dismissed the force (Daley 1979: 342); and the use of policemen to
spy on fellow policemen. Policemen may be denied the civil and
constitutional right to counsel and the right to remain silent (Juris
and Feuille 1973: 142; Reiner 1978: 88). This lack of due process
may have the effect that the men are 'terrified' of Internal Affairs
which they fear more than external control; one response may be
to deny legitimacy to Internal Affairs whereby the cover-up
becomes an 'act of integrity' and the lie becomes an 'act of political bravery' (Muir 1977: 202–06). In addition policemen frequently attack the credibility of investigations and of Internal
Affairs (the men in the latter being referred to in America as
'shoe-fly squads', 'goons', or 'Gestapo' – Fogelson 1977: 99). In
New York the police unions fought Knapp at every stage and
policemen called it a 'charade' and a 'Roman circus'; the State
Commission of Investigation looking into corruption within the
Albany PD (NY) was labelled 'political', 'a circus', 'un-American',
and a 'Star Chamber'; in the Met 'Operation Countryman' was
referred to as 'that long-running farce' (Alex 1976: 107; Christianson 1973; Will 1980d: 402).

Furthermore, in perusing the literature pertaining to Britain,
the United States, and The Netherlands, it seems quite apparent
that the police organization in these three societies does not
normally invest a great deal of energy in internal enquiries and
that external investigations are exceedingly rare (Sherman
1978: 63). In London for almost a century the only agency empowered to examine wrongdoings in the Met was the detective
branch of the Met itself, while in New York the various overlapping units involved in discipline were 'widely dispersed,
understaffed, and often poorly directed' (Kennedy School of

Government 1977a: 13). This led Murphy to surmise that it was 'almost as if the N.Y.P.D.'s internal justice system had been deliberately sabotaged' (Murphy and Plate 1977: 220). In general, then, one gleans a picture of police departments as having internal disciplinary and investigative procedures that are complex, overlapping, weak in resources, and predominantly reactive in style while, as with so much control of 'organizational' deviance, outside agencies are all too often lacking in manpower and penetration. What this comes down to is that most allegations of police deviance are 'received, investigated, and adjudicated' by *other policemen* and this normally occurs within one and the same organization (Sherman 1974: 26; Box and Russell 1975).

The sceptic might justifiably maintain that the foregoing remarks do not generate an upswell of confidence in the willingness or ability of police to investigate their own misconduct. This raises a number of key issues related to the success or failure of investigations that deserve brief comment here, particularly as the Amsterdam affair proved to be a damp squib which smouldered but failed to ignite. First, one can imagine an understandable reluctance, understandable in terms of solidarity and loyalty (Barker and Roebuck 1973: 13–14), among many policemen attached to internal disciplinary units to prosecute investigations energetically against their colleagues 'who may one day be their partners or superiors' (Goldstein 1977: 212). Second, corruption investigations may simply represent more than usually difficult types of investigation in all sorts of ways such as requiring a proactive style of investigation when the investigators are geared to a case-by-case, reactive style of work; or where officers are socialized into never cooperating with investigations of their colleagues (Sherman 1978: 46); or when a fearful victim does not wish to cooperate against an extortioner policeman who may later take revenge; or because, in the last resort, juries are reluctant to believe the testimony of known criminals and to convict a policeman (Wilson 1978; Mark 1978: 98). Third, strategically placed policemen may have the power to deflect, undermine, or sabotage an investigation. In London it was said that a senior officer was able to use his position at Scotland Yard (responsible for several specialized detective squads) to deflect six sets of complaints against the Porn Squad (Cox, Shirley, and Short *et al.* 1977: 209). In Amsterdam I was told by middle-ranking officers that Litjen's pivotal role at Headquarters may have been partly responsible for the failure of the investigation. Indeed, on two occasions key moves were only made when he was safely out of the country (once when the 'Chinese experts' were arrested – and Litjens told me that if he had been around he could probably have prevented them being arrested – and once during the 'secret' investigation against him when his safe was opened). And fourth, police investigators of deviance may face the supreme irony that they cannot achieve results by 'clean' methods and may feel forced to adopt the conventional bag of operational 'dirty' tricks. Accusations on this can readily be used as a defence by policemen under suspicion but New York policemen were scathing about some of the methods used following the Knapp 'hysteria' (Alex 1976), McNee (1983: 195) commented critically on the 'unprofessional conduct' and 'double standards' of the Countryman team, and the Chief Constable of Amsterdam was reported as saying 'you can't tackle corruption with honest means'. While some are reluctant to pursue internal investigations others may feel they have to do so even more vigorously, and unscrupulously, than usual.

Bearing the above points in mind I now wish to turn to a classification of the accusations made against policemen in Amsterdam in the light of the categories developed in the Introduction. This is designed to clarify the nature of the suspicions raised against the Amsterdam Police. The major source used in this chapter is the 350-page corruption case dossier containing witnesses' statements and the interrogations of suspects. The State Detectives who compiled many of the reports in the dossier remind me of Wilson's (1978: 26) description of FBI agents as primarily smartly dressed, desk-bound, reactive investigators who are no longer closely involved with street work. They were called in after the event, relied almost entirely on interviews, faced a difficult job with unreliable witnesses and with linguistic barriers, and did not go out actively looking for evidence of police deviance. A senior officer commented, 'They're willing, clean, but their cutting-edge is nil. In a corruption case you have to lie in the gutter as well, get out on the ground, but in a State Detective case that's already ruled out.' I cannot read their minds but it is possible to interpret their motivation as one of merely going through the motions in a case where they did not expect confessions from experienced policemen and where it was perhaps politic not to point too strongly in the direction of senior officers. This is only surmise on my part but I wish to alert the reader to the fact that we are reliant on what the State Detectives considered important enough to write down while there are all sorts of clichés and filter mechanisms that are employed when detectives construct a report. There may well have been an 'hidden agenda' to the investigation, conveyed to the State Detectives in signals during the negotiations between the parties concerned (Mayor, Justice Department, and police), which is impossible for me to decipher, but the possibility of its existence should be borne continually in mind when interpreting the weight to be put on statements from the dossier.

Internal and External Control in the Amsterdam Police

The material presented above aids in focusing on the dilemmas and effectiveness surrounding the institutional arrangements for investigating police deviance in Amsterdam. The general points made in the previous section also held true for the situation in Amsterdam where internal investigative arrangements were complex and messy. Disciplinary action against a policeman can be taken internally at a number of levels (district, branch, or Internal Affairs) but if a suspected criminal, or serious disciplinary, offence has to be followed up then the investigative work is done in Amsterdam by the Misfeance Department. In contrast to the United States, 'Internal Affairs' is for disciplinary cases only, and crimes of officials, including policemen, are the province of the Misfeance Department (*Ambtsmisdrijven*), which may, however, also cooperate in a disciplinary enquiry. At the stage that it looks fairly certain that a criminal offence is involved the State Detectives will be brought in and they may continue to cooperate with Misfeance. There is no uniformity in The Netherlands on these procedures and my picture is unique to Amsterdam.

As the Amsterdam Police had officially experienced relatively little police deviance of this nature, the machinery for dealing with it was largely dormant and manpower was inadequate particularly once the investigation got underway. When the corruption cases came to light the Misfeance Department comprised *one* man in a department of over 3,000 personnel. (In the Met A10 had over eighty staff while in the NYPD there are 134 supervisors in Internal Affairs and an 'integrity control officer' in each precinct – *Vrij Nederland* 21 January, 1984). That man had no special resources, no separate office space, shared an office with other units, and was also responsible for cases of deviant public officials other than policemen. And, in practice, he was answerable to a confusing number of bosses (i.e. his direct boss – a chief inspector in charge of three squads – the Chief Constable, indirectly to the four branch heads, but especially to the Head of the Detective Branch, to which he formally belonged, and who himself came under suspicion). In addition, he was a senior 'NCO' in the rank of adjutant which made him sensitive and vulnerable to senior officers who not only outranked him but were also his social superiors making it difficult for him to interview them. This man was placed in an unenviable position, suddenly swamped with work, when ironically he had been led to believe that this job was something of a 'cushy number'. He went on to outline the predicament of his work situation.

> 'There only used to be about 3–4 cases a year. So I'm here all on my own. When a suspect comes in I wander around looking for a place where I can talk to him because I share a room with the Fraud and Forgery Squad. If I want to search a house then I have to ask Sergeant Romeijn [from the Fraud Squad] if he'll be so good as to come along or else I just grab anyone who is handy and available. But it doesn't work very effectively here. You start a line of enquiry only to find that Internal Affairs have been working on it for months. So it's really a bit of a mess here and it badly needs streamlining. It's laughable really that I have to go around looking for a room to interrogate someone and that first A. is involved and then B. is also involved in the investigation. It's not efficient. And this work is lousy. You shouldn't stay too long in this department because it wears you down in the end.'

If internal procedures and resources were shaky and inadequate then the State Detectives were hardly more effective. In The Netherlands the State Detectives are appointed by the Ministry of Justice to investigate criminal cases against public officials as well as cases involving the State (such as war crimes) and are attached to the regional offices of the law courts headed by the Attorney Generals. Most of the people I spoke to were generally less than enthusiastic about the efficiency of the State Detectives. They were virtually strangers in the inner-city underculture and were almost totally reliant on others for guidance there. Several officers were convinced that they could have achieved more internally but that calling in the State Detectives was unavoidable given the sensitivity of the issues involved.

In Amsterdam, a policeman-suspect could be subject to several levels of enquiry at different points in the organizational hierarchy. The general procedure for investigating police deviance is laid down in a circular from the Ministry of Justice (dated 17 January 1967). A distinction is made between a criminal and a disciplinary enquiry (of course, the former may end up as the latter, and vice versa). If it appears that a 'reasonable suspicion' exists that a policeman has committed a crime then the Chief Constable must inform the Mayor and Public Prosecutor. The Public Prosecutor, following discussion with the Mayor and/or Chief Constable and his own boss the Attorney General, decides whether the investigation should be conducted by the State Detectives or, the usual course, by the department itself. The major criterion in taking this decision is whether or not any doubt exists about the objectivity of the investigation and, in cases of doubt, it is recommended that the State Detectives be used. The final decision on this rests with the judicial authorities. The Mayor has final responsibility for disciplinary enquiries, which in principle are conducted within the department; but, again, in cases of doubt about objectivity the State Detectives may be called in to assist. This makes it plain that the Chief Constable has little direct control of serious cases, either criminal or disciplinary, and is subordinate to the Mayor and Public Prosecutor particularly in relation to the utilization of State Detectives.

A case of suspected corruption involving a policeman may be prosecuted in terms of criminal law, the rule-book for all civil servants, and the official instructions for police (Perrick 1982: 116–22). In none of these is the word 'corruption' used. However, there are three possibilities for prosecution. First, there are two articles (362 and 363 of the Criminal Law Book) which, in essence, forbid a policeman (or other official) from receiving a gift or promise in order to do, or not to do, something in conflict with his duty. The official has to know the reason why the gift or promise was made; the initiative comes from the corruptor; and the policeman has to *reciprocate* by knowingly doing, or failing to do, something which is against his official obligations. The second possibility relates to misuse of authority either in order to force someone else to do or not to do something, or to commit an offence himself – such as stealing at the scene of a burglary (articles 365 and 44 respectively). Thirdly, the Official Instructions for City and State Police (1958) forbid the acceptance of money, gifts, or reductions in relation to the policeman's official function (especially if these might make it difficult for him to carry out his obligations effectively or 'damage the reputation' of his office). Indeed, as part of those instructions every policeman takes an oath in which he swears not to accept gifts or promises in order to do, or not to do, something (Rookhuyzen 1978).

Of particular importance here is that technically a policeman in The Netherlands cannot accept *anything* that might be related to his position without breaking regulations; that in Amsterdam the criminal cases revolved around articles 362 and 363, while the disciplinary enquiry was concerned with breaking Official Instructions; and that the prosecution had to prove *knowledge* of the reason for the gift or promise and *reciprocation* for it (either action or neglect to act). Furthermore, three central features of the disciplinary investigative procedures in Amsterdam need to be taken into account. First, the situation was complex and untidy so that a policeman in trouble could pass through a whole range of actors in the hierarchy (in fact, no-one could adequately describe to me the lines of authority in Amsterdam regarding internal discipline). Second, depending on the seriousness of the offence, there was considerable potential for discretion in interpreting procedures at each level. Indeed, research carried out in the Amsterdam Police came to the conclusion that there is no unanimity in defining what is precisely a disciplinary offence and what constitutes a crime when committed by a policeman (van Laere and Geerts 1984) while another project revealed that policemen themselves were unclear as to what exactly constitutes a complaint from a civilian (Geerts 1982). And, third, virtually all levels adopted a predominantly reactive control strategy.

The Witnesses' Statements and the Allegations

Grave suspicions were raised against members of the Amsterdam Police and virtually every conceivable offence or practice covered by Barker and Roebuck's typology and by my own classification were mentioned (see Introduction). These accusations, however wild and implausible, are important for three main reasons. First, they shaped the public's image of the nature and extent of police deviance and fuelled the suspicions of the investigators. Second, they formed the basis of the evidence for a criminal prosecution and a disciplinary enquiry. And, third, they comprised an assault on the character and reputation of the suspects against which they had to defend themselves both formally and in their private lives. Precisely what happened remains tantalizingly elusive and I cannot precisely answer the questions 'who bribed whom, how, where, for how much, for what purpose, with what result, and with what consequences flowing from refusal to pay the bribe?' (Reisman 1979: 13). But the essence of the transactions revolves around the nature of the interaction of the main actors – what were the Chinese (among others) hoping to achieve in offering money and gifts to the police; on what understanding did the policemen accept them; what sort of power did the policemen actually have over the people concerned; and what did the policemen do or not do in return? The latter, for instance, forms the crucial element in proving 'corruption' in Dutch law.

MISCONDUCT/CRIME

This category concerns misconduct and criminal activities not (ostensibly) related to corruption. The distinction hangs on whether or not the behaviour is part of a corrupt relationship (e.g. is selling a weapon meant simply as a business transaction or is it part of a *quid pro quo* of mutual advantage between a policeman and others?). A number of statements contained accusations that policemen sexually harassed suspects, stole from suspects, stole from premises, sold heroin, gave drugs to friends, possessed and dealt in illegal firearms, misbehaved themselves under the influence of drink, carried out robberies, illegally disposed of a dead body, and even committed murder.

For example, one policeman in a supervisory function was accused of sexually abusing prostitutes. He sometimes threatened them with prosecution and, in the case of foreigners, with deportation. It was even alleged by an officer to me that he was 'fed' these women by his own personnel in order to keep him preoccupied and out of their way. One prostitute made a statement to the authorities that he had sexually molested her and also supplied her with heroin (Corruption Case Dossier, hereafter CCD with date of document; Witness's Statement, 23 September, 1976). There were several reports containing similar remarks which appear to involve rather pathetic unconsummated gropings around the erogenous zones of women in seedy hotels or during 'searches' while actually in the police station (I shall not bore the reader with the repetitive details – there are some fifty pages of evidence on this alone). But there were also some containing denials that the women concerned had ever been to bed with policemen.

The precise nature of the relationship is important. A policeman who goes to bed with a prostitute is not necessarily committing an offence and some policemen had genuinely friendly and affectionate relationships with prostitutes. But when some element of extortion, such as sexual services under fear of arrest, is concerned then the matter becomes serious from a disciplinary point of view. The material does suggest, however, that some prostitutes were subjected to sexual harassment. If this took place under threat of arrest or deportation (several of the women involved were foreigners), or if sexual services were rewarded with drugs (some of the women were users if not addicts), then this would involve serious offences, disciplinary and criminal, which would also shade over into 'abuse of power'. If a policeman encouraged or protected a prostitute in the exercise of her trade for some form of reward, monetary and/or sexual, then this would constitute a form of 'straightforward' corruption.

There were rumours in circulation that some policemen dealt in illegally confiscated firearms. Then one of the men under suspicion reported that his flat had been broken into and his service pistol had been stolen. Shortly afterwards two young men were arrested for the burglary but they mentioned stealing *several* firearms. When investigating officers subsequently searched the flat they discovered the following: hashish, LSD, methadon, opium, heroin, eight knives, various types of ammunition, several fire arms (revolvers, gas-pistols, alarm-pistols), nunchaku sticks, opium pipes, weighing scales, injection needles, and a tear-gas grenade (fully detailed in documents in the CCD). The buying and selling of firearms by policemen, moreover, was raised earlier in relation to a number of policemen (CCD, Witness's Statement, 23 November, 1974). Several reports also emerged of bizzare behaviour by policemen in bars when under the influence of drink. In a bar a 'dead drunk' detective pulled out his pistol and shot four times into the ceiling and the people were 'scared stiff and dived for cover' (CCD, Witness's Statement, 24 March, 1977). On another occasion, in a night club, an incident was said to have taken place in which a drunken policeman forced a woman on to a sofa and 'made movements as if he was having it off with her'. The woman was a complete stranger, she resisted, but no-one intervened because 'it was clear for all to see that he possessed a pistol' (CCD, Witness's Statement, 24 March 1977). This evidence suggests that the 'cowboy culture' among some policemen could involve heavy drinking, the display of firearms, the collection of weapons and drugs, sexual harassment (and perhaps intimidation), and the private collection and even use of drugs (one member of the PCS told me that he went on an LSD trip and it proved to be 'the greatest night of my life' while several respondents told of other policemen using drugs). Some of these accusations might constitute forms of police crime which do not necessarily, but may well involve forms of corruption.

However colourful and insinuating many of the press statements were, suggesting a wide range of deviance, most of the documentary material points to fairly 'straightforward' corruption in terms of relationships of mutual advantage between policemen and criminals. Those policemen who became involved appear basically as 'grass eaters'. Implicitly or explicitly a bargain is struck whereby policemen perform, or do not perform, certain activities in exchange for some form of reward from people engaged in illegal activities. Generally, in return for money, goods, and services policemen do not enforce the law against illegal enterprises and may also offer them a measure of protection against other policemen. Under these circumstances certain crimes established as a continuous business operation (McIntosh 1975) can be guaranteed a measure of continuity and predictability while policemen can profit both financially from the agreement and also in terms of gaining a degree of control over crime (e.g. prearranged arrests of 'strawmen' to keep up appearances, information on rivals, etc.).

In Amsterdam relationships had developed between policemen and Chinese criminals, and, within this world, policemen might expect drinks, meals, fruit-baskets, the services of 'hostesses', trips abroad, and money, while underworld figures could ostensibly expect some measure of cooperation or protection. For example, the wife of a Chinese bookkeeper who had worked for the Chinese gambling-house 'Club Number One', translated from photocopies of the cash-book kept by her husband. 'On page 10 is recorded "16 January – police – 700 guilders; 17 January – police – 700 guilders; 19 January – police – 700 guilders; 21 January – police – 700 guilders"' (CCD, Witness's Statement, 7 April, 1977). This statement was followed by ten pages of Chinese symbols from the bookkeeping. The payment of money to the police in the gambling-houses appears to have taken place on a routine basis but often the statements did not specify a direct eye-witness account of the money being offered and being accepted. One eye-witness, however, did claim that the passing of money occurred for all to see. The policemen would come in and would be offered a drink. They would sit next to Freddy, drop something by 'accident', and when they bent down to pick it up Freddy would pass money to them under the table; 'this happened more or less covered up but still it was possible for everyone to observe it' (CCD, Witness's Statement, 24 March, 1977).

Why did the Chinese give money to the police? The motivation for paying the policemen emerged clearly from the statement recorded from the owner of one of the gambling-houses, 'Freddy'. If a Chinese acquaintance was arrested then he might have to wait some time in the cells before his case could be processed and he could be deported. Friends of the man would come to Freddy with money and he would pass it on to policemen in order to speed up the process and get the man out of the country quickly. Also when Freddy wanted to open his gambling-house he approached Kramer and Hoogenkamp and they told him to go ahead because one gambling-house had just closed down (the number allowed to operate had been set by the Justice Department). He became friendly with the two men, made them shareholders in the game of 'fan-tan', and went out on the town with them including visits to sex-clubs where he picked up the bill (CCD, Witness's Statement, 18 April, 1977).

A Chinese croupier with experience in several gambling-houses explained that money to the police was simply considered to be one of the recurring overheads: 'Under him [the boss] there was Chan Chi Lun who mostly dealt with all sort of taxes. Among these there were included the expenses of the house such as rent, gas, water, electricity, upkeep, and so on. Included in the expenses of the house were payments to the police.' The payments to policemen were aimed at putting them in a 'positive frame of mind' with regard to the gambling-houses in case of fights and also to leave the clientele (mostly illegal clients) in peace.

> 'Finally, we expected that the police would allow the Chinese world to carry on in its own way in the gambling-houses, let it conduct its own business there, and allow it even to undertake illicit matters there such as the heroin business. I was told this by the bosses of Club Number One, in particular by Li Hung Fat, Chan Chi Lun and Hung Ka Wing.'
>
> (CCD, Witness's Statement, 2 May, 1977)

Here is the classic motivation as to why it is worthwhile to pay off the police. They can guarantee order in potentially disorderly establishments; can help to keep dishonesty within honest bounds; and can selectively enforce the law by simply failing to enforce it. For any businessman running a dodgy enterprise it is a reasonable investment. In Amsterdam, there can be little doubt but that the police were recipients of Chinese hospitality but it is often far more difficult to pinpoint precisely what they did *in return*. Some received money, food, cognac, cigars, golden cigarette lighters, expensive watches (two detectives were known popularly as the 'Rolex Men'), green jade jewelry and white-gold necklaces for their wives, busts of Buddha, sexual services, trips abroad, chocolates, and the notorious fruit-baskets (with or without envelopes containing money): but what precisely did the givers expect in return and how did the receivers interpret these gifts?

The statements of witnesses on this area are frequently long-winded, circuitous, circumspect, and difficult to pin down on concrete details. The view of a prominent witness, Freddy, sums up probably what went on. Initially he was nervous and did not want to cooperate with the two officers questioning him early on in the investigation. But he told them that giving presents was normal in the Asiatic world, that Chinese will offer gifts to policemen to make them friendly towards them, and that he went on to do the same in Amsterdam. He did so primarily to get the police out of the gambling-house as soon as possible because most of the clients were illegal immigrants who became nervous about possible controls of permits if policemen were hanging around. What emerges from later statements and interrogation is that the aim of ridding his place of policemen as quickly as possible misfired and his gambling-house began to *attract* policemen while he himself became quite friendly with some of them. For instance, one of the police suspects remarked on how busy Freddy's place became and once it was so 'chockfull of policemen' in uniform and plain-clothes that he 'just kept on walking and did not come back on that day' (CCD, Witness's Statement, 12 April, 1977).

Freddy admitted that as the relationship developed he began to pay policemen.

'As I told you previously I had heard from the owners of other gambling-houses that they gave money to the police. I also knew this from Chung Mon. [He identifies two detectives from photographs – MP]. I've given both of them money, sums varying from between 100 and 200 guilders. I heard that money was given to them at set times in other gambling-houses and so I did it as well. They didn't ask for it; I gave it of my own accord.'

He mentioned other policemen who would be given a cognac and a handful of silver guilders to play the fruit-machine. But he did not give them sums of money as with the men from Aliens who 'were in my opinion more important people who could use their influence as to whether or not certain Chinese people could stay in Holland. In all honesty I feel obliged to tell you that I was even a little bit scared of them.' He went on to describe a trip to Paris with two members of the PCS and their wives in which he viewed them as his guests and consequently picked up practically all the bills: 'I would like to repeat here, in full honesty, that following my trip to Paris I did not import any heroin' (CCD, Witness's Statement, 4 April, 1977).

Reciprocation is the essence of this form of corruption; it involves two-way traffic related to some implicit or explicit agreement in a power relationship of mutual advantage. Some of the Chinese people involved may have understood that they were paying for protection from enforcement and for freedom from controls (raids and inspections of passports), and they may have been encouraged to believe this by certain policemen, although much of the material suggests that the policemen did very little in return. Freddy, for example, claimed that he expected nothing concrete for himself in return but wanted the policemen to view him favourably and to help friends involved in deportation procedures by passing on the 'speed' money. But this definitely made it look *as if* policemen could intervene in some way to help illegal Chinese immigrants under threat of prosecution and deportation. For example Freddy accepted 1,000 guilders from a Chinese acquaintance without a residence permit; he promised two detectives that the man could work for him and would cause no trouble and one of the policemen covered his face with his hand and said in English, 'OK, I'm not responsible for what other policemen do but he won't have any more trouble from us' (CCD, Witness's Statement, 8 April, 1977). The witness did not see that the money was paid to the policemen. And the detectives did not offer protection from enforcement by others. For a vital question is whether or not they could in practice guarantee protection. Unravelling the expectations and understandings of the actors involved is no easy matter. What is patently clear, however, is that police interference in the Chinese inner-city world was minimal, which must, at the very least, have raised the idea that the police had been bought off. The witnesses stated that none of the police suspects in question ever carried out a control, made an arrest, or asked to see a passport in the casinos although they were often full of illegal Chinese immigrants.

In practice, the reality of the situation was that policemen could help individual people at a fairly incidental, *ad hoc* level but could not ultimately guarantee the protection and continuity of say the gambling-houses. The number of gambling-houses was regulated by the authorities (police, civil, and judicial). The Aliens Branch could not cope with the number of illegal immigrants and was not interested in arresting and deporting the large number of aliens who lived openly in the city. Furthermore, I suspect on the basis of my experience in Amsterdam that it is quite difficult for police-men to interfere in a case conducted by other policemen. But this might be small comfort to an illegal Chinese without papers who lived in apprehension of arrest and deportation. For he was vulnerable to exploitation from other Chinese and the police. And the owner of a gambling-house, even one with excellent relations with the police, must have asked himself if tolerance was limitless. It proved not to be, in fact, because the gambling-houses were closed officially on 1 October, 1976. Those that con-tinued to operate illegally had then even more reason to pay the police.

PREDATORY (STRATEGIC) CORRUPTION

As far as I can tell, fully fledged predatory 'strategic' corruption did not exist in Amsterdam. The police did not encourage, stimu-late, and organize crime because generally they followed events and did not control them. The justice system was not corrupt and it is almost inconceivable that the dominant coalition of the department could be interlocked with organized crime given the nature of public and political life in The Netherlands. Apparently there were no bag men making regular pick-ups of money, there was no 'pad', there was no severance pay on transfer out of a lucrative assignment, and the police did not routinely help to run the heroin trade. In short, policemen did not systematically organize and dictate the standards and levels of corruption in 'strategic' agreements with the organized underworld as in London, New York, Chicago, and Hong Kong. Apart from the Chinese triads, which were international, syndicated criminal organizations of considerable sophistication, the Amsterdam underworld consisted of a criminal fraternity that was largely small-scale, individualistic, and entrepreneurial.

Probably the most that can be said is that some relatively low-level policemen could be typified as 'meat-eaters' in that they sought out corruption and were parasitical on criminals. Some of the rumours, revelations, and accusations did suggest this and raised the cases from the level of free meals and drinks to far more serious offences such as planting, selling heroin, diluting drugs, transporting heroin, and ripping off prisoners ('shake-downs' for money or drugs). In this relationship the policemen are involved in exploiting criminals for their own gain. But what precisely were the terms of the relationship between policemen and criminals? Was it merely a question of mutual advantage, or of policemen consciously preying on criminals, or of policemen using dubious means for 'higher' ends? Motives and practices can be mixed for it is clear that policemen could come to agreements with gambling-house bosses, guaranteeing them (with various levels of specificity) freedom from interference, while also picking up Chinese suspects from the reservoir of illegal immigrants in the inner city. And when does passively receiving a hand-out move over into actually soliciting a hand-out? The essence of predatory corruption is who is in the driving-seat; in other words, who initiates and organizes the corruption and who profits and who loses – police or underworld?

And, obviously, relationships could change over time so that an agreement arrived at one stage, say in terms of mutual advantage, could alter to the detriment of one party who suddenly realizes to his surprise that it is *he* who is being exploited or that he cannot escape the newly negotiated terms of the 'contract'. Freddy, for instance, paid the police to get them out of his gambling-house but, instead, they found his company more and more congenial. For, although Freddy emphasized that he had given money of his own free will (perhaps he had been coached, because this element was essential to the defence and, needless to say, to the prosecution), another source painted a somewhat different picture. A strategically placed witness, a 'bouncer' in Freddy's casino (the 'door-men' were the only Europeans to be found in the casinos), maintained that two policemen offered Freddy protection, were seen to take money from him, would push him aside and play poker with his money, turned up on the two 'pay-days' per month (the 2nd and 16th), and went out on the town always at Freddy's expense.

'They regularly received money from him and just like the others they milked Freddy completely dry. To tell you the truth, Freddy wasn't really strong enough to be able to cope with them. The other porter and myself once told Freddy that he was crazy to behave like this. Then Freddy dropped the hint that he was scared in case his business might be closed down. Freddy could never say no. Because of this he got into deep financial difficulty and the more it went on the more he began to take heroin, something he'd done before but not in such a serious way.'

(CCD, Witness's Statement, 24 March, 1977)

This clearly portrays Freddy as victim and the police as predators (even if Freddy was a 'willing' victim and the police were 'friendly' predators).

Two major series of accusations, indicating that policemen were perhaps 'meat-eaters', focused on stealing, planting, and shaking-down Chinese and other suspects and also on advantageous arrangements with drug dealers leading to the arrests of minor purchasers, low in the drugs hierarchy. First, there arose a whole series of statements that Chinese suspects were vulnerable in the hands of the police. It was said to be common knowledge in the Chinese community that some policemen would arrest people and then let them go free for payment while also confiscating their heroin. Similar statements, recounting comparable incidents, were also made by *policemen* either to the press or while under interrogation (and also to me). For some policemen, then, Chinese suspects in possession of heroin were apparently an easy prey. Second, there were indications too that certain policemen had an intimate relationship with dealers. Again the nature of the exchange involved is crucial and, as with the Chinese, it could operate on two levels; one level was that of mutual advantage between police and dealer while another level concerned preying on lesser fry 'set up' following information passed on by the dealer. But did the dealer get his heroin back via the police and did he pay them? And did he cooperate because of fear of prosecution?

Several witnesses clearly implicated the police. One had lived with the dealer Fynaut' and stated that two policemen came almost daily, that Fynaut paid them money (on one occasion 3,000 guilders comprising three 1,000 guilder notes), that he tipped them about buyers of heroin, and that after the arrests the heroin would flow back to Fynaut (CCD, Witness's Statement, 15 October, 1976). Another witness, who had also shared a flat with Fynaut, claimed that the two policemen came regularly to the flat, that packets of heroin lay visibly on the table (but they ignored these), and that after a deal Fynaut would signal with the curtains to the waiting policemen who would then follow the buyer and arrest him later. He also said that once, when opium was extremely scarce, Fynaut went to the Warmoesstraat Station and came out with ten slices of opium. Yet another witness stated that he visited Fynaut when the two policemen were present and noticed weighing scales on the table (and, when the policemen were gone, Fynaut pulled out a box of heroin from under the table where the policemen had been sitting and began to weigh it); that the policemen had helped to dispose of a dead German by throwing him in a canal after he had died of an overdose in Freddy's place; and that when Fynaut was robbed, as occasionally happened, he could rely on the policemen to resupply him with money and heroin. This picture was confirmed by a woman who had lived with Fynaut for a time but who stated 'I never actually saw such a transaction because Fynaut was much too clever to involve anyone else' (CCD, Witness's Statement, 9 April, 1977).

Fynaut himself had started peddling in 'speed' and 'hash' in the early seventies and later graduated to larger deals in opium and heroin which he obtained from Chinese suppliers. He was frequently subject to controls conducted by the two policemen but the relationship, based originally on conflict, gradually developed into one of cooperation and he began to pass on information to them. If he knew of a deal, or had a buyer he was no longer interested in, then he would go looking for the two men on the street or phone them at the station. But he denied paying them or ever receiving back from them drugs confiscated in an arrest.

'Obviously both of them knew that I was a dealer. In the days of heroin I was really the big man in the inner city. I had good contacts with the Chinese. And in the whole Warmoesstraat, I mean the station, I was known as the biggest heroin dealer in the inner city. My relationship with Kramer and Toxopeus was such that as return on their part, I expected not to be nicked. And obviously that has never happened. In the end it was Headquarters that arrested me.'
(CCD, Witness's Statement, 12 November, 1976)

If these statements can be accepted then this could constitute a relationship of 'straightforward corruption' where Fynaut receives protection from arrest and information on raids in return for providing money and 'good collars'. But the good collars are victims of exploitation by both police and fellow criminals. A one-time friend of Fynaut described his experience of being ripped off by the police and being conned by them and Fynaut. Once he was arrested by the two policemen with ten slices of opium on him but on the way to the station they just told him to 'get lost' and kept the opium. He then began to deal on his own but had a client passed on to him by Fynaut; 'I walked into it with my eyes open' because after he had supplied the heroin he and the buyer were arrested in what he saw as a 'con set up by Fynaut and the two cops'. He saw this as a reprisal for mentioning the policemen's names at headquarters. When working with Fynaut he had been warned several times by Fynaut to stop dealing because of impending raids from headquarters and, indeed, the raid would occur promptly at the time mentioned. He assumed the tips about raids came from the two policemen because Fynaut would say 'it's alright with the police, that's been fixed' and would mention the two men, but he added 'I can't prove it'.

This material suggests that lesser criminals were vulnerable to predatory behaviour by some policemen in combination with other criminals. The names of two policemen were mentioned continually in this respect and they were said to have built up a similar relationship with a series of dealers. If these stories are true then the policemen were engaged in criminal activities themselves as opposed to just profiting from them passively. I do not feel that this deserves the classification 'strategic' but it is undoubtedly predatory. The arrangements appear opportunistic and personal because the two policemen concerned could not guarantee dealers immunity from arrest by detectives from headquarters, apart from warning about raids.

COMBATIVE (STRATEGIC) CORRUPTION

Most of the research material, and most of the case dossier, appears to pertain to fairly unorganized deviant practices that scarcely deserve the term 'strategic'. In a later phase, when the Drug Squad came more into the picture, there were intimations of dubious activities at higher levels which could be interpreted as deviant means aimed at serving institutionally approved ends. No members of the Drug Squad were ever arrested, no senior officers were ever prosecuted, and none of the accusations against Litjens were able to generate any great judicial force. But they did have a considerable impact in raising suspicions of high-level skulduggery (see below pp. 113–120, and Chapters Five and Six). It is possible that combative corruption occurred at a higher level involving major international deals but no concrete evidence ever emerged on this, although it was frequently hinted at.

PERVERSION OF JUSTICE

The central ambivalence in the concept of corruption is that it implies both gaining materially from deviance as well as the abuse of authority itself, of which 'perversion of justice' is one aspect. The Amsterdam cases conveyed the notion that perversion of justice did take place. First, the deviant practices themselves led to falsifying statements, tampering with evidence, and arresting suspects as a reprisal for informing on police deviant practices. Second, the investigation was said to have sponsored defensive reactions that included illegal telephone-tapping, blackmail, intimidating witnesses, perjury, and false statements to the authorities. For whatever motives, abuse of power and perversion of justice were clearly present in the Amsterdam situation.

CREDIBILITY OF WITNESSES

For the vast majority of Dutch policemen the 'evidence' presented above would be considered nothing short of derisory. As such they are probably little different from most policemen in wanting to have their cake and eat it; in other words, policemen routinely rely on evidence and information from criminals and 'disreputable' characters in making their cases but object strenuously to such evidence when it is aimed at policemen (Cox, Shirley, and Short 1977: 52; Laurie 1972: 52). Their objections centre focally on the disreputable and unreliable nature of the informants (while they also discredit policemen who testify against colleagues: Maas 1973: 83; Cox, Shirley, and Short 1977: 60). And it has to be said that many of the 'witnesses' in Amsterdam were prostitutes, gamblers, ponces, drug dealers, junkies, illegal immigrants, bouncers, underworld figures, car thieves, fences, dealers in stolen weapons, and even murderers, while many key statements were made by foreigners leading to subsequent cultural and language barriers. However plausible one may find their stories, one has to recognize that such characters may have ulterior motives for wishing to 'shop' policemen (Goffman 1969: 39). They may be anti-police in general, may wish revenge against individual policemen who have previously arrested or harassed them, may wish to remove greedy policemen in order to replace them with cheaper ones (*Sunday Times* 16 September, 1979), may desire to eliminate policemen hot on their trail, or they may seek to settle scores against old partners or rivals in crime via accusations about them in relation to criminal activities with corrupt policemen. It may also be that the criminal subculture encourages bragging, exaggeration, cheating, and lies (Sherman 1974: 98; Reisman 1979: 9).

This is of importance to the nature of the investigation because investigating officers, put on the scent of highly suspect behaviour, have to come up with evidence that constitutes judicial *proof* for a prosecution in a court of law. In Amsterdam, due to the rather cumbersome, reactive nature of the investigation, no policeman was caught '*in flagrante delicto*' (except for the man with weapons and drugs in his flat) and hence the investigators had to rely on either witness's testimony or suspects' confessions. Indeed, even if a policeman had been observed actually taking money that would not necessarily constitute proof of 'corruption' which in Dutch law has to involve reciprocation 'in conflict with duty'.

But what value could be placed on the testimony and what difficulties did the investigators face? Chinese witnesses had to be interviewed using a translater (or else in English which was later translated in to Dutch). Some translators were threatened with death (*Time Magazine* 29 November, 1976); one man rejected his statement later when it was read back to him in Chinese; some Chinese witnesses were deported and could no longer be traced; others clammed up because they feared reprisals from policemen and/or the underworld; and the two men with the most to tell, Chung Mon and 'Mao', were murdered (while all Chung Mon's papers containing evidence damaging to the police apparently 'disappeared'). Some witnesses were inconsistent and had conspicuous lapses of memory (cf. Ball, Chester, and Perrott 1979: 81); much of the testimony was hearsay and of little use in court; people who made statements refused to sign or failed to turn up for a second interview. A weekly magazine noted that it was a strange coincidence that the police clamp down on illegal Chinese immigrants had removed most of the potential witnesses in the case (*Vrij Nederland* 3 December, 1977). Some simply retracted earlier statements (this was a particular problem for the Countryman investigation: McNee 1983: 189); and, finally, some evidence was palpably weak – 'I held all these envelopes against the light and made out that in some envelopes were sheaves of 1000 guilders' – and some could just not be taken seriously (such as the accusation that the policeman known as 'the Hippie' murdered a dealer in an alleyway when no other source mentioned this and no body was ever found).

Furthermore, on 24 March, 1977 someone who had worked for Freddy as a bouncer/doorman had stated to State Detectives that Freddy had accompanied two members of the PCS and their wives on a weekend trip to Paris. On the way back the policemen drove part of the way in Freddy's Mercedes while Freddy took the wheel of their car when crossing the French–Belgian border. Two kilos of heroin were transported during this journey and the proceeds from its sale were distributed among the three men. The bouncer said that he *saw* the heroin being moved from the boot of Freddy's car. A week later, on 31 March, 1977, the same witness *withdrew* this last part of his statement and said that it had been deduction based on hearsay and was not something he had witnessed himself. Another witness was visited in prison for a follow-up interview but refused to cooperate further. There are all sorts of reasons for this sort of non-cooperation with the police. But two are doubtless crucial. First, a witness will not want to incriminate himself. For instance, a witness said that a Surinamese dealer had been arrested but in return for 3000 guilders from a friend his drugs were switched in the station for 'bull-shit' and the real heroin was returned to another Surinamese dealer for resale. When contacted the friend hotly denied the whole story, which is quite understandable because otherwise he would have to admit aiding to bribe a police officer and possession of heroin (CCD, Witness's Statement, 7 January, 1977). And the key witness, Fynaut, simply went through all the testimony, on his paying the police and setting up deals with them, and roundly denied each statement as lies, falsification, falsehood, and fiction. For an acknowledged and self-proclaimed drug-dealer, already sampling the pleasures of imprisonment, that seems a very sensible thing to do.

Second, some witnesses were frightened of reprisals (Beigel and Beigel, 1977: 23). I was told by an investigating officer, 'We know that some witnesses have been threatened and have withdrawn or changed their testimony.' A woman who had made a first summary statement never turned up for a second appointment to confirm and sign it because she had received threats from Surinamers and Chinese and 'did not want to know' anymore. One Chinese witness asked for police protection and this too is highly understable in that informing in the Chinese world was sometimes punished with death. One of the police suspects told me that he was accused by a Chinese witness of taking 1,500 guilders in a gambling-den, so he openly challenged him, calling him a 'filthy dirty slimy rat'. The witness was found later floating in the river Amstel with six bullets in his body (probably for informing about a murder but the policeman's denunciation may have hastened his demise). There was a reason, however, why some Chinese were prepared to make statements against the police. The crackdown on the Chinese community, and the numerous expulsions, meant that they were no longer left in peace by the authorities but faced raids, imprisonment, and deportation. One policeman suggested a sinister reason for some of the retractions (although his conspiracy theory is impossible to verify). He stated that a senior officer returned from the Far East, following the arrests of eight policemen, and, accompanied by three bosses from the gambling-houses, he personally demanded that statements be retracted. The bosses did not want conflict with Headquarters but a full retraction was impossible so it was agreed to implicate a few of the 'little guys' and the 'big nobs can stay put'.

In short, the legal evidence, however colourful, suggestive, and insinuating, was not strong. Were there envelopes in the fruit-baskets; did the envelopes contain money; did the envelopes disappear en route to the policemen; who actually saw money changing hands in the gambling-houses (it was often a private transaction in an office); did entries in a Chinese cash-book mean that the money was actually paid to the police; did some Chinese middle-men in drug deals tell their bosses that they had paid the police, or had had their drugs confiscated, simply as a way of making extra money or keeping the drugs for themselves (*Nieuwe Revue* 7 June, 1978); and who saw the heroin being returned to the dealer–informant following the arrest of a buyer set up in a shakedown? The case, then, was weak. And it would remain weak as long as the suspects, and key witnesses, denied their involvement in criminal and corrupt activity.

Conclusion

'There are two things you'll never cut out; prostitution and corruption.'

(Interview with Commissioner, headquarters)

In this chapter I have examined the nature of the accusations made against the police, principally in the light of the suspicions that were aroused among investigating officers during interviews with witnesses and among the general public via the media. In classifying those accusations it appeared that most of them boiled down to low-level, opportunistic practices of the perks, free meals, mutual services variety, and that most of the policemen emerged as 'grass-eaters'. However, there were some elements in the statements that suggested that possibly several policemen went after corruption almost as a style of life and these could be typified as 'meat-eaters'. In effect, the allegations dealt largely with misconduct and straightforward corruption but also hinted at combative and predatory corruption, and also perversion of justice. Genuinely strategic corruption, at the level of the SIU in New York or the 'Dirty Squad' in the Met, where the police, either for profit and power or for combating organized crime, came to high-level, long-term arrangements with the underworld, did not seem to exist although it was hinted at occasionally. The incidents were largely confined to a 'bribal zone' (Reisman 1979: 31) in the inner city which presented particular problems for the investigation because the predominant ethnic group, the Chinese, were difficult to penetrate because of their language, culture, and syndicate organization (Reiss 1983).

At the same time the Amsterdam Police had no bureaucratic rivals in the inner city competing for territory, which gave considerable freedom to the detectives operating there. The geographic and cultural isolation of the Chinese made low-level Chinese vulnerable to enforcement while, as a minority group not tied into the mainstream of Dutch society, they did not protest actively about their victim role. The often flamboyant and suggestive statements of witnesses all too frequently provided weak, inconsistent, contradictory, or unprovable testimony and the investigation was hampered by the vulnerability of that material as the basis for a juridical prosection. At the time, and in the eyes of investigating officers, it must have seemed, however, that they were gathering potentially damaging information on some very serious offences involving policemen and criminals. This is reinforced when we consider that an investigation can generate a snowball effect whereby witnesses, of 'low repute' and low credibility, discover that their stories are suddenly being given credence and, for a number of reasons, come forward to testify against policemen (Beigel and Beigel 1977: 130). Corruption scandals have a nasty habit of not lying down gracefully but of getting out of hand.

At this stage it is worthwhile to subject the allegations to closer scrutiny in order to read between the lines of the documentary evidence. For instance, in endeavouring to decipher the precise nature of the power relationship and the mutuality between policemen and the Chinese underworld, it is essential to raise the question – who is conning whom or who was pretending to let himself be conned by whom? If we assume that nothing is quite what it seems to be and that relationships in the underworld are characterized by exploitation and dependency, then there may be more going on here than meets the eye or than appears in statements of witnesses and suspects. Let us examine three possibilities. One is that the policemen pretended that they were more powerful than they actually were. Civilians often do not understand the hierarchy of authority in the police and may not appreciate the distinction between a detective and a senior officer. Furthermore, Freddy may have believed that the plain-clothes policemen he knew had materially influenced the opening of his gambling-house because, quite amazingly, he never consulted anyone in authority at all. And a policeman with inside knowledge could pretend to influence a case which had already been decided; as one informant told me, he could not help a Chinese to get a friend released once he had been arrested, 'But what I can do is take his money and pretend I've done something for him because I've just seen on the telex messages in the station that his mate has already been set free.' The two detectives from the Aliens Department could obviously turn a blind eye to the hundreds of illegal Chinese hanging around the restaurants and gambling-houses but, once an alien had been arrested, the most they could do was speed up the procedure so that the person spent less time in custody or else delay the moment of arrest as there was always a backlog. Yet again, however, they may have appeared, or made themselves appear, more powerful than they actually were.

A second possibility is that the Chinese were ripping off one another. The fruit-baskets were supposed to contain envelopes with money but one police respondent told me, 'Yes, I've had a fruit-basket, but there was no envelope in it when I got it; maybe there was one in it when it left the gambling-house but it wasn't there by the time the basket reached me.' Twice a month Chung Mon used to ask for 2,000 guilders to 'pay the police' but did he actually use the money for that purpose? The cash-book in 'Club Number One', with entries recording payments to the police, proved to be as reliable as conventional 'creative' book-keeping. Before the profit was distributed to the share-holders in the gambling-houses a percentage was skimmed off for 'expenses' and not entered in the records; in one case a witness suspected the book-keeper of keeping 10,000 guilders for himself and then trying to cover this up by entering 8,300 guilders as 'paid to the police' (CCD, Witness's Statement, 7 July, 1976). Then there was the potentially damning evidence against two detectives that they had taken 1000 guilders from Freddy to allow an illegal alien to remain in the country. Freddy had overcome their reluctance by putting a roll of notes, bound with an elastic band, in the pocket of one of them; only later did he mention that the detective took out the money and left it behind. He kept the money and could not admit this to his acquaintances otherwise he would 'lose face' (while he denied that he was now changing his previous statement because he was frightened of the detectives – CCD, Witness's Statement, 25 April, 1977). In effect, so-called 'payments to the police' may have been a means whereby some Chinese exploited other Chinese to their own advantage.

The third scenario is that the real business was heroin and the gambling-houses were just a front. For example, there was some confusion as to who drove which car on the trip to Paris. According to Freddy he drove across the French–Belgian border on the way back and his car was searched for twenty minutes by customs officials (a red Mercedes with a Chinese driver was then a likely target for a search for drugs). One statement claimed that a policeman drove the car over the border. Even if Freddy's story is correct then it would have been convenient for Europeans in a less conspicuous car to bring something across the border in relative safety from control (particularly if they let fall, had they been about to be searched, that they were policemen). And it would not be the first time that wives provided an excellent cover for crime (Ball, Chester and Perrott 1979: 89). Perhaps the real *quid pro quo* for lucky money was not leaving the aliens or the gambling-houses alone but tip-offs about forthcoming raids for drugs and weapons.

If the underlying basis of power in the Chinese world was the import and distribution of heroin then the Chinese paid very cheaply for a form of protection. The cigars, cognac, and handouts were a small price to pay for a measure of immunity. On the surface, it appears as though we are concerned primarily with low-level policemen who could be classified as 'grass-eaters' and who engaged in standard, 'straightforward' corruption of a fairly unorganized kind (i.e. on a limited and personal rather than widespread basis, for *ad hoc* cases rather than for blanket coverage, and of a sporadic nature rather than a refined, regular system of payments). If, however, the fruit-baskets were only the 'tip of the iceberg' and if the policemen had managed to conceal from investigators the real nature of the rewards, then there may well have been a very lucrative 'iceberg' hidden from view. While many of these questions remain unanswered, and probably unanswerable, it is nevertheless perfectly clear that at the time of the investigation there were strong indications and serious suspicions that the cases concerned far more than just lucky money and fruit-baskets.

This view is magnified if we examine the more serious suspicions raised throughout the affair. Now detectives used to say, if you asked them whether or not a suspect had committed a crime, 'I don't know; I wasn't there when it happened.' This half-humorous remark reveals the detective's reliance on accounts as he is rarely an eye-witness. Here we are faced with the same dilemma; how do we interpret these statements? For instance, a highly respected senior officer in Rotterdam stated unequivocally of The Netherlands 'that there is no question of structural corruption in our police departments' (Blauw 1982: 539). Yet a member of the State Detectives wrote a paper in which he not only documented an increase in corruption cases (from twenty-five in 1978 to seventy in 1982) and the number of policemen involved (from eighteeen in 1978 to sixty-three in 1982) but also argued, on the basis of his professional experience as an investigator, that it was no longer possible to speak of 'rotten apples'. For example, he pointed to the fact that in some cases 'extremely close contacts' existed between corrupt policemen in The Netherlands, Belgium and West Germany and that over the years the same criminals were continually named in corruption cases in those three countries and the criminals themselves also kept frequently in touch with one another. This suggests, he argued, that hidden corruption exists in relation to organized crime (Lentink 1983: 21–25).

There is no doubt that in Amsterdam several sources pointed in the direction of more serious incidents than receiving a warm turkey in a fruit basket. These accusations may be part of mutual mud-slinging and they overlap with attacks on senior officers but I deal with them here to try to indicate what may have been taking place. For instance, a senior officer assured me that heroin had been transported from France by policemen and that one of the suspects 'supervised shipments and also sold the stuff (but don't write this down)'; another worked out that the men from Licensing may have been taking *f*25,000 a year (then roughly £5,000 or $10,000); and Freddy claimed to have given money to some fifty policemen. Indeed, a crucial source with considerable inside information, believed that as many as 150 policemen were involved in corrupt activities. The rumours about close involvement of policemen with underworld characters – particularly in relation to contacts with prostitutes, warning criminals of police intervention, buying and selling firearms, and supplying drugs – had circulated for several years before 1976 and frequently the same names of policemen were mentioned suggesting involvement in a period of over five years. In one statement a policeman recalls that he was drunk in a bar with another suspect when the suspect asked to borrow his pistol and went off with a Chinese acquaintance. Why did he need the pistol? The same suspect was also alleged to have committed an armed robbery of a Chinese restaurant in another town. I was told by an 'eye-witness' that he secretly observed that one suspect tried to cover up the loss of his service pistol by smashing the window of his car and reporting the theft as if from his car; if true, this must have failed because he was forced to report its loss from his flat. Yet another officer informed me that the men from the Aliens Department could have been taking money for ten years. Indeed, in one of the few remarks in which a suspect admitted an offence to me, he hinted that accepting money was regular and systematic. His partner, he said, 'knew his people. I mean every bar that stayed open late gave him a *tientje* [ten guilders] or a bottle and at first he kept me out of it. I cottoned on to this and then one evening I asked him "What are you going to do about it?" and he said "You've realized what's going on." From then on we were partners.'

A number of sources do indicate, then, that there was an iceberg, although its dimensions are unclear. A senior officer at headquarters had 'serious suspicions and indications that there was the beginning of an organization' and believed that there was a measure of cooperation between the main suspects and between them and Litjens. There was always a connection between Litjens, the eight suspects, and the Chinese; and I overheard an officer telling detectives, 'Let's face it, if Litjens hadn't been a commissioner they'd have taken his shoe laces away' (i.e. arrested him). For instance, the advice to the Justice Department on which gambling-houses to tolerate and leave open was crucial to the Chinese and who knows how that advice was delivered and for what reward. I was told that the Chinese experts and Litjens organized it and were paid for so doing. Was it merely a coincidence that Chung Mon's casino did receive permission? And what was the relationship between Litjens and Chung Mon, who 'wore a hole in Litjen's carpet'? Was it not suspicious that Chung Mon was used by the police as a translator in cases involving Chinese suspects? Was it not suspicious that Chung Mon had a travel agency and that deported Chinese had tickets bought for them with police mediation at that agency? And apparently all Litjens or one of his minions had to do was phone the Aliens Department and say that a Chinese prisoner awaiting deportation was a 'good informant' for him to be released. One source spoke of an incomplete jig-saw puzzle but that when 'Mao' was murdered Litjens turned up half-drunk, messed around, and for hours nothing was committed to paper because he insisted on waiting for the Chinese experts, who were out of town. The detectives extensively questioned witnesses who

> 'told everything in detail, about appointments in the Marriott Hotel and the weapons used, and the identity of the killers was completely known. But in the official dossier their interrogations are not included. Somebody had messed around with the documents. Litjens must have known about the statements from Hoogland and Lighthart, who took them down.'

There was a case of protection and intimidation involving a Chinese 'heavy mob' and an hotel owner who came to the Warmoesstraat to file a complaint. Two detectives in the Warmoesstraat tipped headquarters and, through the intervention of two detectives there, the suspect concerned, a member of the 14K triad destined for deportation, was released and the case disappeared in the *doofpot* (or 'cover-up can').

How does one interpret this material? Are we dealing with honest but maligned men or with an evil conspiracy that far exceeds the legally acceptable proof brought to light by the investigation? Some of the investigating officers were convinced that most of the accusations were valid. Some of the suspects also thought so too, with one telling me, 'I can mention three more names with regard to firearms', and 'I know that Chinese suspects were set free for money, but not by me.' Another said that he was positive that the money noted in the Chinese cashbook was paid to policemen. One feature which does emerge strongly is that policemen had built up very close links with characters in the underworld and that they had almost unrestricted power in terms of arrests, deportations, and turning a blind eye. And I am pretty sure that an inspection of lockers in the Warmoesstraat would have brought forth illegal truncheons, confiscated pornography, samples of drugs, and even the occasional firearm. Some men kept collections of drugs and weapons at home 'to show their friends' and I recall a junior officer scouting eagerly around for 'souvenirs' after raids for his collection of grenades, knives, and firearms. There are strong indications that drugs were kept back following raids and arrests, that informants were rewarded with drugs, and that informants were protected. For example, a newspaper report spoke of a CID detective visiting an informant who openly displayed firearms, while on another occasion a different informant, caught in a raid on a night club, was helped to escape in the car of a detective (*De Telegraaf* 16 February, 1980). Policemen are habitually suspicious and say that where there is smoke there must be a fire. In Amsterdam the source of the fire may not have been uncovered but there were smoke signals in abundance.

It is tantalizing not to know exactly what took place. There are indications, for instance, that policemen transported drugs, blackmailed and intimidated witnesses, perhaps even aided in getting a Chinese informer murdered, lied, committed perjury, falsified evidence, dealt in firearms, sexually abused prostitutes, and became involved in arrangements reaping 'hundreds of thousands of guilders' (according to one senior officer). But how many were involved, at what level of organization, and with what consequences for deals, suspects, and informants remains unclear. There were all too often indications but these were not backed up with evidence.

For example, on the occasion of the Queen's Birthday (a public holiday celebrated with considerable festivity) I went out on the street with a chief inspector dressed imperiously in ceremonial uniform with white silk scarf and gloves. In the middle of the main street of Amsterdam, ringed by thousands of revellers, we came face to face with one of the suspended suspects out for a stroll with his wife and daughter. In this embarrassing and incongruous confrontation the man complained that the business was dragging on for so long and why did not the officer come around to see him sometime, 'I'm nearly always at home, aren't I, and I won't eat you.' We walked on and the officer said almost as an aside, 'He's supposed to have taken 70,000 guilders.' Did the man really take the money? The officer added, 'I don't know. I wasn't there when it happened.'

5
Labelling, Rationalizations, and Accounts

Police Views on Deviance and the Experience of Labelling

In this chapter I examine how policemen themselves define deviance and react to the experience of labelling while in the following chapter I explore how this definitional process ignited a prolonged and acrimonious institutional clash. As a brief preface underpinning these chapters I wish to focus on five central features of the police occupational culture.

First, studies of policing almost universally accentuate secrecy and solidarity as core elements of police values and practice (Westley 1970: 56; van Maanen 1978: 119). This defensive and introspective culture, which approaches the structure of a secret society (as etched by Simmel, Wolff 1950), is powerful, swiftly encapsulates newcomers, condones occupational deviance, and can be punitive if the 'rule of silence' is broken and solidarity is threatened (Smith 1973: 220). But the 'blue curtain' has been penetrated and, under certain circumstances, police do expose their colleagues' deviance as in Newburgh (NY), Chicago, Oakland, New York, London, and Amsterdam. Also the sentimental view of police comradeship and fraternity has to be tempered with the fact that some policemen may implicate other policemen in deviance and then blackmail them into not revealing anything, may collect incriminating evidence on colleagues as an insurance in case things do go wrong, and may single out a scapegoat to feed to the authorities in time of need (Cox, Shirley, and Short 1977: 157; Beigel and Beigel 1977: 8; Davies and Goodstadt 1975: 10). How deep is loyalty in these instances? I recall a senior officer contemplating seriously the possibility of 'cocking up the chances' of a colleague receiving promotion to the rank of commissioner and a constable explaining to me how, if he really wanted to, he could 'set up' a chief inspector should the man be seen walking alone in the red-light district:

> 'It's so easy to plant suspicion. If I know when he's walking about in the district then I've the date and the time, and I could get a tart to swear that he visited her and even get another tart to swear blind that she came in and saw him at it, "There he was getting stuck in and going at it like a bull in a china-shop," something like that. What could he put against that? He'd have a hell of a job denying it if he had to admit he was there on that day at that time.'

According to the arch-cynical detective Terry Sneed in Newman's novel (1978a: 230), 'In the final analysis, loyalty doesn't exist.' It is worth bearing in mind here what one informant said to me in Amsterdam, 'Police work is dominated by fear and distrust. Everyone distrusts everyone else. It's the same all over in this force.'

Second, one can perceive the policeman's occupational and moral 'career' as involving adaptation to perks and 'gilding the lily' and to backing blindly the behaviour and accounts of colleagues (Smith and Gray 1983: 71). For example, one explanation of a policeman's involvement in deviance may be the unwillingness to forgo membership in certain subgroups, as where accepting bribes is seen as the only way to continue in detective work. Deviance can be justified, either in terms of readily available perks that no reasonable person would refuse or as essential means of achieving results in a system weighted against the policeman's view of justice. Ethnographies of policing frequently reveal a high level of tolerance for deviance among colleagues although there are limits to this (as in condemning premeditated theft or in reporting gratuitous violence by colleagues: Sherman 1978: 123; Reiner 1978: 224). The existence of scandal does not necessarily mean that all policemen are involved, even when deviance is widespread and is condoned by the culture, and there are different adaptations to the dilemma of what to do about it (Birch 1983). Some can seek careers through positions that avoid it by not providing opportunity, while others can respond with 'resignation, ritualism, inaction' (Barker and Roebuck 1973: 31). But, typically, policemen refrain from judging colleagues because they may feel that a strong-man or a devious investigator is needed under certain circumstances – 'well, I wouldn't do it myself but maybe we need people like him' (personal communication, Egon Bittner; Reisman 1979: 145). Of Philadelphia, an ex-patrolman recalled, 'I don't remember any Serpicos in my department. A live and let live attitude existed. "Don't make waves" seemed to be the cops' favourite cliché' (Birch 1983: 83) and in Amsterdam some men justified not reporting deviance by saying 'am I my brother's keeper?' (van Laere and Geerts 1984: 20).

Third, police may develop an occupational 'logic' that helps to cloak and to rationalize deviance by justifying techniques that amplify presumed guilt into actual guilt. For instance, in the Warmoesstraat two patrolmen found a wallet in their patrol car when bringing in a prisoner and, assuming he had stolen it (he was a Turkish 'guestworker' who spoke almost no Dutch), they wrote in their crime report that they found the wallet when searching him *inside* the station. Unfortunately for them, it belonged to someone who had been arrested earlier and the coincidence was noticed; but a senior officer said, 'in a way they considered it logical and then they wouldn't admit their mistake, but it all came out'. Fourth, socialization to the police world is said to lead to a 'working personality' characterized by suspicion, cynicism, callousness, masculinity, disillusion, and even self-contempt (Rubin 1974). On the one hand, the culture may cynically support the necessity of bending rules and thwarting of legal restrictions (Manning 1980: 69); while, on the other hand, some policemen may revel in 'dirty work' and enjoy contacts with dirt, obscenity, and lawlessness, which represent danger, risk, and power (Douglas 1966: 77), and may become indistinguishable from criminals (*Newsweek* 27 February, 1984).

Finally, policemen in their daily work may violate people's privacy, reveal their secrets, and harm their reputation (Becker 1970: 108). They have a tendency to assume that suspects are guilty, to be derogatory to suspects and witnesses, to discredit routinely other people's accounts, to interpret ordinary behaviour as incriminating, to degrade and demean prisoners, and to use suspicion as a weapon against both guilty and innocent (and as retaliation besmirching those found not guilty by the courts). Police can become insensitive and immune to how wounding these semi-conscious techniques of imposing moral stigma can be.

Indeed, when policemen are exposed to them themselves they find them almost unendurable.

POLICE DEFINITIONS OF DEVIANCE

Deviance is a 'contingent, processual, and relativistic' concept that has to be defined and attributed in an interaction between rules, situations, definers and defined (Manning 1973: 127). A curious difficulty arises, however, when we turn to how police set normative limits on occupational deviance because these professional labellers and stigmatizers do not routinely discuss certain delicate aspects of their own professional activities. In effect, the nature of occupational deviance is a taboo subject. Policemen may refer to the dark areas of their work obliquely, through story-telling or humour (Holdaway 1981), but evidence indicates that they avoid open consideration of occupational hazards, pitfalls, and 'trade secrets' related to the dark side of the work (Goffman 1959: 141–42). Murphy says that 'wiring' him as a rookie in New York would not have worked because 'not a single word about the system of graft was mentioned directly' (Murphy and Plate 1977: 45), while, in London, Laurie (1972: 276) referred to the subject of police taking bribes as 'rather like masturbation in a Victorian public school – denounced in public and evasively discussed in private'. The aversion to touching on critical areas can be seen simply as a professional unwillingness to divulge too much information to colleagues on specific cases (Daley 1979: 196), or on 'dodgy' incidents that might backfire, but the defensiveness seems to go deeper. In certain predominantly masculine professions that involve risk and danger there is a tendency to display role distance, to adopt a laconic, off-hand style, and not to account for behaviour in other than base, deflating, or unduly modest terms. This adaptation seems to be related intimately to the individual's perception of self as a hardened exponent who can take what is coming, who does not need to justify conduct in pretentious or ideal terms, and who does not need to lean emotionally on others. The compensation for this inability to articulate about the core experience of their lives is the feeling of fraternity with close colleagues who are tied by an unspoken appreciation of their mutual predicament and their unbridgeable separation from straight society and outsiders. This pattern has been noted among test-pilots (Wolfe 1980), combat soldiers (Ellis 1982), and criminals (Ball, Chester, and Perrott 1979), and appears to be central to the concept of their manhood.

One major consequence of this is that policemen are unable to ventilate their problems because they are frightened of appearing weak or 'soft'. In London, for instance, one officer described in court his mixed feelings of remorse, loyalty, and helplessness on being confronted with corruption.

'You had to adhere to this bloody system. . . . You have to know what it was like, this banding together. I'm not saying any of the people I could go to [senior officers outside the squad] was corrupt. What I'm saying is it just wasn't done. You swallow it. It goes on but no one wants to admit it.'

He admitted that the corruption 'preyed on his mind', he felt 'disgusted', and became 'neurotic' about it until it reached an 'obsession' (*Sunday Times* 21 November, 1976). To mention this to colleagues, however, might be interpreted as not being able to shoulder the strain of the work. As a result of this potential negative sanctioning, pivotal features of the work situation, such as coping with fear and dealing with deviance, are not brought out into the open and emotional problems about them are bottled up. Of course, not discussing deviance may be an avoidance mechanism for policemen who would have difficulty facing up to the reality of their wrongdoing if it was spelled out to them openly (Daley 1979: 196; Maas 1974: 156).

During my second and third research projects in Amsterdam, however, the matter was widely discussed because the subject dominated the department. Remarks were, then, a reflection on past events and respondents were usually careful to distance themselves from those cases. No one came out and told me straightforwardly that he had been involved in serious incidents – how he went about it and how he justified it – so that these reflections indicate merely how the policemen set about categorizing deviance generally. What did emerge clearly, in many discussions with policemen in Amsterdam, was that they experienced considerable difficulty in applying the term 'corruption' to these particular set of cases. They viewed corruption as something large-scale, systematic, involving large sums of money, and as almost wholly pernicious. When it came to non-criminal deviance then two researchers in Amsterdam found that there was no unanimity in defining it, although everyone claimed to know what it meant ('it's everything that's not allowed' was often heard), and between police forces in Holland they elicited considerable discrepancies in defining internal disciplinary offences; they concluded,

'It soon became clear to us, on the basis of our interviews, that in Amsterdam consensus does not exist as to what is unacceptable and what is acceptable. The concrete definition of what is unacceptable is an individual matter and is also often unclear because by no means is everything specified, or can be specified, in written rules available to everyone.'

(van Laere and Geerts 1984: 19)

Most of my respondents felt that that you *had* to take something. When I told a senior officer about an incident at 'Modderdam', a small town where police saved a man's life following an accident and a gift of flowers for the constables concerned was returned to the sender, he considered it outrageous, offensive, and as driving a wedge between police and public: 'It shows a form of fear and the public will curse you if you do things like that.' But technically the leadership in 'Modderdam' was right – policemen may not accept *anything*. And, if you do accept things, where do you draw the line? In Amsterdam the line was drawn by finding sporadic 'grass-eating' acceptable and that meant the passive acceptance of minor perks and symbolic gifts, the 'cadging' of presents for raffles at Christmas time, and 'mumping' for drinks and snacks (the so-called *naggen*). But systematic, financially based transactions were viewed as dangerous, unadvisable, or even unacceptable.

For most people that I talked to, the cases were part and parcel of relatively low-level and innocent relationships with businesses and even criminals which did not seriously challenge the integrity of the police but which were seen as constituting a perennial problem in police work (money, drink, and women were seen as the predictable stumbling-blocks). Senior personnel too, who often deal with foreign visitors and guests of the Amsterdam Police, may find the giving and receiving of hospitality unavoidable in relationships with people and may receive drinks, meals, and presents. Given this perspective – that some reciprocation is inevitable – it is perhaps not surprising that some of the suspects were seen as victims caught in an exaggerated reaction to technically illegal, but customary, practices. In the eyes of many policemen, then, the cases did not involve 'corruption' and the suspects were not 'corrupt'. Some policemen apparently refused to accept anything at all from civilians, others drew the line at low-value symbolic gifts of drink and food, while others were even prepared to see small sums of money as acceptable. Often, however, there was the feeling that money altered the relationship and placed the policeman in a potentially vulnerable position. The suspects tended to be seen as unlucky scapegoats who had been led astray by a combination of weak supervision and personal ambition;

> 'They're not corrupt as far as I'm concerned. I don't call this corruption. It used to be called 'cadging'. But we've sent back-woods gamekeepers in against the Mafia to cope with prostitutes and heroin. And they've gone to work like Kojak and they've been taken in by their own enthusiasm.'

One difficulty in interpreting these fairly general statements about the policeman's own definition of corruption is that most of them do not emanate from people who admit to having been involved themselves. In fact, there may be a tendency for outsiders to overestimate the extent to which many policemen have opportunities for, and knowledge about, corruption. For it is clearly a largely secret activity that may be concealed from *other policemen* and, in a 'segmented' organization (Koot 1983), knowledge of deviant practices is likely to be differentially distributed (Birch 1983: 84). Policemen themselves may simply not know exactly what is going on in their department (and, of course, may not want to know). Those with the best knowledge of corruption are likely to be corrupt themselves but unlikely to talk about it.

However, my questions to the suspects as to what they considered to be corruption did elicit specific references to corruption within the Amsterdam Police. These statements have to be approached with caution; for it was sometimes a case of the kettle calling the pot black with policemen suspected of corruption accusing others of precisely the same charges levelled at them (where pointing the finger is part of a technique of counter-accusation against senior officers this will be dealt with in the following chapter). One of the suspects in the affair told me, of a Chinese suspect who entered the Warmoesstraat with 3,000 guilders but left with only 800, of confiscated heroin that was never reported by the policemen concerned and, of two detectives taking 400 guilders in a gambling house and dividing it between them. He and his partner put a Chinese contact in touch with a detective at headquarters who was handling a drug case involving several Chinese suspects;

> 'But then we heard that the suspects were due to be deported to Hong Kong. Now the detective also knew that of course but he

pretends to do something about their case and receives 5,000 guilders. We only got to hear about this later and I went out for a drink with the detective. I said "you're a nice one pulling a stroke like that" and he said "Och, why don't you just have another drink". Then in a way I'm corrupt too. It sounds a bit crude but I'm telling you as a way of making clear what the climate was like.'

Two other sources suggested that certain serious forms of deviance were not only institutionalized in Amsterdam but that they were enforced with the sort of group pressure and intimidation reported elsewhere (Stoddard 1968; Barker 1977). A report on measures to deal with unacceptable police conduct raised the possibility that some of the following practices were present in Amsterdam – removing parts from confiscated cars, taking clothing from property recovered after a break-in, stealing material from patrol cars, stealing from colleagues, and dipping into the coffee-money, and that the threat of physical force was used to sanction one 'whistle-blower' (van Laere and Geerts 1984: 11). A key informant, with considerable access to inside information, told me of two policemen in uniform who went to an illegal casino where one of them sees his partner lose 600 guilders.

'Back in the patrol car he tries to say something and is told, "Keep your mouth shut, sometimes I get good information there and in return I fix their parking tickets for them." The partner confides in a chief inspector but it gets around that he's been talking. He's been threatened to keep quiet or else and as a result he's now decided to leave Amsterdam.'

Although it is extremely difficult to decipher precisely what went on, the material in this section suggests that the policemen simply did not see many of the perks and presents that come their way ('grass-eaters') as objectionable, that they viewed acceptance of money as crossing a potentially dangerous boundary, and that they carried a strong negative stereotype of active deviants involved with criminals ('meat-eaters').

THE ARRESTS AND INTERROGATIONS

'At Headquarters Volmer [investigating officer] shouted at me, "You're sitting there lying, I can be mean you know, and I know a lot more than you think." Well, of course, I just said,

"Well then, if you know so much, why don't you just put it down in your report?"'

(Interview, suspect, PCS)

The arrests of the police suspects took place in April, 1977. All of the suspects were soon released after their arrests except for Kramer, who had to spend thirty-eight days in custody. Later doubts were expressed about the wisdom of so many arrests within such a short time as this exaggerated the magnitude of the problem while making the Justice Department look rather foolish when it proved less than easy to make the cases stick. A major facet typical of this sparring match prior to the trials was the attempt to shift blame from the suspects to a number of senior officers (dealt with in Chapter Six). Two of the suspects had themselves demanded a new investigation which would include scrutinizing the performance of the force leadership (*De Volkskrant* 3 December, 1977) while allegations were made that officers in the Warmoesstraat must have been aware of the somewhat irregular use which drugs were being put to by their subordinates because a message on the station's notice-board called for an end to 'messing around with drugs for informants' (*Haagse Post* 8 October, 1977).

The suspects themselves began a long and difficult period of waiting, first for the culmination of the criminal investigation at the trial and, then, second, enduring the subsequent internal disciplinary investigation. They were almost immediately faced with interrogation by State Detectives and/or investigating officers from headquarters (Misfeance and Internal Affairs). One assumes that they must know intimately the rules of the game surrounding interrogations and that this makes them potentially difficult suspects to interview. For, to a man, all the suspects fervently *denied corruption*. Now every policeman worth his salt knows that the best form of defence is a denial (indeed their professional lives are largely devoted to persuading people to change their initial denials into confessions). And, not unnaturally, the suspects knew this to be the basic rule for any prisoner. Nevertheless, the arrest and investigation was a considerable trauma for them and some of them soon 'coughed' to minor offences. It is possible to see from the dossier that several of the men began with a defiant denial; but a night in the cells, as with most people, brought a rapid change of mind. But all the serious accusations – of sexual harassment, dealing in firearms, transporting drugs, letting suspects go in return for money, recycling drugs, and so on – were consistently and emphatically rejected. Indeed, the two 'Chinese experts', who steadfastly refused to admit *anything*, were released from criminal prosecution and were never brought to trial.

Aware of the criminal definition of corruption, the suspects couched their statements carefully. One reacted initially to his arrest with a straight denial: he had never taken money, received a fruit-basket, or let prisoners go free (CCD, Suspect's Statement, 25 April, 1977). The very next day, however, the story had changed to a cautious admission. He explained that during his detective training he teamed up with a former colleague from the Warmoesstraat and they used to go out on the town in their spare time. They also began to visit Freddy's casino regularly. Following one of these visits his partner gave him fifty guilders and he assumed that the money came from Freddy and that the partner 'simply divided it honestly with me'. Probably in total he had received 250 guilders from Freddy but, he added, Freddy could not expect anything in return from him because he no longer performed any duties in the district. The suspect denied passing on any information gained during his periods in the Aliens and Drug Squads. In addition, he had taken between 150–200 guilders at another gambling-house. The two policemen did not frequent the Chinese casinos specifically in anticipation of obtaining money but merely because his partner had close contacts with a lot of Chinese people. He denied letting a prisoner go free who was in possession of heroin – 'This story is a pack of lies from beginning to end' – had never kept back drugs confiscated from a suspect, and had never accepted money in relation to his official duties. He concluded with words that avoided responsibility for a criminal offence, but clearly anticipated a disciplinary offence.

> 'In summary I can state that I have in fact received money from Chinese people, but that in return for it I have never done, or neglected to do, anything that was in conflict with my duty as a policeman. In my opinion, then, I have not been guilty of committing a criminal offence. Looking back now I can see that it was very stupid of me to do these things. I am aware that one or two things may have been in conflict with my official instructions and that I, from a disciplinary point of view, was doing wrong.'
>
> (CCD: Suspect's Statement, 26 April, 1977)

In admitting to having received around 600 guilders in Chinese casinos on various occasions, he later explicitly used words that reflected a conscious denial of corruption by refusing to admit that he did or did not do something in conflict with his duty in return for a reward or gift (the crucial element in the law on 'corruption' in The Netherlands). He saw the sums of money as presents and certainly not as bribes (CCD: Suspect's Statement, 28 April, 1977).

Similar elements were forthcoming from the other suspects. For example, one of the policemen made a limited admission; again it appears as if he was endeavouring to avoid the accusation of a criminal offence by opting for a disciplinary charge. He claimed that he had only received money to play the 'one-armed bandits' in Freddy's gambling-house, that this had not prevented him from carrying out controls in the place, and that Freddy could expect nothing in return. But the more serious accusations, such as setting prisoners free and keeping back confiscated drugs, were emphatically rejected, 'with the greatest conviction'. There follows a systematic evasion of responsibility for the list of offences suggested by witnesses. Some small quantities of opium might have been kept back from prisoners because the quantities were below the permitted limits set by the Justice Department (to avoid being swamped by trivial cases); these drugs were routinely tossed into the wastebasket in the Warmoesstraat. He had not appreciated that Fynaut was a dealer (anyway, the relationship ran through his partner), had never seen weighing scales on Fynaut's table (in fact Fynaut did not have a table), never gave money or drugs to Fynaut and never received money from him. As for the alleged 3,000 guilders from Fynaut he knew nothing about it – 'in any event I never saw a cent of it' – and never offered him protection although he received information from him.

The story about throwing a dead junkie in the canal was 'complete nonsense'; he cannot remember anything related to a theft of 2,000 guilders from a witness ('when I knew him he was always broke'); and, as for setting up a cocaine deal in Central Station, that was the work of Headquarters and 'not us'; and he was completely unaware of the term 'lucky money' and that certain days were 'pay-days' in the Chinese gambling-houses. He could not recall how six packets of heroin, found in his coat pocket on arrest, got there, and was unaware that a cigar in a foil case had a 100-guilder note wrapped around it. In short, the suspect covered himself against any possible criminal charge:

'In summary I wish to state that I deny having received gifts or promises from anyone in order to behave, or neglect to behave,

in ways that are in conflict with my duty. Also I deny that I have ever been guilty of theft, or embezzling money or drugs or in fact of any sort of goods.'
(Quotations from CCD, Suspect's Statement, 27 April, 1977)

Part of the tactic here is to suggest that perhaps others knew more and also to refer to orders or discussions with superiors.

The other partner in this twosome also emphatically denied the serious charges levelled at him in almost identical terms and claimed that his direct boss, the sergeant in charge of the PCS, had ordered him to keep an eye on the gambling-house. He had never been a share-holder in Freddy's gambling-house, had never kept back drugs from prisoners, and had not received a gold cigarette-lighter. The trip to Paris had cost him around 500 guilders and was not related in any way to drugs; he did not drive Freddy's car, would never place his wife in such a predicament, and he considered the trip 'purely a private arrangement' (CCD, Suspect's Statement, 13 April, 1977). He had, however, received lucky money, had been given a fruit-basket (but without money in it), and, as for visiting a sex-club, he had merely gone up to the room where he 'only talked to the girl'. On his arrest he was in possession of someone's identity papers and a photo of a naked prostitute taken in the Warmoesstraat, while two packets of heroin were found in his attic.

The two detectives from the Aliens Department also began with complete denials but soon after their arrest were making limited admissions. They acknowledged receiving small sums of money but brushed aside the notion that this influenced them in giving favourable treatment to aliens. One of them explained their relationship with Freddy. Freddy was useful because he spoke English and would help to find a Chinese suspect's passport for them. Once a week there was a KLM plane to Kuala Lumpur and the government designated this as the official flight for deportations to the Far East (but then with a limited number of seats as the government was footing the bill). The detectives claimed that they could not arrange for a deportee to leave on an earlier flight, thus avoiding an unpleasant and lengthy stay in the cells awaiting his turn, but on their advice friends or relatives of the person in question could buy a ticket with an airline which had an earlier flight (thus also reducing pressure on the cells). But there was no question of allowing illegal Chinese immigrants to remain in Holland in return for presents or bribes; 'to put it briefly: I deny that I have in any way at all allowed myself to be bribed' (CCD, Suspect's Statement, 28 April, 1977).

In their statements five of the eight men admitted receiving money and/or various types of presents while one claimed to have kept a few guilders won on the 'one-armed bandit'. But, in effect, the long-drawn-out investigation could be summed up as lots of statements but few witnesses and little proof. And the confessions were limited, no doubt deliberately, to admitting only a number of minor offences which did not constitute corruption but might be classified as disciplinary offences.

THE TRIAL

The trial of the suspects took place in May, 1978. Facsimiles of the witnesses' statements appeared in the newspapers with the names of the suspects blacked out and these were consumed with relish by the public. One respondent complained that these leaks were so selective that it almost seemed as if they were designed to help the prosecution, 'then in the press you only saw the witnesses' and not our own interviews with our denials. It was a dirty business. Everything against us appeared in the papers. It was all one-sided, designed to blacken our reputations, and there was nothing positive about us'. Court procedure in The Netherlands tends to be sober, clinical, and expeditious and the Public Prosecutor presents his case (which is highly pre-digested in largely documentary form with few witnesses and few histrionics) and demands a level of punishment which is then decided on several weeks later at a separate sitting by the judges (there is no jury system). The defence launched an immediate attack which virtually claimed that the policies of the Justice Department should be on trial because, in relation to the crime–drugs–Chinese complex, they had been 'utterly random, careless and panic-stricken' (*De Volkskrant* 18 May, 1978). In addition it was stated that the then force leadership had seriously failed. Objection was also made to the methods used in the investigation which were said to parallel those employed against the Baader–Meinhof terrorists in that some of the policemen had been hauled out of their beds and had been kept isolated from each other in diverse police stations. Furthermore, all the defence lawyers demanded freedom for their clients on the ground that they had already been sufficiently punished. They more or less portrayed the cases as a storm in a tea cup because the men had to behave as they did in order to do their work and never considered such practices to be corrupt.

Policemen themselves are often sceptical about trials and one of the suspects reflected this in his criticism of the quality of the proceedings: 'The trial was a joke. I mean every trial is a joke but this was a real laugh. It was all so trivial.' He added, 'We never met to discuss the trial together, not at all'.

A different version was recounted by a senior officer who informed me that the suspects and their lawyers met together for a rehearsal, 'there were about fifteen people altogether and they had to learn their parts reciting their lessons, just like in Sunday School, in order to all have the same story', and that this emerged because the telephone of one of the lawyers was being tapped by the State Police. The performance of senior officers at the trial was also a subject of derision, contempt, and counter-accusations. In short, the suspects were convinced that senior officers had committed perjury in court in order to make the cases stick. A respondent recalled that Litjens had interviewed Freddy at Headquarters but the Commissioner denied this under oath in court.

The Public Prosecutor launched a strong plea for stiff sentences ('No Pardon for "Corrupt" Policemen', *De Telegraaf,* 1 June, 1978). He argued that with the current legislation it was difficult to prove corruption and lamented that in The Netherlands 'it was extra-ordinarily difficult for an official to be found criminally corrupt'. Furthermore, he argued for better disciplinary measures and a stronger personnel policy within the police to cope with the fact that the legislation was out-of-date. He demanded prison sentences for all the suspects ranging from four months for Kramer to three weeks for Toxopeus. These prison sentences would have meant the automatic sacking of all six policemen from the force. But when the judges met to pass sentence two weeks later they were lenient (police habitually complain that they *always* are lenient with criminals), and reduced the Prosecutor's demand. Their decision was to fine five of the suspects while the sixth was found not guilty (while the fines were reduced to compensate for the days in custody).

The judges outlined the reasoning behind their lenient decision with four arguments. The suspects had already been heavily punished because of their exposure to negative publicity: they had all been kept in protective custody; they now faced an uncertain future; and they had fallen foul of the law as a result of uncertain policies. They suggested that an internal disciplinary investigation be mounted as soon as possible (*De Volkskrant* 15 June, 1978). In effect the judges had returned the hot potato into the reluctant lap of the Chief Constable. In place of a decision which would have rid him of the six suspects (although probably they would have appealed and some were told by contacts inside the Justice Department that they had a good chance of getting off on appeal), he was faced with eight suspended policemen whose behaviour had to be rescrutinized in terms of force discipline. This marked the shift from Enquiry 2 to Enquiry 3. Suddenly the attention switched away from fruit-baskets, lucky-money, and the ritual of the court-room and towards the internal functioning of the Amsterdam police. The scandal was not going to die down easily, as might have happened if the six men had been found guilty of 'corruption' (involving reciprocation for the money/gifts received) and had been dismissed, but was entering an even more bitter stage.

THE PREDICAMENT OF THE SUSPECTS

In Amsterdam, the eight police suspects were all highly active policemen and when they fell it was a searing experience for them. One informant said the Amsterdam Police acted like some 'medieval town, casting the people out and closing the gates behind them' while a union representative encountered them as vulnerable isolates, almost without legal protection against the department (in terms of suspension and reduction in salary), and having to hear decisions on their fate from the radio or read it in the papers because the force ignored them. It does seem that policemen have considerable difficulty in accepting the role of suspect despite the fact that they are familiar with it, albeit in other people. In New York, for example, one of the prosecutors found that he could not restrain a measure of compassion for policemen under investigation for corruption. '"Don't you see?" Leuci said, "we're not criminals. We're policemen, and we can't cope with being criminals. When was the last time a Mafia guy committed suicide because he got in trouble? It isn't criminals who kill themselves, it's cops"' (Daley 1979: 316–17).

Informally, then, the suspects experienced a considerable blow to their pride and reputation. And formally the sanctions imposed on them were far from light. The suspects were suspended from duty for almost three years (Honeycombe 1974: 211), had their salaries cut by a third, were confined to their homes, were not permitted to go on holiday (and certainly not abroad), were not allowed to visit a police station or consort with their former colleagues, faced constant publicity (some of it self-induced), eight of them experienced arrest and incarceration, six went on trial, and all eight were subject to two successive investigations – a criminal one and a disciplinary one. When a policeman is arrested this constitutes a stripping process (Goffman 1961) – in which he surrenders the symbols of his occupation, namely his uniform, pistol, and warrant card – that can be perceived as an extreme ceremony of personal and social degradation whereby the stigma almost precludes the chance of further positive relabelling.

In addition, 'once a suspect always a suspect' holds true not only for criminals but also for policemen who have come under serious suspicion. The four suspects that I interviewed all seemed to believe that they would not be arrested, and certainly not detained following questioning, although they did anticipate that they would be questioned. They knew from their contacts inside and outside the force that they were under suspicion but were unsure as to whether or not they were to be questioned as witnesses or as suspects. Here one begins to experience the 'Rashomon' effect of hearing stories from different perspectives. For a criminal investigation is a battle of wits, bluff, and psychological staying power and the sensible suspect keeps calm and says as little as possible. A normal tactic of the police is to play someone along as if he is a witness until they can confirm that he is a suspect. In Amsterdam the suspects clearly felt that once they had been singled out as suspects then they were made *to look like suspects*; for example, instead of being allowed to walk voluntarily into a police station to give themselves up, they were arrested. Yet this is precisely the sort of technique that a policeman might use against a suspect criminal. This ambivalence was also revealed with clarity by a respondent who claimed never to have been arrested correctly.

> 'It was still a terrible slap in the face. I'd never counted on being arrested. There's obviously not much point in making a fuss about it now but technically I was never arrested. I went up to van Thiel's room and the State Detective said, "Jan, you've got to come along for a while" and I said, "That's fine with me." So formally I wasn't arrested but of course *we never say it formally to a suspect either.*'

(My emphasis)

He was searched in the cell by a local sergeant who discovered several packets of heroin on him but one of the State Detectives reported that *he* found it,

> 'yet he never came near me. So one of the State Detectives committed perjury but of course there's no way I can prove it.

[After four days custody he was set free.] For six months I was put under house arrest. I mean house arrest doesn't even exist in Dutch law but never mind. So I had a few packets of heroin in my pocket, so what? Everybody had some stuff in their lockers in those days, you know that yourself. I'd just forgotten it and could easily have thrown it away several times on the way to the station.'

Another suspect explained how he had been arrested in the station as if he were a dangerous criminal. He knew for eight months that there was a case pending against him because his Chinese contacts told him.

'They came with six men. "You're under arrest." I had my pistol in my belt and went to take it out but I wasn't allowed to take it out myself and they did it for me. Then I was taken to the Public Prosecutor and then to the Commissioner of Enquiry, Homan. He told me, "if nothing more turns up then I've got nothing much against you". His exact words were, "if I could prove that it did happen then I'd string you up by your balls". He also said that getting a fruit-basket happened in business, and businessmen had it off with their secretaries, and that only for policemen was it not acceptable.'

He then went on to describe his uncomfortable experience in prison where he had encountered prisoners that he had arrested himself, where hot tea would be poured over his hand when he held out his cup, and where he avoided recreation because he was derided as 'Kojak'. Most people find the experience of being locked up more or less traumatic; when your personal possessions have been taken off you and the cell-door slams shut – leaving you to the graffiti, the smell of sweat and excrement, the drab and depressing decor, the grunts and wailings from other cells, and the scrutiny through the peep-hole – then even the most hardened must feel a pang of fear. One respondent told me that the most difficult aspect of the whole ordeal was having to go in a cell.

The interest of the above accounts is that they detail precisely what a 'normal' suspect undergoes when subjected to arrest and prosecution. Furthermore, many a criminal claims that the police were out to get him and this was exactly echoed by my respondents. The investigation was seen as slanted against them.

'The whole business was selective. Well, I've seen some of the statements, which I got from my lawyer, and someone has messed around with them. In the statements there are lies and also the names of others who took more money than us but they were interviewed and nothing ever happened to them. They knew they could get at me because they knew I'd get some form of punishment for the weapons and drugs. And to be honest I'd really counted on being sacked as a punishment for possessing firearms. But they were out to get me.'

This material is valuable in that it suggests two things. On the one hand the policemen's own perceptions of the investigation as biased against them provided fuel later for counter-attacks against the nature of the enquiry; while, on the other hand, policemen are no more immune to the pains of arrest and detention than 'ordinary' criminals, and, indeed, may be more vulnerable to them. The publicity and the investigation inevitably had consequences for the private lives of the suspects. Policemen clearly have problems with the stigma attached to the suspicion of being involved in crime and this can affect their wives and children (Sherman 1978: 65). The men and their families may be subject to humour, innuendo, and sarcasm (Alex 1976: 120). Some policemen reacted with a form of gallows humour and used to say 'I'm sleeping on the sofa these days so I won't have to get out of bed when they come for me'. In fact, the strain on the domestic lives of the suspects was considerable. For they were condemned officially to inactivity, financially handicapped (especially the detectives who had lost their considerable overtime payments), facing stigma in their neighbourhood and among acquaintances, and with a criminal prosecution, a prison sentence, and dismissal from the force hanging over their heads. One member of the force took it upon himself to attend to the welfare of the suspects and he told me.

'It's just simply impossible to describe the circumstances the suspects had to go through. No-one would listen to them and I feel that they've been treated unjustly and then in quite an unbelievable way. One wanted to commit suicide, another was alcoholic, their kids were pointed at in school, and Jan always used to see a colleague at the bus-stop but suddenly this colleague starts using another bus-stop in order to avoid meeting him.'

All the suspects found the experience of suspension and investigation trying and burdensome. Several people were said to have been virtually broken by the experience. But perhaps the most galling aspect of this period was the feeling and experience of banishment and abandonment, of being thrust out of the police community as if they were lepers. They were forbidden to mix with their old colleagues and policemen were not permitted to approach them. All contacts with the organization ran through formal channels and these were tardy, remote, and cold. It was as if the organization did not want to own up any more to having anything to do with them. The organization's way of dealing with deviants was to accord them pariah status. Anyone who tried to help them became discredited and was, in turn, viewed as a suspect. In defining them as outcasts the force leadership drew a line and crossing it meant that one placed oneself in the danger zone, exposed to moral pollution. This attitude launched the notion that the organizational representatives did not remain neutral but actively penalized the outcasts in a manner that some considered to be rancorous. The suspects felt that the organization was out to get them and waged a form of psychological warfare against them: 'It's quite impossible to describe what I've been through; they just set out to break us psychologically and they kept on needling us and messing us around in all sorts of ways.' This may be exaggerated, and may be explained by the distortion caused by the emotionally strained position of the suspects in which they might interpret bureaucratic shortcomings on the part of the organization as deliberate and malicious, but stories along this theme circulated within the force and were given wide credence.

The organization saw them as criminals who had forfeited the right to help whereas the suspects basically perceived themselves as falsely accused, or unlucky to be accused, and perceived the situation as though they were ill and therefore temporarily off-duty until they recovered and returned to normal work. Isolated, aggrieved, and wallowing in an unaccustomed sea of time, with no prospect of an early settlement, they resented the abandonment by senior officers and the lack of support from their employer. Indeed, the banishment, abandonment, and prolonged suspension in a state of anxiety and insecurity also meant that the suspects had quite some difficulty at the thought of returning to work. The suspects felt that they had been placed in limbo for almost three years, had been punished, and should now be allowed back to continue their old work with honour. But how would they be received? Would people in the organization forgive and forget or would the conflict continue after re-entry? Would they be positively relabelled or would the stigma remain?

Of the eight suspects two eventually left on grounds of ill-health and the other six were in effect 'demoted', with four being given administrative jobs and two being put back into uniform on patrol.

Part of the continuing personal struggle for rehabilitation and reacceptance was the wish to return to their previous positions as a symbol of moral victory but this was denied to them all. One man explained that he wanted to go back to the Warmoesstraat. He phoned Maartens, who he had no objection but then later said, ' "Maybe it's not such a good idea, it might lead to conflict." It's just an excuse, it's van Thiel who's behind it. But they're just a bunch of stupid shits. They can't face up to you. They can't cope with a confrontation.' Once more the lower ranks' view of the organization as rancorous and resentful of their return was re-inforced, as another suspect maintained. On his first day back a young inspector had wished him good luck and said 'do your best'. Then later a senior officer called him in and said,

> ' "I've been digging into your past work and one thing seems clear, and that is that you're a bit too quick with your fists. So I'm warning you to go on tip-toe from now on." What a bloody offensive remark! Then I asked him, "You haven't by any chance seen Maartens and van Thiel in District Two lately?" They can't stand the fact that I'm working again. That makes them rancorous and that's typical of the climate here. They're still trying to get back at me.'

CONCLUSION

Policemen are professionally concerned with reconnoitring their outside environment for signals of deviance and usually are not geared to picking up those signals from within their own ranks. When they do so they may feel betrayed because, as with a gar-rison, the enemy within not only forms a greater danger than the external enemy but his behaviour is an act doubly condemnable because it constitutes a form of treachery. At the same time, a policeman, who perhaps in his daily work life approaches most people as if they are suspects (by discrediting their accounts, sub-jecting them to scrutiny, and viewing informal punishment and retribution as legitimate – Smith and Gray 1983: 78), and who routinely deprives people of their freedom, may find it almost unbearable that he himself becomes an object of suspicion and that he be exposed to the humiliation of arrest. One way to retaliate is for police to view the organization as the 'enemy' which in some way is getting back at them for they may feel it is not just the courts and the media, but even their own department, which is 'persecuting' them.

We could argue that it is salutary for policemen to undergo the experience of being arrested. Yet this should not blind us to the fact that it is a wounding torment for a policeman to be subjected to a criminal investigation by his own colleagues and for him to have to go through the debasement that he normally associates with disreputable, and often morally reprehensible, characters. Policemen, once caught, may experience guilt, shame, and remorse (Daley 1979: 32). And, yet, one assumes that they must have been aware of breaking rules. What happens is that they define certain forms of deviance as acceptable and/or harmless (Beigel and Beigel 1977: 275). Like businessmen involved in crime they may come to argue that what they did was 'Illegal? Yes, but not criminal' (Geis 1982: 131). But unlike deviant executives, whose consciences 'do not ordinarily bother them' (Sutherland 1982: 55), bent policemen do seem to have difficulty coping with stigma, shame, and guilty consciences; and, unlike businessmen who are often not stigmatized by their profession (Vandivier 1982: 122), policemen can face severe sanctions for their infractions (Daley 1979: 275). This forces them to rationalize and justify their misconduct to a greater extent than 'ordinary' people.

Dirty Hands and Muddy Shoes; Rationalizations and Accounts

'If you ask me Litjens has done it [used illegal methods – MP] a couple of times. Now they say he has dirty hands. But if you ask a gynaecologist to make a caesarian cut, then his gloves will also be covered in blood. Who can dig out a cess-pit without tools and yet not get his hands dirty? And believe you me, heroin is the dirtiest business that exists. Heroin is hell.'
(Detective, in *Extra* 29 December 1978)

In defending, justifying, and excusing deviant behaviour, a noticeable ambivalence emerged from policemen's reactions to the scandal in Amsterdam. On the one hand there was a tendency to express sympathy with the suspects yet, on the other hand, this was often combined with an attempt at distancing oneself from the phenomenon of corruption. The crude, even coprophiliac, imagery used was that of disease, pollution, and contamination (shit, mud, dirt, cancer, etc.) which not only shaped a rhetoric of mitigation for dirty workers but also seemed designed to establish the honesty and purity of the speaker. Policemen, faced with the shock of entrapment in reprehensible conduct, reacted with accounts reflecting their involvement in the dangerous and dirty zones of society where it is impossible to operate without becoming soiled – 'if you walk around in a swamp in patent leather shoes then you'll come out with dirty feet' (*Elseviers Magazine* 27 May, 1978). The giving and taking of accounts, and the assessing and honouring of their credibility, is a critical process in maintaining the 'reality' of organizational life (Altheide and Johnson 1980: 39). This is amplified by the nature of police work where uncertain incidents, open to multiple interpretations and later subject to scrutiny by several audiences, may 'bounce' and bring opprobrium down on the head of the policeman concerned; 'in this job you are always in the shit. Sometimes you're up to your eyes in it, at others it's only up to your ankles, but you're never completely out of it' (Chatterton 1979: 93). Skilful accounting may, then, be an essential part of the policeman's working world and this requires us to examine the rhetorical resources brought to bear when he is forced to articulate formulas of mitigation and extenuation (van Maanen 1980).

These 'accounts' (Lyman and Scott 1970) are verbal articulations of defence and attack engaged in by people who perform acts and which provide them with 'vocabularies of motive' (Mills 1940). Matza and Sykes (1957: 251), for instance, have analysed how deviants endeavour to 'neutralize' the negative connotations associated with their behaviour and most writers argue that the 'moral career' of the bent policemen involves some progressive accommodation and neutralization to illicit behaviour. Both Ditton (1977) and Henry (1978) have analysed how people engaged in 'part-time crime', i.e. occupational crime at work which is tolerated and legitimated within certain limits, can retain a conception of themselves as non-deviant by a process of rationalization. Henry (1978: 15), for example, holds that all jobs contain some 'fiddling, stealing and dealing'. Furthermore, employee offenders may often resemble the 'stereotypically perfect' worker, while the 'zealot' who exceeds the norms of tolerance, say by pilfering from the company rather than fiddling from the customer, is stigmatized as a 'morally defective individual, unable to resist temptation, and liable to infect others' (Ditton 1977: 87f.). This helps to explain how corrupt policemen can in some senses be 'good' policemen, how they may be rewarded by the formal system before their fall, and how they may condemn dubious contacts vehemently in others even when their own behaviour is not lilly-white (e.g. by making distinctions between 'clean' and 'dirty' money or by refusing graft from 'murderers, pushers, the Mob' – Beigel and Beigel 1977: 175). Niederhoffer (1969: 74) also captures this apparent contradiction in outlining some counter-arguments used by policemen to explain the erosion of norms and standards of law-enforcement:

'the strange thing is that a policeman can take the pay-off and still consider himself an honest or innocent man. Such psychological prestidigitation can be accomplished only by artful casuistry based on cynicism. The policeman rationalizes with twisted logic. I am not hurting anyone, everyone is doing the same thing, most people are much worse, the public thinks a policeman is dishonest whether he is or not, therefore I am not doing anything wrong by taking graft.'

The 'twisted logic' of vocabularies of motive is analysed by Scott and Lyman (1968) in terms of 'justifications', where some responsibility is accepted, and 'excuses', where responsibility is denied. These verbally articulated defences are difficult to unravel analytically precisely because of that casuistry and because of their uncertain relationship with genuine motives and behaviour. However transparent accounts may appear, deviant policemen faced with the challenge of exposure are forced to justify their behaviour and tend to grasp at relatively standardized formulas of defence as if they really do believe in them as accurate representations of motives. They may even come to believe them as 'real' explanations. Indeed, they would be foolish to do otherwise.

JUSTIFICATIONS: ACCEPTING SOME RESPONSIBILITY

Everybody is Doing it

One can endeavour to reduce guilt, spread blame, and present a defence by suggesting that the deviance is widespread, both within the organization and perhaps also in the wider society, which conveys the possibility that the behaviour was so normal that it would be 'deviant' to refuse while condemnation from outside is hypocritical. One of the police suspects, for instance, legitimized his acceptance of 'lucky money' by saying that everyone standing around the gambling table was given twenty-five guilders for bringing the successful player good luck – 'we were standing there too so we took it as well' – and that if he had won money on the lottery he would treat all his friends in some way. But it was not corruption because he would arrest the man concerned the next day if necessary. Here 'grass-eating' is justified in terms of normal, everyday conduct which had no psychic consequences for the performance of the policeman's duty. One element in this defence is that it effectively implicates a broader category of policemen ('every narcotics detective he had ever known gave drugs to informants': Daley 1979: 280), or else describing it as virtually universal police behaviour (like the widespread feeling among businessmen 'that the "other fellow" was regularly cheating': Stone 1975: 250; or the argument 'everyone is at it and if I don't do it someone else will': Henry 1978: 46). Perhaps as a mitigating element for this, the deviance is also attributed to wider circles outside the police; in Amsterdam policemen were wont to say, 'Prince Bernhard does it as well' (*Nieuwe Revue* 28 January, 1977).

He Had It Coming

Criminals may be 'fitted up' (Parker 1981: 13) or ripped off with the justification that they had it coming to them, there was no other way to prosecute them, or they deserved informal punishment because the formal system was too weak to tackle them effectively. In New York stealing money from drug dealers was for the SIU justifiable because,

> 'they would buy boundsmen, district attorneys, judges. They were so rich they could buy anybody. Most could be hurt, could be put out of business, in one way only, and that was by stealing all their cash at the moment of arrest. . . . The SIU detectives, Leuci explained, having conceived an overpowering hatred for these peoples [Latin American dealers – MP], began to dispense their own justice. Sometimes they talked of killing one or another prisoner, though this had never been done to Leuci's knowledge. Instead, they simply began to rob them. They would take whatever money the dope dealer had, order him on the next plane to South America, and applaud themselves for accomplishing what no court seemed able to accomplish, a heavy fine followed by instant deportation.'
>
> (Daley 1979: 280, 312)

And, if a policeman takes money off a criminal, it is not as if the criminal 'were being deprived of something that was legitimately his' (Goldstein 1977: 199).

We Could Not Refuse

A central bulwark in the policemen's defence in Amsterdam was that it was in the nature of their relationship with the leaders of the Chinese community that they were obliged to accept food, gifts, and small sums of money and could not refuse these without offending their contacts (Birch 1983: 83).

> 'In answer to your question, as to how I interpret these gifts, I have to declare that I saw this as an expression of esteem for the work we performed, and it goes without saying that we are paid a salary to do this, yet nevertheless we were rewarded for this work as an Eastern token of gratitude.'
>
> (CCD, Suspect's Statement, 26 April, 1977)

These 'friendly gestures' were viewed then as an 'Eastern gesture of respect' in a relationship of 'mutual cooperation' (*Het Parool* 18 May, 1978). It was further suggested that the offer of Chinese hospitality was particularly insistent, that the Chinese were deeply offended when one endeavoured to refuse, and that 'we simply could not refuse, because then we would have lost our contacts' (*De Volkskrant*, 18 May, 1978). Indeed, in certain ethnic communities cultural views about food and presents may reflect long-standing traditions that it is in the nature of food to be shared, that you cannot refuse presents, and that gifts bind contracting parties in perpetual interdependence. The Chinese, for instance, believe that it is dangerous to receive a gift precisely because of the dependence it creates in the receiver (Mauss 1970). Perhaps the detective, accepting a Rolex watch under protest from a Chinese acquaintance in order to maintain the relationship and to identify with his contacts, was not fully aware of the depth of social obligation which the Chinese person implied with his gift.

It Was Part of the Job

Almost as an extension of the above argument was the mitigating defence that the relationships with criminals and informants were simply part and parcel of the daily routine which was, in turn, essential to fulfilling one's task effectively (*Elseviers Magazine* 27 May, 1978). The men were required to enter regularly the Chinese gambling-dens in order to glean information and to carry out controls; indeed, without the cooperation of the Chinese bosses it would have been 'almost impossible' to carry out their task. The predicament for the PCS policeman, for instance, was that he had a highly diffuse responsibility for keeping an eye on matters while, at the same time, being almost handcuffed in terms of his possibility of intervening in certain cases of crime. This did allow unlimited licence for hanging around in the area but it was precisely this that later came to look suspicious.

> 'Of course I took something. But Chinese people will only agree to talk to you if you eat and drink together and they pay the bill. And the whole point is to build up a relationship with them. You have to remember that the two opium dens were allowed, Chinese gambling was permitted – "Oh, take no notice, we don't have any trouble from them," people said – and if you went in to a gambling den then you weren't allowed to do anything anyway. We weren't allowed to touch illegal aliens because that was for the Aliens' Department. Then they accuse us of having contacts with dubious characters!'

In effect, the only way to collect information was to consort with criminals; outsiders may find this questionable but it was simply part of the job.

We Did Not Do It For Ourselves

A strong theme among the police defence was that they did not accept things from a base, mercenary motive but rather that they acted as a form of altruism (Matza and Sykes 1957: 251). They were doing it to make 'justice' work, to complete cases, and to get convictions (Daley 1979: 280). Indeed, several suspects, and particularly the two 'Chinese experts', emphasized the sacrifices they made in order to invest their energies in police work without a thought for personal advantage. Here the imagery was of the relentless, dedicated detective, abandoning his family and social life in order to pursue criminals, and incidentally taking a gift or a meal merely as a means to achieving higher ends.

EXCUSES: DENYING RESPONSIBILITY

Age and Financial Circumstances

In attempting to deny or reduce responsibility two 'excuses' were put forward in terms of the youthfulness and inexperience of the policemen concerned and also of the policeman who has got himself into financial straits and finds it difficult to resist temptation. Representatives of one of the police unions informed me that policemen can easily get loans and may be led into overextending themselves financially. One told me of constables deep in debt:

'Policemen are often not particularly very adult persons. A lot of them are just children, that's all they are really, and they can be very vulnerable. Previously you had people in the police who'd already had some experience in society and had learnt to put up with a lot of things.'

Yet by Amsterdam standards the men concerned were *not* young and were *not* inexperienced; indeed, the reverse was true. A senior officer said they kept emphasizing the age issue, which he admitted was not relevant to these suspects, to try and get more personnel, and more mature men, for key positions. (Incidentally, another argument continually raised by policemen, especially those outside of Amsterdam, is that the Amsterdam Police is too large and that this leads to impersonality and lack of control. Size is, of course, purely relative as Amsterdam may be large by Dutch standards but the NYPD has as many detectives as there are policemen in Amsterdam, around 3,000, and the *total* number of city policemen in all of The Netherlands is about 23,000, which is less than the establishment of either the Met or the NYPD – Perrick 1982: 55). Also Dutch policemen seemed to be reasonably affluent at the time of the research (certainly compared to British policemen in the middle 1970s) but there was a pattern of detectives working very long hours in order to buy their own homes. The accuracy of such statements is not so much the point here as the fact that deviant behaviour was explained in terms of the individual under pressure who momentarily succumbs to temptation. A detective explained,

'Some of the lads are paying back 700–800 guilders a month on cars or mortgages. Then they come to work in this area and see people walking around with thousands of guilders in their pocket. They nick someone with heroin and he offers them 1,000 guilders and there's just the two of them, no other witnesses. And then it's a difficult choice.'

The Suspect as Victim

One of the most persistent mitigating arguments used in Amsterdam was that a long process of 'erosion' in standards of police work had created a situation where it was easy for some policemen to drift into deviance. As such they were perceived as, and presented themselves as, 'victims' rather than as perpetrators. They were victims of ambiguous policies, weak leadership, unscrupulous criminals, and the unquestioning search for success. One officer explained the growth of a laissez-faire situation by tracing developments back to the trauma of 1966 when the Amsterdam Police was publicly humiliated by intense press criticism, by exposure to a critical external enquiry, and by the sacking of the Chief Constable. The City had become 'intoxicated with a toleration based on postponement' where it was almost 'obscene' to consider expelling an illegal Chinese immigrant or it was 'authoritarian' to control squatters. Enforcement often led to interference from the mayor, derision in the media, and cries of 'SS' from the public. The police had been made a laughing-stock and 'so we crept into our shell and said "Let well alone." The police became frightened off and said, "OK, if that's all too much bother, then leave it alone, and let's be careful." ' Another officer spoke of the suspects as,

> 'victims of a system that failed in which no one ever talked about informants. Informants were received with open arms and given a shot [of heroin] in return for a tip, informants were protected, heroin was kept in lockers as a curiosity, and all of this was never even discussed in any way by senior personnel.'

Within this lax structure some policemen began to set their own standards of success. One theme was that they were victims partly of a desire to achieve arrests and partly because they were not sufficiently astute to avoid the snares set by cunning oriental criminals. The suspects could argue that they were used and that they were easily led astray in an organization where significant actors adopted a 'couldn't care less' attitude to supervision and control. One key suspect summarized several of these themes in his account to me.

> 'I was taken in by them. You'd come in a gambling-den and the Chinese fellows would be so friendly and give you a cigar and sit you down. At first it didn't occur to me who is doing something in there that they want to conceal. I only started to cotton on afterwards, after I'd been doing the rounds for some time

and now I'm much more suspicious and ask myself, "Why do they want me to sit down and drink cognac?" Do I feel guilty? Look, I'm a policeman through and through. I don't like it when the police are attacked and I'll defend them. But what has come out – a couple of fruit-baskets! To use an Amsterdam expression "I've been conned." I've been used because I didn't understand exactly what was going on. I did it under their [i.e. senior officers'] command.'

Perhaps because of this the suspects rarely expressed any guilt. There was clearly shame involved (one suspect was religious, regularly attended church, and was a leader in the Scout movement, so his arrest was a 'shattering blow' according to a colleague) and also personal expressions of regret – 'Obviously this was incredibly stupid of me' – but no guilt. As one suspect put it, 'I may have failed as a person but I have not messed around as a policeman. But I was singled out. And I have it all to blame on the combination of police work and bosses.'

We Were Nobbled

A variant on the above theme – the policeman as victim – was the claim that criminals deliberately fabricated accusations against policemen in order to remove them from the scene because they were getting to know too much. This was the defence particularly of the two 'Chinese experts' whom, it was said, the Chinese bosses wanted out of the way because they knew too much ('Policemen Nobbled by Opposition', *De Telegraaf* 30 April, 1977). One of these men argued that following the dual assault on the Chinese underworld, involving a ban on gambling and a crack-down on illegal aliens, there was a good deal of rancour among the Chinese against the authorities in general (while they now had less reason for keeping quiet about police deviance) and this lead some of them to spread stories besmirching the reputation of certain policemen (CCD: Suspect's Statement, 29 April, 1977). This theme was repeated by one of the detectives from Aliens who claimed that the story about his receiving jewels was 'rancour' because some Chinese had had to leave the country (CCD: Suspect's Statement, 26 April, 1977). This form of account has the advantage that it portrays the policemen as being subject to suspicion not because they are doing their job badly but rather because they are doing it all too well. It was even suggested that some of the Chinese were ripped-off by underworld characters posing as policemen (and using a warrantcard from a drug squad detective – *Haagse Post* 4 November, 1978). Litjens dismissed stories about him as 'bluff'.

> 'I pay my way wherever I go. I know there are people in the city-centre who say, "Litjens and X were in here the whole evening knocking it back and they didn't pay a thing." That's all bluff. There were stories of Chinese being robbed by policemen but later it proved to be villains claiming to be policemen. It's all a tactic of these people to discredit the police. There are stories going around, "Litjens has taken a million", but I never took anything. It's just that the journalists have to have a story.'

Finally, corruption is judged on universal, rule-bound criteria of bureaucratic rectitude. But for the participants rules are situationally problematic and have a different meaning for members at different levels of the organization (Chatterton 1979) so that the plea for the suspects was to view their behaviour in the light of their personal predicament in the concrete setting of the inner-city. For them the discipline code was simply not appropriate to a gambling-den in Amsterdam's 'Chinatown' where they were trying to elicit information on an unsolved murder and were having egg-rolls and cognac waved temptingly under their noses. Yet rules are rules and the question is to what extent are we prepared to exonerate actors from following the rules because of specific conditions?

> 'Our respondents conclude, then, that those who criticize them for being corrupt fail to make allowances for the many social pressures, contingencies, collusions, and compromises that oblige some policemen to break the law. . . .
>
> Thus, from the police standpoint, a proper perspective on police corruption must recognize how the web of social pressures and individual differences make strict compliance to police codes extremely difficult.'
>
> (Alex 1976: 110)

Like the manager who says, 'You follow the rules when you can – maybe that's half the time, not a hell of a lot more' (Dalton 1959: 82), the policeman feels that he has to bend or break the law in order to enforce it. But, when he is caught out, he has to acknowledge the validity of the rules (and has even sworn a solemn oath to uphold them); and, to excuse his departure from them, he is forced to justify and to rationalize.

6
Resistance and Repercussions

'In many respects, police organizations represent a hodge-podge of cliques, cabals, and conspiracies. Since members often do not trust each other . . . deceit, evasiveness, duplicity, lying, innuendo, secrecy, double-talk, and triple-talk mark many of the interactions in police agencies.'

(van Maanen 1978: 322)

For more than four years the Amsterdam Police was in the grip of an institutional crisis sponsored by the corruption scandal and the crisis led, in particular, to the crystallization of conflict within the department. Indeed, I would argue that a central feature of policing which has not received sufficient attention is the divisiveness between ranks which becomes explicit at times of crises. For example, the emphasis on the police occupational culture's characteristics of solidarity and secrecy arose from taking the perspective of lower participants and particularly in relation to their attitudes to outsiders. Less interest has been aroused by that cohesion in relation to senior officers and, from that viewpoint, the police organization as a whole is not so much characterized by solidarity as by a divisiveness which can vary from mutual indifference and distancing techniques to predatory control from above and hostility from below. In short, a major conflict of interest is latent in virtually every police department, which mirrors that between bosses and workers in many organizations

(Hill, 1981), but which becomes acute when moral blame is being distributed because the dynamics of investigation inevitably tend to focus the spotlight *downwards*.

There emerged in Amsterdam a complex pattern of resistance, defence, cooperation, and conflict between the ranks and factions within, and between the factions and interested parties outside. This conflict is of especial interest because of what it reveals about the nature of the police organization and police work but also as a case of industrial conflict between employers and employees in which both just happen to be policemen. For, 'when the shit hits the fan', the organization reacts by dubbing the deviance as individual and incidental. The response of those accused, feeling let down and singled out as scapegoats, is to argue precisely that police deviance is *organizational*. In order to do this they have to expose the operational code, as to how things actually get done, as routine practice. In other words, the major defence of the lower ranks is to lift the veil of secrecy, and the mystique surrounding police work and, in so doing, they provide a glimpse of what 'really' happens. But in embarrassing the organization and in pointing upwards they make powerful enemies. In Amsterdam this process sponsored a bitter battle of definition. The top of the organization counted on loyalty and closing the ranks, the middle demanded change, and the lower ranks bitched and often passively, or actively, supported the suspects, who felt they were fighting for their lives. The latter defended themselves, counter-attacked, and decided to lift the veil.

Resistance: The Lower Ranks Strike Back

'When I joined up an old copper told me, "In this job you've always got one leg pointing to the sack and the other to the cell." We used to say, "You've got two opponents. The first is the public and the second is the police force itself. Because if you get into trouble then they'll try and destroy you." '
(Interview: experienced constable in Amsterdam)

Conflict in organizations may arise between units, between 'staff and line', or between superiors and subordinates. Workers' relationships with employers may range from 'low-key, begrudging acquiescence' to 'full-blooded resistance and opposition' (Salaman 1979: 155). In Amsterdam, for example, the corruption scandal ignited bitter internal struggles which led one to the conclusion that, in a time of crisis, the Amsterdam police as a whole was most certainly *not* characterized by a high degree of secrecy and solidarity. When senior officers attempted to reassert managerial control they uncovered deviant behaviour and elicited resistance. The next four years witnessed a constant guerilla warfare in which the lower ranks resisted the deviant label, and the attempt at control, from above. A corruption investigation will promote divisiveness because it will inevitably uncover the easily traced non-criminal occupational deviance of the lower orders (the perks, privileges, and work manipulation), who, in turn, will feel that they have been made scapegoats in that these practices are also located higher in the hierarchy, but that senior officers have the power to deflect attention away from themselves. The hostility of the lower ranks and resistance to being investigated is explicable and understandable in terms of an occupational group whose autonomy, and definition of self, is under threat.

There are two main reasons why scandal can cause internal strife and both are related to the impact of the word 'corruption', which is insidious and suggestive. First, the police are intimately involved in attributing labels to individuals and groups in society yet clearly experience great difficulty in accepting moral labels attributed to themselves. This is acute with 'corruption' because the very term implies something mysterious and all-encompassing. In short, corruption makes *every* policeman a potential suspect. And, second, because corruption is largely hidden and difficult to detect and to prosecute, a scandal plants the impression of a submerged, widespread system which may successfully escape investigation. In effect, it suggests that the force cannot adequately control a number of its members. A corruption scandal is a public exposure of senior police officers' impotence at controlling and supervising their own personnel. In Amsterdam, I would suggest, the acrimony and tension was caused by the senior officers' attempt to locate blame as far down the hierarchy as possible, and by the lower ranks' endeavour to return the compliment by pointing accusingly upwards; and also by the leadership's conspicuous attempt to display their *reimposition* of control over the lower levels which was met by resistance and recrimination from below. The effect was to activate latent inter-rank hostility and to divide officers and men into two mutually antagonistic camps.

For the latter, the conduct of the investigation had fuelled counter-accusations of bias, perjury, and scapegoating and these were reinforced by the treatment meted out to the suspects in terms of banishment and abandonment by the organization. The senior ranks, and to a certain extent the organization itself, were perceived as the 'enemy within' (Harris 1973: 43). Elsewhere during scandals the department is seen by the lower personnel as having a long memory, as setting out to get back at people through informal means, while Internal Affairs is not accepted as neutral and fair but as 'harsh and crazy' leading to counter-productive demoralization and disillusion (Muir 1977: 202 and 248). In Amsterdam, people felt that old-style solidarity, where senior officers backed you up against complaints from civilians, had been replaced by a system weighted against the ordinary man, 'nowadays if something happens its the Complaints Advisory Centre, Neighbourhood Law Centre [both subsidised legal agencies to assist citizens, including complaints against police], Internal Affairs, State Detectives, and the whole show'. Scandal symbolizes the change in the style of control and the lower orders resist by a grievancy pattern (Gouldner 1954) of bitching, gossiping, and rumour that aids in blunting and subverting the senior group's attempt to regain control and to diminish the lower ranks' autonomy (Salaman 1979: 145).

SOLIDARITY

Initially, however, the scandal did succeed in uniting policemen. Following the intense negative publicity surrounding the arrests in 1977 it was perhaps rather provocative of the socialist television company, the VARA, to put out in mid-May a sketch which depicted a policeman sharing the contents of a woman's purse with a thief (cf. the *New Statesman* cover of a policeman with a stocking mask over his face and holding a sawn-off shot-gun, 18 January, 1980). The men in the Warmoesstraat that evening were so incensed that they refused to go out on patrol and the duty-sergeant informed Headquarters that he could not take responsibility for the consequences of sending highly emotional men out on the street. The men further decided that they would make a formal complaint against the VARA via the Public Prosecutor and sent out a telex to this effect. This message was picked up by many police forces who responded spontaneously. The first to react were the State Police at Schiphol Airport who sent back a message of support through the teleprinter. This was followed by messages from all over the country so that by the next morning the Warmoesstraat was festooned with teletype pledging support. The police union canalized the sense of outrage by organizing a protest demonstration of policemen in the RAI conference centre in Amsterdam. This was attended by around 2,000 policemen from all over The Netherlands who noisily condemned the VARA and equally noisily displayed their sympathy with the Warmoesstraat. The chairman of the Dutch Police Union objected to the police being described as 'a gang of corrupt, head-cracking sadists and fascists' while another spokesman said that the VARA programme was the last straw leading to an explosive situation. 'It is really an assault on democracy when organs of the press abuse their freedom by suggesting that the whole police apparatus is corrupt' (*De Telegraaf* 13 May, 1977). A plea was made not to pass the buck of mistakes caused by faulty policies on to the backs of a few of the lower ranks. This was the high point of police solidarity with a conspicuous display of support for the Amsterdam Police.

KEEPING SILENT

Policemen, in keeping with other closed groups (in boarding schools, prisons, the criminal fraternity, and secret societies), operate by a code of silence which dictates that you do not 'rat on your mates' (Lambert 1969; Sykes 1958; Ball, Chester, and Perrott 1979). Serpico did so and he was ostracized, threatened, and perhaps even set up in a shooting: 'he had broken an unwritten law that in effect put policemen above the law, that said a cop could not turn in other cops' (Maas 1974: 21). He appears to have acted out of idealism but some policemen supplied information on errant colleagues as part of a deal for immunity from prosecution in return for being 'turned around' to spy on their colleagues (Daley 1979). Self-interest, then, may be stronger than the hold of the occupational culture and there are betrayals as well as keeping quiet (Sorrentino 1980: 279). Indeed, in Chicago a policeman must cooperate in a departmental investigation or risk being fired; one who takes the Fifth Amendment before a court may also be dismissed from the department (Beigel and Beigel 1977). In the Chicago corruption cases, furthermore, two arrested policemen remained resolutely silent until they heard that some colleagues had stolen the proceeds of a raffle held to assist their families; another testified when it dawned on him that his superior officer had lied to him, betrayed him, was prepared to 'dump' him, and that he might suffer alone for the corruption and for protecting his boss (Beigel and Beigel 1977: 170 and 190).

In Amsterdam the silence was broken for mercenary reasons. For example, an ex-policeman sold his story to a popular weekly in order to finance a move abroad. One suspect obtained copies of witnesses' statements from his lawyer and sold them to the press so that just before the trial extensive extracts were published in several weeklies. But, once the investigation got underway, it became clear that policemen did talk and named names. I heard on several occasions from investigating officers that questioning police suspects lead to the reaction 'What are you looking at me for? You ought to be taking a look at *him*.' The Licensing Officials pointed to the PCS, the PCS complained about the district detectives, the Warmoesstraat pointed the finger at headquarters, and headquarters retaliated with counter-accusations. One of the suspects named 'all and sundry', according to a senior officer at headquarters, and although the man claimed that 'he would not let anyone hang' he put the authorities on to the two detectives in District South who were arrested and convicted for corruption (cf. Chapter Two). Two of the couples 'knew a lot about one another and were frightened of one another and Kramer and Toxopeus thought they had been screwed by Lighthart and Hoogland.' There were two other reasons for this, both related to their defence. The twin planks of the suspects' counter-accusations were, first, that 'Everyone was doing it so we went along too,' and second, 'The governors were doing it as well so why just pick on the small fry?' Codes of silence are only effective when everyone keeps them, out of loyalty and/or fear, and are likely to be undermined where one group carries the can for another and where the intimidation of that other group is not powerful enough to silence loose tongues.

NON-CONSENSUAL SOLIDARITY AND INTER-RANK HOSTILITY

It may seem obvious that an investigation into corruption will stimulate inter-rank antagonism because, if it is formal and internal (as opposed to externally imposed in which case the ranks may unite against it – Christianson 1973), the force leadership can use official authority and facilities to deflect the attention downwards. The lower ranks, in contrast, are relatively impotent in that they cannot formally direct the investigation upwards and are wary of testifying against a boss who may avoid conviction and then later take vengeance on the 'loud-mouths'. 'When the shit hit the fan' in Amsterdam there was strong resentment of bosses who were seen as culpable. On the one hand those who did not want to know, and who insulated themselves from the burden of guilty knowledge (Hughes 1958), implicitly condoned the growth of deviant practices while those who did know (generally a number of detective chiefs keen on results) actively stimulated the practices. The first reaction of a senior officer caught with corruption on his patch is to deny knowledge of it (how could he do otherwise without implicating himself?). His men are, in effect, abandoned by him and they resent his self-interest and hypocrisy because, in their eyes, a good boss is one who backs you through thick and thin.

In Amsterdam there arose counter-accusations which focused on the bosses' culpability both for their laxity and for their own involvement in 'dirty tricks'. In trying to gain more control over the functioning of the lower ranks the two senior officers in the Warmoesstraat, for instance, initiated enormous unrest, heated personal emotions, powerful informal sanctions, and helped bring the station to a crisis of confidence and to the verge of mutiny. In particular, considerable hostility was generated against senior officers. Serpico referred to the bosses as the 'real culprits' (Maas 1974: 176). Reus-Ianni (1983) argues that in the wake of Knapp there was an accentuation of the 'two cultures' separating higher and lower ranks; in London detectives under suspicion were seen as 'victims of dishonest superiors' (Cox, Shirley, and Short 1977: 123); and in Chicago a policeman broke his long silence with a letter from prison asking the prosecutors, 'what about the Captains? Didn't Frank tell you about the Captains?' (Beigel and Beigel 1977: 259). One informant had mounted a one-man campaign, following an incident several years earlier when he felt the department left him in the lurch, in which he set out to 'wring the necks' of senior officers and presented himself as 'a wolf in sheep's clothing' to infiltrate positions from which he carried out his vendetta, part of which involved taking the side of the suspects against the department. When he approached me he was highly frustrated and said, 'There's no one I can go to with my knowledge.'

INFORMAL SOCIAL CONTROL

Policemen who gratuitously broke the code of silence (as opposed to those who 'coughed' under investigation – see below), witnesses, and investigating officers were exposed to informal social control from colleagues in the form of physical threats, blackmail, and ostracism. The senior officers in the Warmoesstraat were physically threatened, ostracized in the canteen, and treated as pariahs who had 'screwed their colleagues'. One of the officers said,

> 'In the last year there have been real personal dramas here and we've been singled out as the cause of all the misery. When Wouters died [of a heart-attack following questioning by State Detectives] we were subjected to aggression from the relatives [his son was also a policeman and stormed into the officer's room claiming they had contributed to his father's death]. According to some our handling of the issue was responsible for his death and that we drove him into his grave. We weren't allowed to attend the funeral. Now his son could shoot us dead. Some people really hate us. They say we destroyed people's careers. We've almost become untouchables.'

One officer claimed that his telephone was tapped by one of the suspects, who also threatened his wife and children. Another officer was apparently threatened by a constable with the words, 'You broke your leg once at football, but if it goes on like this I'll break both your legs.' A key witness, the hapless Freddy, was visited by policemen and beaten up for saying too much. Policemen who might have given evidence were allegedly blackmailed into keeping quiet for fear of facing counter-accusations. An investigating officer was ostracized in the corridors at headquarters and met a 'solid wall of incomprehension' when he lectured trainee-detectives on the nature of his work:

> 'Policemen see themselves as different from civilians and cannot accept the idea that their own colleagues can be subject to investigation. When I mentioned the State Detectives there was a completely irrational response. I was seen as someone who screwed his own mates, and people stopped acknowledging me in the corridor.'

A detective, who actually was sympathetic towards several of the suspects, explained how rumour and gossip could be used to darken your reputation if you were suspected of providing information on deviance:

> 'When I heard about Frank's trip to Antwerp, when he was supposed to have brought back heroin (something like that gets around quickly and I picked it up from my Chinese contacts), I just went up to him here in the detective room and said quietly to him that if I was him I'd use my own car instead of a Mercedes

belonging to a Chinese and that what he brought back was his own business. He began ranting and raving and he would do this and that and started shouting in front of my mates why I didn't go to the governor if that was what I thought. The next day I had to go to Headquarters to pick up a photo from the Information Centre and this colleague says, "What's all this then, John? Trying to screw one of your own mates?" About two years later Frank phones up and thanks me for not saying anything to the boss. So I said, "OK then, and I suppose now you're going to phone all those people who accused me of screwing one of my mates because of your loud mouth and put the story right." You see if you get a reputation in this job it takes years to get rid of it.'

This material suggests not only that informal social control could be powerful and persuasive but also that it could merge into 'perversion of justice' whereby the investigation was materially hindered by blackmail and intimidation.

BLACK PROPAGANDA

A powerful weapon that the lower orders have is the use of gossip which, next to official information, keeps up a supply of unofficial information to combat the organization's formal view. In Amsterdam this took two principal forms: one was to blame the bosses and to point counter-accusations in their direction and the other was to criticize the nature of the investigation itself.

Throughout this study we have consistently seen examples of lower ranks forthrightly condemning their senior officers for negligence, incompetence, careerism, etc.; far more damaging, however, were the revelations and rumours that highly placed policemen were themselves involved in dubious practices including theft, perjury, and endangering the lives of informants. What this means is that in order to remove blame, or some of the blame, from themselves policemen are forced to point the finger at other policemen. One the suspects told me (in 1980),

'It's still not right with the P.C.S. Things are still not straightened out. Philips [member of 'reformed' PCS] for instance, took a thousand guilders from a Chinese bloke in the San Kwan [gambling house]. First he refused, then he accepted. One of the bosses knows it but nothing has been done. It's really nonsense that things are better. I've still got my contacts in the area and I know. But what I've seen is only a fraction of what's really happened and it reaches to Public Prosecutors as well. So much has been covered up. There's watertight evidence that a Chief Inspector committed theft but nothing happens about it.'

And some of this material does accuse other policemen of corruption and criminal practices thereby reinforcing the allegations made by witnesses but not proved in court or substantiated in the investigation. I was told of a detective who had left Amsterdam because of difficulties with a senior officer but had taken up a new job that made it important that he not be involved in any controversy so that he was not prepared to make a statement. He was involved in a case where 300 grammes of cocaine were placed in the safe of a senior officer. When he went to collect it in order to present the case to the Public Prosecutor it was no longer there. The senior officer said,

> ' "tell the Public Prosecutor that the cocaine has been destroyed and put that in the crime report". van Tol [detective] says, "how can that be arranged, and who's supposed to arrange it?" Because he's getting worried about carrying the can himself. Then . . . [senior officer] phones up the Public Prosecutor in his presence and fixes it.'

Practically all the main actors were surrounded by gossip which cast suspicion on the investigators in the same way that they had raised doubts about the suspects (Goldstein 1977: 205). The Chief Constable had remarried and was supposed to have received free travellers cheques from a travel agency for his honeymoon; one of the State Detectives was stopped for driving under the influence and it was said that he was not only paralytic drunk but that the woman with him was not his wife; the senior officers in the Warmoesstraat were being paid by a gambling-house; and most of the officers and former officers in the Warmoesstraat were tainted by rumours (when van Thiel went to eat with 'Mao' there were immediate stories that he had received a gold Parker pen set). In particular, the lower ranks claimed that senior officers had persistently ignored the warnings and signals of deviance so that their inattention and/or inactivity amounted to negligence:

> 'There was no leadership, and they laughed about __ [police-man accused of sexual offences] but nobody did anything about it. Now they'll say they didn't know, but they did. The top knew as well but they've washed their hands of the affair. This business hasn't come as a surprise to me but I was angry when I

heard the governors say, "But we knew nothing about it," when it was pointed out to them on several occasions. But nothing was done about it.'

One detective got hold of an earlier report warning of corruption in the Warmoesstraat and shoved it under the nose of a senior officer, asking why, if his signature was on the report, he had subsequently done nothing about it, and the officer replied lamely, 'But I sign so many papers.'

Another method of counter-attack was to denigrate the nature and quality of the investigation itself and clearly policemen can be particularly effective in their criticism because of their practical and professional knowledge of criminal investigations. Throughout the four years there were persistent attempts to undermine the credibility of the investigation. Its methods were described as unethical or incompetent or both. In particular the enquiry was seen as slanted against a number of 'small fry' and as a cover-up for 'big fry'. It was said that Chung Mon's books had disappeared after his death removing material damaging to senior officers; reports had been 'doctored' at Internal Affairs and Misfeance; why were so many names mentioned in statements yet there were so few arrests; Freddy was forced to talk to the authorities under pressure of deporting him and his common-law Japanese wife but taking their child into custody for adoption in The Netherlands; and the dossier had been fiddled with before it went to the Mayor (*Haagse Post* 13 May, 1977; *Elseviers Magazine* 18 May, 1978). One of the suspects strongly formulated this scapegoat theory.

'They tried to break us psychologically by dragging it out so long. And one of the women who accused me came to the station and her statement was already typed out and all she had to do was sign it without even an interview. It was all arranged from the top – "we'll nick eight of them, kick them out, and we're rid off the problem". But it didn't work.'

Rumours persisted of hard interrogations, psychological pressure, and crude searches of suspect's houses by the State Detectives.

THE COUNTER-MYTHOLOGY

Two different policemen described one of the suspects in the PCS to me. An investigating officer said, 'he's a bad one, a real villain, he has contacts with the Chinese and is involved with the 14K [triad], he's sold crime reports to the press, and he's blackmailed colleagues into keeping quiet.' Yet a colleague of the man said, 'I was talking to Chief Inspector Withagen [former head of Detective Branch in Warmoesstraat] the other day and we agreed you'll never find another one like . . . [member of PCS], he's one of the best' and a detective said of the same person that he was a 'really good copper and I'm convinced he's done nothing to the disadvantage of the force.' The discrepancy helps to reveal one of the tactics used to counter suspicion and that was to build up the suspects as above-average, hard-working, dedicated policemen whose motives were positive and who had become victims of a hypocritical system. The informal culture relabelled positively their own errant members as a mechanism against stigma. In fact, the deviant may approximate closely to the 'stereotypically perfect employee' (Ditton 1977: 87), while corrupt policemen often have exemplary records. Members of the Met Drug Squad had received commendations for 'initiative and ability' (Honeycombe 1974: 240); while two of the suspects had received commendations for their work and it was said of one of them that he 'brought more heroin in on his good days than the whole of the Drug Squad at Headquarters' (*Haagse Post* 8 October, 1977).

Another function of the counter-mythology was to excuse the fact that some policemen did open their mouths, breaking the code of silence. In effect, some of the suspects did talk in an effort to save their own necks and to spread the blame. But breaking the code of silence was so palpably in stride with the norms of the occupational culture that a mythology developed to help explain the fact that policemen as suspects would readily confess. All sorts of rumours began circulating – which ironically echoed precisely the critical accusations of outsiders in relation to dubious police methods – about suspects being put under pressure. An informant claimed that, 'Ton Kater [policeman convicted of stealing money from a suspect inside the station] was taken at 4 am to HQ after a night's work and with no food, no drink, no fags, he was interrogated in relays as if he was a great villain. I can imagine that after a whole day of that you'll confess to anything.' One of the suspects received the witnesses' statements from his lawyer and saw that a colleague had mentioned his name to the State Detectives. He called the man's colleagues around to his house and read extracts from the dossier to them. When they accosted their colleague and put it to him he denied it hotly and this led to the idea of fabrication and falsification in the statements in the dossier. The function of these rumours was to protect the image of the policeman as someone innately superior to ordinary citizens, to darken the reputation of the investigators, and to offer an excuse for the fact that some policemen gave information about their colleagues. Another possibility was that the suspects were admired for *not* talking. In other words, their admissions were limited to a small circle who were already known to be under suspicion, so that they could be seen to be cooperating with the enquiry, whereas in fact they were covering-up for a number of grateful colleagues who were prepared to reciprocate in various ways. It is highly likely, for instance, that the two Chinese experts knew enough to put Litjens in jail but kept quiet on really incriminating matters.

COLLUSION WITH SUSPECTS

There was a good deal of sympathy for the personal predicament of the suspects, and formal and informal attempts were made to help them. They were seen as victims of near universal deviant practices, such as accepting free meals and gifts, and as scapegoats for illicit enforcement condoned by superiors. The police unions, certain lawyers, prison officials, social workers, and court officials all displayed varying levels of above normal sympathy and support. As we shall see below, some members of the press also sought to aid the suspects although their concerns were more self-centred. Assistance was particularly forthcoming when the men faced a disciplinary enquiry following the judicial investigation and therefore were exposed to 'double jeopardy'. The eight suspects were subjected not just to arrest, publicity, suspension, and decrease in salary but were denied access to police stations and were not supposed to fraternize with former colleagues. In response they received help and information from their mates and from former contacts in the inner city. In brief, they received information on the movements of senior officers and State Detectives (other police would look in their diaries), they were sent copies of documents related to their cases (policemen would photocopy reports while the officers were out for meals), they were made welcome at certain stations and never had their entry barred at others, and one was encouraged to take up 'black' employment by a doctor who worked for the city:

'I was the first to be considered for return to duty and I wanted to wait and see what happened to the others so I reported sick.

The doctor said the best therapy was that I work as much as possible! So I worked flat out [on a "black" job] although officially I was down as ill with the force. He said, "We'll just keep our mouths shut and they can all get stuffed".'

One suspect (how typical of the police bureaucracy) was placed in the Misfeance Department for a period as part of his training as detective although he was under suspicion. 'When I was at Misfeance all I had to do was pull open a drawer and I could read all the statements made about me. At the end of the period we celebrated as usual with a drink and this adjutant says, "Well, you've worked pretty well here," and he's sitting on the desk containing my file! What a wanker.' Clearly he had access to documents but even after his arrest the documents were available to fellow detectives because Misfeance shared an office with other units and I was told by a detective who worked there that it was a simple matter to look at them. Perhaps the most active piece of collusion was the plan of a suspect to escape temporarily from prison in order to visit his family and 'sort some things out' (a plan which was not in fact carried out); colleagues had placed his car at a prearranged spot and had told him where he could find the keys.

LEAKS TO THE PRESS

Following the arrests in April, 1977, a good deal of inside information was leaked to the press either through carelessness with documents at headquarters, or for money, or via regular relationships between policemen and journalists (Chibnall 1977), or even through the suspects themselves. In any event, the contents of crime-reports and witnesses' statements were almost literally reproduced in the press. The whole scandal was played out almost daily via the papers. Leaks were probably made for purely mercenary ends but much of the provision of documents appeared to be done in order to help the suspects' defence and to embarrass the force leadership. The suspects leaked documents obtained from the lawyers (one, as mentioned earlier, for financial reward), gave interviews, and one appeared on television. They were frightened that public attention would wane as the investigation dragged on and were determined to keep their cases in the public eye. This played into the hands of the press, who were delighted to receive so much ammunition from within the force and who, in return, helped the suspects' defence by scrutinizing closely the deficiencies of the police top. In terms of a journalistic scandal, the technique was to suggest and insinuate that what had been revealed was only the 'tip of the iceberg' and that the top of the hierarchy was also involved (for example, the series 'The Mortally Ill Police Force' in *Het Parool* January.–March, 1979). Between them the suspects and the press were highly successful at directing attention away from the lower ranks and refocusing it in the direction of senior officers and the nature of the investigation itself.

Repercussions: Stirring the Shit

'It's a bit like handling a pot of shit. I can take off the lid and start stirring around in the shit. But then some of it might stick to my own fingers.'

(Investigating officer, Amsterdam)

If earlier phases of the investigation tended to be dominated by the errant members of the PCS in the Warmoesstraat then the final phase saw a shift in emphasis to Headquarters, to internal rivalries and tensions within the force, and particularly to the functioning of the Drug Squad. In essence, the focus shifted to the 'factory' (Headquarters) and the material replicates some of the features revealed in earlier stages, namely rivalry, distrust, jealousy, intrigue, factionalism, scapegoating, and the difficulty of obtaining water-tight evidence on police corruption from underworld characters. Attention was now turned full square on the internal functioning of the force, on the methods used by the Drug Squad in combating crime, on the disciplinary enquiry, and on four key figures. If van Thiel and Maartens in the Warmoesstraat had been the 'villains' of the piece earlier then now the headlines were captured by Commissioner Litjens, Chief Inspector van Rossum, and the two 'Chinese experts' Hoogland and Lighthart. To understand how this came about it is necessary briefly to touch on three elements which help to explain the resilience of the scandal and why it continued to cause seismic reverberations in certain parts of the force.

First, it was in the interests of the press to keep the story alive by suggesting that the incidents recorded were far more than incidents and that not only 'small fry' were involved. One element in this journalistic labelling was to suggest continually that senior officers were also involved (one weekly magazine used the headline 'Police Top Also Widely Corrupt', *Accent* 7 May, 1977) and many newspaper accounts were spiced with gossip about senior officers to suggest their involvement in deviant practices or in relationships with underworld characters. Second, once the trial was over and the internal disciplinary enquiry began, the path was open for a great deal of manipulation within the force to influence the outcome of the investigation now that the external element was reduced. Some people feared that the enquiry would neglect to probe the conduct of certain senior officers and would also prove to be too lenient towards the eight suspects now subjected to an internal enquiry. The representatives of this 'clean party', who believed in pushing the investigation remorselessly to its conclusion, were principally three young chief-inspectors (Maartens, van Thiel and particularly van Rossum who found support in Chief Inspectors Collewijn, Schippers, and Bakker). They forcefully and continually lobbied the Chief Constable not to ease up against the 'dirty party' around Litjens which, in turn, drew strength from the 'sweep it under the carpet' lobby (the older defensive bureaucrats). This 'clique' from middle-management, in effect, supported an enquiry within an enquiry, against Commissioner Litjens in particular, and stood for a hard-line against the suspects (e.g. that they should not be accepted back in the force).

And, third, there was not only considerable internal sympathy for the eight suspended policemen but also a degree of external support. This came particularly from their position as civil servants. Civil service status in The Netherlands is strongly protected by law, and the Civil Service Court which arbitrates in disputes between employee and employer is renowned for frequently championing the rights of the civil servant (while some employers would rather come to a compromise than face the court, even when they have a good chance of winning, in order to avoid the negative publicity). It is most unlikely that the court would have supported dismissal on grounds of accepting gifts and money if the suspects had appealed to it. In addition, the Mayor is the official head of the Police and it was he who, in the last resort, would decide the fate of the suspects.

To illustrate his ultimate control over personnel questions within the force there was the example of a policewoman, employed in the Criminal Intelligence Branch, who was found to be having a relationship with a German suspected of sympathizing with the 'RAF' terrorists. She was moved by the Chief Constable to an obscure administrative job in the Traffic Branch for security reasons (*Vrij Nederland* 13 May, 1978). The woman took her case first to the Mayor and then to the Civil Service Court. At the last moment the Mayor decided not to face the court and, arguing that the woman had been unjustifiably deprived of her position, ordered her reinstated in her old function within the Detective Branch. This indicates not only the strength of a civil service appointment in The Netherlands but also the relative powerlessness of a police chief in removing or sanctioning members of his force (Muir 1977: 202).

If anyone within the Amsterdam Police hoped that the case could be swiftly terminated with a surgical house-cleaning operation then these three major factors ensured that the affair would not only be prolonged but also that it would open the field for tough in-fighting and bitter power-struggles within the department. The material in this section depends considerably on the interviews given to the press by the two 'Chinese experts' and while their accusations overlap considerably with previous sections I have decided to treat them here separately for several reasons. They were widely considered to be honest and dedicated cops; they opened up the situation at headquarters and in the sensitive power centres of the specialized squads; and they pointed unambiguously at the antics of senior officers. They were well qualified and well placed, then, to say what went on in areas difficult for me to reach and previously left untouched by the investigation.

LITJENS, THE DRUG SQUAD, AND THE SECRET ENQUIRY

'A clean conscience makes the most comfortable pillow.'
(Senior officer under suspicion)

In the early 1970s the Amsterdam Drug Squad was always good copy and the man responsible for it at that time, Litjens, was not shy of grasping publicity and was usually good for a pithy quote or jovial interview (direct control of the Squad was in the hands of a Chief Inspector but Litjens controlled several units including the Drug Squad). The early amateurism and set-backs in drug enforcement in the beginning of the Chinese power-struggle were followed by successes, and Litjens clearly enjoyed basking in the limelight. He flew to the centre of the international drug trade in the Far East, attended a DEA course in the USA, and espoused American methods as necessary to book success in the face of Holland's antiquated legal system. His highly personal, soloistic, and 'unorthodox' style involved conducting himself like

an ordinary detective by running his own informants and by leading from the front even after he was promoted to head the Central
Detective Branch. He built up around him a group of policemen
who more or less worked for him on a personal basis and they
would frequently be involved in cases behind the backs of their
direct chiefs and outside of formal channels. Later the man in
charge of the Drug Squad was Chief Inspector van Rossum who
also was not averse to publicity but who was more systematic and
managerially oriented than Litjens. Under his leadership, the
Drug Squad went to book even more success.

The two 'Chinese experts', the detectives Hoogland and
Lighthart, had played a vital role in all this. They worked for the
CID, which came under the authority of the senior officer responsible collectively for the Drug Squad, the Shadow Squad, and also
the CID. This meant that they worked under Litjens and later
under van Rossum. When arrested they steadfastly denied everything and the cases against them were dropped in November
1977. But they remained suspended pending the outcome of the
disciplinary enquiry. Unlike some of the other suspects they did
not seek publicity and initially refused all interviews with the
press. Towards the end of 1978, however, it became common
knowledge that, on the basis of the disciplinary enquiry, the
Chief Constable was recommending their dismissal to the Mayor.
The Chinese experts decided to talk. They launched a counter-
attack which not only exposed some of the methods used in
detective work at headquarters in Amsterdam but which also
aimed principally to discredit 'the bosses'.

The press responded by using the same imagery that had been
used against the Warmoesstraat to depict the symptoms of decay
and disarray at Headquarters. The magazine *Extra* asked 'Is the
Capital's Drug Squad Rotten to the Core?' (29 December, 1978)
while *Panorama* (26 January, 1979) promised to reveal a 'ruthless
x-ray of a mortally ill police apparatus that is suffering from frustration, prejudice, jealousy, and especially the thrusting imperial-
ism of the puppet-master of the CIA's drugs department, the
Drug Enforcement Agency.' When it was reported that the Chief
Constable was recommending the dismissal of both detectives
because of 'very serious dereliction of duty' (related to accepting
money and jewelry, having too intimate relations with Chinese
criminals, and withholding information) they retaliated by claiming that Chief Inspector van Rossum had himself covered up
certain lines of enquiry and had even advised a number of fellow-
officers about how to avoid being suspected of corruption. In

addition, the Central Detective and Information Branch (a state coordinating agency for crime enforcement) in The Hague was reputed to have knowledge in 1976 that the leadership in the Warmoesstraat had been 'bought' by a Chinese gambling-house and they demanded a new enquiry from the Chief Constable into these allegations (*De Volkskrant* 4 November, 1978).

Now the two Chinese experts set out both to elicit sympathy for their predicament and also to turn the spotlight on the rivalry between van Rossum and Litjens of which they had allegedly become the victims. The two detectives spoke out in graphic terms, 'They're embittered, feel they've been sacrificed, and have made counter-accusations' (*Extra* 29 December, 1978).

One of them, Lighthart, elaborated on this.

'All of a sudden I was picked up. Even my wife wasn't allowed to know where I was. I was put away for a couple of days and my wife wasn't even given the chance to fetch my dirty underpants. We were treated like pigs. In comparison with us Litjens has had the VIP treatment, but then he's a commissioner and we're only a couple of street cops. Damn it, now we're treated as crooks but I swear to you we never took a thing. May be now and then an egg-roll but you have to go along with the Chinese. Give and take, win their confidence, otherwise you won't get a shred of information. We were Litjen's experts. His Chinese boys. Now he's in the shit himself but he'll get out of it alright. But not us. When I think about how we used to sweat blood on the pavements, how hard we worked, seven days a week. My wife had breast-cancer. One breast had to be cut off. I'm sitting next to her in the hospital when I get a call from the station. And then you're off again, back on the streets, leaving your critically-ill wife alone. Now I ask you, is that corruption? And yet, who knows, given the chance I'd probably do it again, perhaps, if I get the chance. Because being a cop is rather like having an incurable disease.'

Initially, Litjens had functioned as their protector, but had dropped them when the going got rough. 'We did the work and Litjens sold it to the press. But in the end we got the brush-off as thanks. When we needed him he said he was not at home' (*Haagse Post* 10 February, 1979).

They launched into a string of serious accusations against their former bosses, van Rossum and Litjens. They objected to the fact of being caught between rival bosses who demanded to be informed of everything in case the rival gained an advantage.

Litjens was depicted as practically incompetent, as a 'TV-copper' who was too busy playing to the press, and they referred to 'Derrick' (a popular German television series about a commissioner) as 'a load of rubbish, of course, if only because you see a commissioner actually doing some work. We have never, at any time, seen a commissioner who ever did any work' (*Panorama* 2 February, 1979). They claimed that the Drug Squad and the Warmoesstraat resented their successes and their close contacts with the Chinese. They claimed, further, that Chinese contacts complained to them that they lost money during police searches; that money for informants in the Drug Squad never reached the informants; and that informants were short-changed by detectives (receiving only a portion of their reward money). But when they pointed this out to colleagues (one of whom said, 'Well, so what, he [the suspect in question] will only go away and buy heroin with the money') they were attacked for 'screwing their own mates'. Van Rossum was said to have signed blank search-warrants to cover the period when he was away on an FBI course in the USA, to have kept a collection of keys to gain access to the houses of Chinese people, and to have 'stolen' opium pipes after a raid on an opium-den. Litjens also damaged their relations in the Chinese community, where they had been initiated into some of the secret practices of the triads, by loudly publishing details of the triads on his return from the Far East. Furthermore, a number of informants were allegedly brought into danger and six of them perhaps even murdered because of Litjens, van Rossum, van Thiel, and Maartens; in particular Litjens and van Rossum were said to have talked too much to the press in order to get publicity for themselves, and this endangered informants. This offended the detectives' code. 'The informant must always be protected. If necessary from colleagues and bosses. That's why we've always made sure that nobody could identify the informant from any of the papers' (*Panorama* 26 January, 1979). The Drug Squad may even have deliberately betrayed some informants to the underworld.

All this was enough to focus attention on the Drug Squad and on the personality of Commissioner Litjens, who, in a book entitled *Manhunters* (Deeley 1970), was ranked among some of the best detectives in the world for a case against diamond smugglers. The magazine *Extra* (29 December, 1978) portrayed him as a sort of relentless Dutch 'Dirty Harry' of the old school, opposed by a new generation of bookish managers who resented him. He was said to have 'used tips, betrayal, clean and not so clean methods in order to break the triads in Amsterdam. He did it with a low budget, handicapped by all sorts of bureaucratic shortcomings, and followed by admiring but more often jealous glances from his those around him.' In exchange for information and money (a couple of 'ton' – a 'ton' is slang for 100,000 guilders), 'Litjens is supposed to have exercised a selective enforcement policy, to put it mildly'.

At this stage there was all sorts of speculation about Litjens – that he willingly did Chung Mon's bidding, that he wrote a letter for Chung Mon asserting that he was not involved in the drug trade, that he helped retrieve Chung Mon's bullet-proof Mercedes from Belgian customs authorities, and that he was little other than an errand-boy in the heroin world (*Haagse Post* 4 November, 1978). Questions were raised as to why the murderers of Chung Mon and 'Mao' so easily evaded arrest and were never convicted. The world of double-agents, giant deals, betrayal, and the elimination of rivals and unwanted informants was bandied about. The suggestion was that the Drug Squad was little more than an enthusiastic and sometimes clumsy amateur in all this and that the real force at work was the no-holds-barred struggle between the DEA and the organized drug traffickers of the Far East. Hoogland and Lighthart, for instance, admitted that they had not told everything they knew about Mao because they did not trust their bosses. Then Litjens told them to leave Mao alone because the DEA was interested in him. But Hoogland and Lighthart got in the way of the DEA and 'had to be eliminated' (*Panorama* 9 February, 1979).

All sorts of byzantine intrigues – involving the DEA, the Chinese underworld, and the Amsterdam Police – were sketched which are impossible to verify. But all this was used to suggest that much of the 'truth' had not come to the surface and that, if told, it would reveal a good deal that was fundamentally wrong inside the Central Detective Branch of the Amsterdam Police, 'Litjens was literally supposed to have been the tip of an iceberg of corruption that covered the whole of the Amsterdam Police. The whole of the capital's detective apparatus was said to stink, from top to toe' (*Extra* 29 December, 1978).

But the fact that a well-known policeman of the rank of Commissioner was involved in a corruption scandal, however marginally and however much by insinuation, was unprecedented for The Netherlands ('never before was a Dutch policeman so blatantly left in the lurch by his bosses in the Police and Justice Departments. Never before was a man with a plate-armoured international reputation as Litjens so mercilessly sacrificed on the block of public opinion' (*Elseviers Magazine* 23 February, 1980). Given his considerable power and high formal status it is likely that he could have deflected suspicion except for the fact that a group of 'young turk' officers were pushing the Chief Constable to mount a secret internal enquiry against him. Because the first investigation had come up with so little the 'vultures' were, claimed Litjens, determined not to fail this time and a 'witchhunt' was mounted against him; in their determination to get him, he went on, information was leaked to the press, reports had been tampered with, and all this had been carried out in secrecy so that he had to learn about it in the newspapers (*Elseviers Magazine* 23 February, 1980). Solidarity and collegial relations had been poisoned by all this and he stated 'I do not trust anyone anymore' (*De Telegraaf* 15 February, 1980). The finale to this phase, with its internal bickering and mutual accusations, reached a climax in January 1979 when Litjens was moved from Headquarters to head a district station. This was, in effect, a humiliating demotion for an interntionally renowned detective. *De Telegraaf*, which had close relations with Litjens, took his side and presented him as the victim of an intrigue in which his jealous arch-rival, van Rossum, was the major culprit. Their offices were on the same corridor at headquarters and relations were strained, doors were slammed, and at one stage Litjens burst furiously into the room of an investigating officer shouting, 'So you want to break a commissioner, do you? Well, go ahead and try it!' But the young turks had presented the Chief with an ultimatum that either 'Litjens goes or we go' (*De Telegraaf* 29 January, 1979). Litjens put on a brave face and claimed that he did not view the move as a demotion and that the Attorney General felt that he had merely been guilty of 'technical errors' (*Het Parool* 30 January, 1979). A supporter of Litjens, Chief Inspector Otten, was also moved from Headquarters to a district station but died of a heart-attack before he could take up his new appointment. There were rumours of suicide, that he shot himself with his service-pistol, and that his death was related directly to the strains of the corruption affair.

In fact, it proved extremely difficult to raise convincing evidence against Litjens, despite serious efforts to implicate him in highly devious practices. The secret investigation was stimulated by three sources. First, the enquiries into the cases of the eight policemen had undoubtedly raised serious question marks about the Drug Squad and pointed irresistibly in the direction of Litjens. The young turks were pushing to avoid a cover-up and this meant that van Rossum was virtually 'spying' on his boss.

Then when Litjens went away on a business trip to Cairo, State Detectives, with the backing of the Chief Constable, opened his safe and apparently discovered drugs and weapons. (His Chinese experts had been arrested while he was out of the country and it is interesting that both Mark and Murphy waited until their detective chiefs were on holiday before announcing important moves (Mark 1978: 117; Murphy and Plate 1977: 210). Second, a 'confidential report' was supplied by the police in The Hague to the Amsterdam Police in April 1978 which initiated an investigation into Litjen's doings by the State Detectives. A criminal in prison had volunteered a statement in which he alleged that Litjens offered protection to certain figures in the underworld and passed on information which, among other things, was meant to lead to the kidnapping, robbing, and murdering of a cocaine dealer in an operation whereby four million guilders were at stake. At one stage, Stein, the Head of the State Detectives in Amsterdam, was said to have had an arrest warrant in his pocket for Litjens (*De Telegraaf* 15 February, 1980). And, third, a number of suspects in drug cases had raised accusations against the methods of the Amsterdam Drug Squad (including the defence of one well-known criminal, nicknamed 'Pimmetje Paf', that he was working as an undercover agent for the police when caught smuggling drugs through Schiphol Airport: *De Volkskrant* 9 February, 1980).

An example of how determined the Justice Department was to push the case came when two convicted criminals were freed temporarily from jail sentences because they were supposed to have access to incriminating material against Litjens and the Drug Squad. Such deals with convicted criminals are officially denied in The Netherlands and this appears to be the first time ever that a senior official (the Attorney General for Amsterdam) admitted openly to an arrangement whereby, in return for information, a prisoner was temporarily freed and also offered a reduction in sentence and a financial reward. The man concerned promptly used his temporary freedom to disappear for three months until he was arrested by chance (the second man was sent to look for him and returned as agreed, but empty handed, to prison). Then he was flown to Zurich accompanied by the head of the State Detectives in Amsterdam because he claimed that tapes, letters, and other incriminating material were located in a Swiss bank safe. At Zurich airport he requested to proceed *alone* and, when this was understandably denied, he refused any further co-operation (*De Telegraaf* 11 January, 1980). The Justice Department eventually concluded that they could not come up with evidence justifying criminal charges, and not even disciplinary charges, and passed on the dossier to the Mayor. He, in turn, felt that there were no grounds for disciplinary action but passed the buck to the Minister of Home Affairs (who is responsible, as representative of the 'crown', for disciplining police commissioners who are technically appointed by the Queen). The minister then announced that no further steps were to be taken against Litjens (*De Volkskrant* 29 February, 1980). Litjens had been under suspicion for more than two years but continued to function as Head of the Central Detective Branch, and later as Head of a district, and was not arrested, prosecuted, or brought to trial.

For a number of obvious reasons I doubt if the information will ever be made available to piece together what actually took place in the major drug deals involving the Amsterdam Police. There is, however, a striking resemblance between Kelaher, head of the Met Drug Squad, and Litjens. There seems to be a common pattern in London and Amsterdam that drug enforcement was new, that it attracted a great deal of publicity, that it lent itself to 'unorthodox' methods, and that its practitioners both excite jealousy from more traditional policemen, and also get themselves into difficulties. (In a fascinating parallel with The Netherlands, Fijnaut (1983), describes the importation of American drug enforcement techniques in Belgium and analyses the demise of the two most important agencies, the NBD and BCI, and the fate of the head of the former, Francois, who sold cocaine to recover money he had given to informants, while some of the Belgian 'narcs' set up drug rings). In particular, in drug enforcement there is often a suggestion of idealism tinged almost with fanaticism whereby means, whatever means, justify the ends ('combative' corruption).

If combative strategic corruption took place in Amsterdam, and I strongly suspect that it did, then there is no convincing evidence in detail as to what actually took place. However, the indications are that Litjens enthusiastically practised some of the methods employed by the DEA and the Met in the 'war' against drugs. But in the end the most that could be laid at his door officially was that he broke department guidelines on relations with informants and on the registering of drugs and weapons and that he did not always keep the Justice Department well-informed on cases. It could be that the force simply could not withstand the repercussions if an officer of his rank was prosecuted for it would surely have led to an external enquiry and enforced change. And who knows whom he might have taken down with him? Perhaps he was also fortunate in not making powerful enough enemies. His external opponents were in the underworld where the Chinese power had been crushed and many had been deported while other accusers were considered unreliable and untrustworthy. Litjens was allowed a relatively comfortable pillow compared to others who came under suspicion; but then it is possible that his conscience was completely clear.

What he seemed unable to do, however, was to let go of his contacts in the underworld because, after four years as head of a district, he was suddenly moved aside to an obscure function at headquarters (and, refusing to go the headquarters, having described the force leadership as a 'medieval Council of Blood', he sequestered himself in a small office in a separate building belonging to the Traffic Department). The incident which sparked this off was his meeting of a Pakistani drug-dealer while he was on holiday (Drury of the Met had called attention to himself by going on holiday with a criminal and a Chicago policeman was discovered on holiday with a Mafia boss: Cox, Shirley, and Short 1977; Maas 1974: 115). He received free tickets from the KLM for the trip and the dealer paid his hotel bill. His defence was that he was helping the Dutch police official stationed in Karachi to form good contacts (*De Volkskrant* 23 September, 1983). But this time the 'vultures' do seem finally to have got their prey and he has announced his intention of retiring early and of writing his memoirs (*De Volkskrant* 18 June, 1984). It has also emerged (at the time of writing) that the new Mayor recommended to the Minister of Home Affairs that Litjens be disciplined and, in response, the Minister sent a letter to Litjens formally warning him of his conduct. There was no evidence of personal criminal involvement but it was considered that he went too far in his relationships with criminals and that this broke both regulations and the ethics for police officers (*Vrij Nederland* 14 July, 1984). It was also announced at the same time that three chief inspectors who represented the 'young turks' had been promoted to commissioner (their fear that one day the 'top' would get back at them proved not to be true and, in the long run, the 'clean party' did not suffer for their efforts).

The importance of this material is twofold. First, it reveals that, when things go wrong, relationships of trust and dependency break down. Protectors suddenly see that their power base is threatened and to save themselves they ditch their acolytes; these in turn, feeling betrayed and exposed, feel that one way to save their necks, or to get revenge, is to implicate their boss or try to show that he needed them more than they needed him. Second, in defending themselves and airing their grievances, the lower ranks have to lift the veil and expose the operational code. In so doing policemen, ironically, are forced to confirm many of the accusations levelled at them by others.

WHEELING AND DEALING

There must have been at this time numerous telephone calls and umpteen appointments involving all the main actors – the Chief Constable, the Mayor, the judicial authorities, trade union representatives, the suspects, lawyers, the young turks, Litjens, journalists, and doubtless even at the level of ministers (of Justice and Home Affairs) – but these endless and secretive machinations are almost completely shrouded in mystery. Clearly 'wheeling and dealing' took place but either people were not prepared to admit to it or else the negotiations were at a level where the participants were too vulnerable to let the veil of secrecy slip (I am thinking particularly of the Chief Constable, the Mayor, the judicial authorities, and the politicians). There are occasionally some glimpses, however, of what was going on behind the scenes.

The difficulty for all the suspects was that, if they cooperated, they could only do so by incriminating themselves. For example, Chief Inspector Schippers offered to make a deal with one of the suspects and to take him under his protection against van Rossum: 'But I said "No, that's impossible." If I told everything that I'd seen then I'd be putting my own neck in the noose. Because if I say "I saw __ [detective] take the money" then I'd also have to explain why I was there and how I was able to see it.' One of them did, nevertheless, agree to a private, man-to-man talk with a senior officer. This incident reached almost farcical proportions but is most revealing as to the nature of the methods employed in the informal investigation. Chief Inspector van Rossum decided to hear for himself what had 'really' taken place and arranged a meeting with one of the suspects, Kramer, in a motel in a small town close to Amsterdam where they would share a bottle of *genever* (gin) and talk 'off the record'. This is what transpired according to the suspect; 'van Rossum had sought a meeting with me using Schippers as intermediary and Schippers stood guarantee for van Rossum. But van Rossum had the conversation taped outside of Schippers's knowledge.' Arrangements to meet in a motel were changed at the last moment and this made the suspect suspicious; after the 'man-to-man' talk he waited outside behind a tree and saw van Rossum emerge with two colleagues he recognized from Headquarters:

> 'When I came out in the open van Rossum saw me and jumped in his car and reversed wildly down the road. I'd had quite a few drinks and ran to my car and tried to chase him – him reversing madly and me half-pissed trying to catch him – but somewhere in the village I lost him. So I went straight to Schippers's house in Amsterdam and around 3.30 a.m. we finally managed to get in touch with van Rossum. At first van Rossum denied it but eventually he admitted it. Schippers said ''That's not honest and I'll give you in black and white a statement saying that this material won't be used against you.'' '

Kramer had apparently opened his heart as to how the low-level policeman worked under pressure and 'messed around', how 'erosion of standards was almost a normal business', and how 'within fourteen days in the PCS you begin to adapt', and how you could 'score' a South American pick-pocket for money or a leather jacket without him putting in a complaint (*Haagse Post* 10 February, 1979). But, once outside, he felt 'conned' when he observed two men coming out of the building with a suit-case which he believed contained apparatus to record his conversation (van Rossum denied this and Schippers confirmed this version). van Rossum allegedly reacted as follows.

> 'During my conversation with van Rossum and Schippers, van Rossum asked, ''Are things really so rotten?'', and I told him a few home truths. Afterwards he rushed back at once to HQ, went into the Drug Squad, locked the door, ordered all the drawers open and demanded that all the heroin be taken out – ''We've got to do it quickly before the State Detectives get here.'' '

An almost unimpeachable source, one of the middle-ranking young turks, told me personally that 126 kilos of heroin (which he estimated were worth 40 million guilders on the streets) were collected in two large garbage bags following this incident. Much later there were still denials to me that the conversation was ever taped but one officer let slip that he had listened to the tape. We were chatting in an unmarked car on a prolonged stake-out when he admitted that the tape revealed just how much 'messing around' really had gone on, that it was 'one big gang' (then he said, 'Now I've said too much, and this mustn't go outside').

The two Chinese experts were also endeavouring to work the informal system. Hoogland and Lighthart were invited to Headquarters in June 1978 where Chief Inspector Schippers (a senior officer in the Detective Branch responsible for discipline and personnel) endeavoured to make a 'deal' with them. He claimed to represent a group of young chief inspectors who had *carte blanche* from an unspecified higher authority to look into the affair. This group was directed against the 'old guard' including Litjens and were prepared to make peace with Hoogland and Lighthart who would be let off with a formal warning (the lowest form of disciplinary punishment) if they darkened the reputation of Litjens and the 'old guard' (*Haagse Post* 10 February, 1979). Schippers then admitted in confidence, but in the presence of their lawyer, that the dossier sent to the Mayor had been doctored to remove all positive references to them and suggested that, as they had been wronged, they should seek support by getting in touch with a representative of the press such as Ton van Dijk from the magazine *Haagse Post*. The two men left the meeting in an emotional state and went to chat with some of their old colleagues in Headquarters. They let slip the content of the conversation with Schippers, and, when van Rossum heard of this, he is said to have reacted as if 'bitten by a viper' and stormed into Schippers's room shouting, 'There'll only be a deal made with Hoogland and Lighthart over my dead body. Those two will be sacked. And that's final!' (*Panorama* 9 February, 1979). These machinations were seen as part of van Rossum's power game to remove Litjens and claim his throne and, in this devious plan, Hoogland and Lighthart were expendable pawns. But by pressure via procedures in the Civil Service Court they persuaded the Mayor not to dismiss them (against the advice of the Chief Constable) and they were taken back in routine, administrative jobs.

To a certain extent in The Netherlands he who complains loudest and longest wins. A culture of coalition politics, moral relativism, use of publicity, attention for minorities, and succumbing readily to pressure seems to have produced a society where you can get your way if you protest vigorously enough. The Amsterdam Police was a microcosm of this because the chance that the suspects would be dismissed was high and yet, by threatening continuous publicity, they did at least succeed in staying in the force (if not quite getting full rehabilitation in their old positions). Of course, in such a battle of psychological warfare the victor needs to be resilient and be prepared to back up his claims and call the other's bluff. One man was not, but his answer reveals that the authorities were informally prepared to make threats of pressuring individuals. He told me that the suspects considered appealing against the sentence.

'The lawyers and the trade union said "Go ahead, let the ball roll, bring in the other forty men who have been mentioned, make them testify." But the Public Prosecutor threatened me that he would put the State Detectives after us for a whole year if necessary until eventually they came up with something against us. I just couldn't face this psychologically.'

Another suspect, of tougher fibre, threatened to keep the scandal continuously on the boil and this produced results. His lawyer took up contact with Labour Party (PVDA) representatives on the town council and with Conservative Party (VVD) members of Parliament. Some members of Parliament came to Amsterdam to discuss the affair with the Mayor and one of the suspects said:

'we phoned them for a chat as well. We met them in the "American Hotel" and I said "we're prepared to keep on going, in front of the TV cameras, before the press, every six months we will bring it up again and again until the case is finally closed, and if necessary we'll undermine the Amsterdam Police and break it up". On a Monday Cohen [Mayor] decided against going to the Civil Service Court on the next Wednesday and that meant no sackings. When he heard it the Chief Constable shouted "then I'll resign!" Then, in the end I got fed up with waiting, and one day when I'd had a few drinks I went along to see Schippers. I said, "where am I going? If I don't find out soon I'm going to open my mouth and tell a lot. If necessary I'll send my wife and kids to the family farm for a year or eighteen months and just concentrate on fighting the case". Then Schippers got in touch with the Chief. The next day Schippers phoned my lawyer and said "I can see him coming back." And, to be honest, I thought I was going to be sacked.'

However frustrating it may be, it is simply not possible to uncover more than a glimpse of these machinations which touch areas that may be simply unresearchable. But they do allow us a glimpse of Headquarters where one officer said,

'The atmosphere among colleagues is sickening. I live in a state of war with my boss, [a 'sweep it under the carpet' man – MP]. Since a couple of months I've been on the verge of a nervous breakdown and have considered getting out of the force, in fact I've applied for jobs in other departments.'

The case took a personal toll, with stress, personality clashes, and nervous breakdowns. They also undermined trust and the same officer said,

'Maartens didn't trust H.Q. so I had to phone Kroon [inspector in Warmoesstraat] and make him promise to send copies of all the reports direct to me. In fact I wouldn't deal directly with the State Detectives myself or even let matters run through my superior, but I sent copies of every bit of paper direct to the Chief so that he was fully informed and nothing could go astray.'

This reveals the belief that there were influences working for a cover-up within the organization and that documents might disappear or be 'doctored'. The young turks argued strongly in interviews that nothing had been learned by these cases and that somehow the 'guilty' had got off lightly.

'The whole business around Litjens doesn't smell nice. When I heard that the city wasn't going to push disciplinary proceedings against the Chinese experts I thought what sort of devious forces are at work here because I had the feeling that in order to protect Litjens it had been decided not to prosecute the others.'

When two internal commissions were set up to look into aspects of discipline and corruption both were chaired by senior officers who were not held in high esteem by some of their colleagues (to put it mildly).

All of this can be taken as signals that the department was not in a position to tackle the issue of corruption. Not one of the suspects had been sacked and several had been taken back. One of the leading actors reflected despondently, but defiantly,

'And if they are taken back what does this mean? That we've been wasting our time? What will the other constables say – "we might as well be corrupt too, because you can get away with it"?

What am I supposed to do about corruption now? The mayor says "take them back" and may be tomorrow I'm the boss of Kramer or one of the others. And what if tomorrow someone walks into this office and starts telling me about corruption? What am I supposed to do when I know that no-one wants to take it any further and that we've scarcely got an apparatus that can successfully investigate a case? Why shouldn't I tell the man to run away and just not do it again? But we're probably block-headed enough to start the whole thing all over again.'

This material can only suggest a fraction of the informal processes that went on behind the scenes. Of interest is that, in The Netherlands, institutions are frequently prepared to cave in to pressure rather than face continuous negative publicity and threats of legal action through the Civil Service Court. And, crucially, the only way some of the suspects felt that they could defend themselves was to attack, damage, and undermine the organization for which they worked.

POWER STRUGGLES, CHANGE, AND 'CREATIVE POLICING'

In every organization there exists an informal organization – 'a shadow organization in which dramas of power' are played out (Kanter 1977: 164); while a scandal which sparks off an institutional crisis is more than likely to act as an agent of change and realign the structure of power (Sherman 1978: xviii). This can occur formally, in terms of proposals for change, and/or informally in terms of factionalism and in-fighting. Amsterdam was no exception. What had happened within the organization was a shift in power from the old guard to the young turks who had gained the ear of the Chief. The young turk clique were for forceful prosecution of the corruption affair, for a responsible and accountable police, and for more effective policies against crime. Now most of these machinations took place at secret or confidential meetings about which little is officially known. What did emerge, however, was an ambitious programme to improve the image of the police, to alter some features of the organization, and to change aspects of how police work was being done and particularly in improving relationships with the public. The details are not important here (see Punch 1981b) but of considerable significance is the fact that the corruption scandal gave rise to a programme of change supported by internal factions and also by external groups. Those most likely to be effected by the change were the lower ranks and it was this two-pronged assault on their traditional autonomy, the scandal *and* the change programme, which helps to explain the defence, resistance, and support for the suspects which was forthcoming from the lower ranks.

Briefly, with considerable financial support from the Mayor and city council and with external expertise from an organizational consultancy bureau, the Chief Constable launched 'Kreapol' (for 'creative-police') in 1977 in a blaze of publicity (cf. six issues of campaign broadsheet: *Kreakant* 1977–79). There is no doubt that the corruption affair hastened the advent of Kreapol and it was used as a display to the outside world that the department was busily putting its own house in order. But, in effect, what happened within the Amsterdam Police in the period 1976–80 was that the investigation into corruption magnified the conflicts which the movement for change wished to minimize. It is highly probable that the Kreapol campaign would not have succeeded anyway for a number of reasons but the scandal, while giving the campaign an initial boost, effectively undermined its chances of succeeding partly because the investigation elicited considerable occupational and bureaucratic resistance and partly because the undercurrents of frustration unleashed by Kreapol began to threaten the very people concerned with change. The complexity of the reaction reveals how an attempt to investigate and to control police deviance can set up such volatile tensions that the investigation itself is blunted and demand for change is undermined.

The Chief and some of the 'new guard' became personally identified with pushing the Kreapol campaign which was resented as an attempt from *outside*, led by expensive 'experts' to change the system from the top (Wycoff and Kelling 1978). It promised a more open, democratic, responsible department with improved communication and with the stimulation of change. At the lowest level, of patrolmen in the districts, this unleashed a flood of criticism which canalized the frustration of the uniformed men against the system of work and authority. Middle-rank officers in favour of change suddenly saw a quite different upsurge of opinion from *below* which began to threaten their position because almost any subject was open to discussion and the nature of the command and control hierarchy itself was viewed critically. At the same time, a number of politicians were endeavouring to use the corruption affair to get more of a grip on the internal functioning of the department (raising once again the spectre of an Enschedé-type enquiry – *De Telegraaf* 9 March, 1979). One of the social scientists employed by the department became co-author of a Labour Party pamphlet that echoed this position. Furthermore, a number of internal reports were leaked via Kreapol to the city council. In effect, Kreapol became discredited in the eyes of many senior officers and hard-line detectives (who had never been particularly open to its arguments anyway) as a political manoeuvre from outside to impose a more party-political control over the organization. The investigation and Kreapol together threatened the established hierarchy at the top and the basis of control and supervision at the bottom. And both failed. The evidence for Amsterdam suggests that the complex world of the police organization is unbalanced by an investigation into deviance and that the subsequent occupational conflict and institutional in-fighting materially handicaps the investigation itself while also undermining the very demands for change which the scandal may elicit.

In 1980 a new chief constable was appointed and he made 'integrity' a cornerstone of his policy. Commissions and work-groups were formed and, once more, radical plans for change were developed ('Nota Binnenspiegel' 1981; 'De Amsterdamse Politie: Een Nieuw Perspectief' 1982). By 1984, with the publication of a research project on the effectiveness of proposals to combat occupational deviance (the so-called *naggen* – van Laere and Geerts 1984) and with a new, tougher mayor, there were determined noises that at last the matter was to be tackled forcefully and the Chief came out with hard words that deviance was not to be tolerated, that the public must be able to have confidence in the police, and that those police who strayed would be sacked (*De Telegraaf* 28 February, 1984). The corruption scandal began in 1976 and petered out in 1980 (but with headlines surrounding Litjens arousing the periodic rekindling of interest). But there can be shadow of a doubt that it still continues to effect the Amsterdam Police deeply.

Conclusion

A major theme of this chapter has been to argue that secrecy and solidarity characterize the occupational culture of policing not only in relation to the outside world but also with regard to *internal* relationships. For instance, when Skolnick (1981: 2) writes, 'Police culture permits, sometimes demands, deception of courts, prosecutors, defense attorneys, defendants . . . *but not of fellow policemen,*' then I would go along with him most of the way except that I would clearly disagree with the statement italicized. In particular, there is a deep dichotomy between the values, styles, and vulnerability of lower ranks and senior officers which is characterized by social distance, mutual distrust, and varying levels of manipulation, control, and acquiescence in deviant practices. Furthermore, when the chips were down some policemen did talk and broke the rule of silence which protects police practice from outside scrutiny. They did so largely out of self-interest – for money and to protect themselves – but they succeeded in deflecting attention on to the conduct of certain senior officers and the force leadership. The lesson of these cases is that in Amsterdam the ordinary policemen did not owe their primary allegiance to the organization but to the 'job', that is their peer group within the occupational community. Breaking the rule of silence was seen as legitimate in so far as it embarrassed and exposed the common enemy, 'upstairs', where the officer caste insulates itself from the dirty work and from the responsibility for daily street and detective practice.

This chapter has also conveyed some of the complexity of institutional life exposed by the corruption affair in Amsterdam which led to vindictive turmoil within the organization. The press had a field-day, personal disputes and mutual incriminations were relayed direct to the papers, some units were almost paralysed with dissent, officers were threatened and were shadowed by their own men, two deaths were ascribed to the affair, there were crises of confidence between lower ranks and senior officers in the Warmoesstraat and between young officers and the top ranks, there was virtually a sit-down strike in the Warmoesstraat where near-mutinous patrolmen refused to go out on the streets, and there were sympathy demonstrations for Amsterdam by many units of the Dutch Police.

But, above all, there was a protracted, acrimonious conflict between the lower ranks and senior officers which divided the organization into opposing camps determined to affix blame elsewhere. My research in Amsterdam, with its accent on the micro-processes of institutional life, does not portray the police organization as a harmonious, integrated entity with a comforting consensus and with unbreachable defences against internal investigation and outside enquiry based on a universal code of silence. On the contrary it conveys a deeply divided pattern of semi-autonomous and conflicting units, a portrait of an ambivalent occupational culure based on the norms of a continually threatened group who must engage in morally vulnerable work, and who bitterly resent being investigated, and an analysis of inter-rank relationships based on suspicion and mistrust. Non-consensual solidarity binds policemen together in complex patterns of dependency until 'the wheel comes off' and relationships become soured by feelings of abandonment and betrayal.

In the police organization there is a 'moral division of labour'

(Hughes 1958) which does not accord with the elaborate, hierarchical rank structure but rather turns it upside down in terms of the social distribution of secret knowledge. The dirty workers at the bottom are the ones who 'really' know the rules of the game and they rely on friendship, trust, secrecy, and team-work (Holdaway 1980: 229). But the hierarchical relationhip is 'moral' in the sense that 'the superordinate parties are those who represent the forces of approved and official morality,' while credibility and the right to be heard are 'differentially distributed throughout the system' (Becker 1970: 127). In the face of scandal there are two levels of counter-strategies to the deviant labelling; the top, in order to keep the organization from being labelled deviant, endeavours to individualize the issue, to scapegoat, and to espouse the 'rotten apple' theory; but the bottom mounts a counter-intelligence of black propaganda that pushes the label back up the hierarchy, suggesting that the deviance is widespread. The organization treats the lower orders as disloyal whereas they perceive themselves as the genuine defenders of the true ends of the organization and believe that they are being accused of precisely what the organization demanded of them (cf. Reisman 1979: 28, 'adherence to the operational code is not a violation of an oath to serve an organization, but rather the ultimate affirmation of that loyalty'). The 'workers' in the police bureaucracy are not deferential and servile actors but, rather, they actively and energetically defend their definition of the situation and their concept of self and are prepared to take on the hierarchy of authority when it loses legitimacy. Feeling betrayed by the organization the lower ranks may feel no compunction about 'stirring the shit' both as defence and as revenge.

The Chinese experts – ostensibly the epitome of the archetypal, dedicated employee – in taking the offensive, accused their colleagues and senior officers of theft, cover-up, amateurism and incompetence, falsifying documents, stealing from suspects, endangering the lives of informants, invading the privacy of people's homes, personal jealousy and rivalry which hindered effective operations, a fixation on publicity and personal reputation, rancorous intrigue against subordinates, using dubious methods and manipulation in internal investigations, and fraudulently obtaining money. A radical critic of the police could hardly ask for more.

7
Conclusion – Everything but Temptation

'I think the boys could resist everything but temptation.'
(Executive commenting on anti-trust case: Geis 1982: 136)

'Nice fellow, Norman. But rather stupid. He couldn't cope with the temptation.'
(Policeman referring to prosecution of head of Triad Society Bureau in Hong Kong: Bresler 1981: 60)

The examination of the nature of police deviance and control in this book has accentuated the view that this is a highly complex matter, embedded in an intricate web of factors. To scrutinize the matter adequately requires attention to several layers of analysis including those of society, organization, work, culture, change, and the interrelationship between deviance and control. A research agenda to tackle this area effectively, in all its variety and with sufficient nuances, would require more attention to the historical, comparative (cross-cultural and cross-national), and organizational levels of analysis in order to take us away from the one society, one language, one department studies which tend to dominate the predominantly North American literature on policing. Comparative research induces the insight that the nature and extent of corruption varies with time, place, actors, and culture. It may be held to be endemic and almost inevitable but that does not necessarily mean that it is universal (Simpson 1977: 46), for the forms it takes are a matter of careful empirical investigation.

Although an impressive amount of research has been done on specific areas of policing, the standard works (some of which are now seriously showing their age) tend to neglect the organizational level of analysis (Reiss and Bordua 1967). In particular, a common fault with researchers is to become mesmerized by the police world and to attribute behaviour uniquely to its culture whereas fruitful similarities, and contrasts, abound with workers in other types of organizational setting. My own preference is clearly for a micro level of analysis, of policing 'on the ground', and I support low-level, concrete studies of institutional life where vital issues, of great importance for society, such as control or accountability, can be illuminated by scrutinizing the interaction between organizational constraints and dilemmas faced in work. To solve these dilemmas workers evolve an 'operational code' (Reisman, 1979), and unravelling and elucidating that code tells us a great deal about the guile, craft, and craftiness with which workers construct and reconstruct their daily reality. Reiss (1977: x) says of the code,

> 'Often overlooked but often the most powerful normative order in any organization is its operating code – that unwritten set of rules and procedures that prescribe what can or must be done and which are enforced by informal peer sanctions and control. Yet what is lacking is a systematic understanding of how operating codes within organizations and peer sanctions subvert organizational goals and sanctions and of how such operating codes may converge with, rather than diverge from, the normative codes of law, ethics, and administration.'

This book has been concerned with the creation, definition, and control of police occupational and organizational deviance in terms of an operational code and in relation to internal processes and relationships with the environment in three cities, with special reference to one, Amsterdam. In the remainder of this concluding chapter I examine the material and analysis presented in this book at three levels which are constantly mentioned by scholars as of central importance; namely, those of society and the 'police problem', of organization and control, and of the nature of police work.

Policing the 'Soft' Society

'Amsterdam is really going to the dogs; I mean, even the police are bent.'
(Attributed to 'Black Henkie Boersma', so-called 'Godfather' of the Amsterdam underworld)

Increasingly, since around the middle 1960s, the police in the three societies under consideration have come to operate in an atmosphere of almost continual crisis and unrelenting pressure (Goldstein 1977). They came under hostile scrutiny and this was often experienced as an outright attack on the traditional ways in which policemen dealt with problems, precisely at a time when they were faced with both rising crime rates and restrictions on their freedom of operation. Generally the 1960s decade was one of considerable social and political change with a new element of youth and minority group emancipation and rebellion directed at authority, including the police (Lipset 1969). Policemen tended to view these developments with dismay and interpreted them as signs of a permissive and tolerant society gone 'soft', which confronted them with near insoluble dilemmas, and which converted them to the underdog role as members of a 'persecuted minority' (Alex 1976: 131). In America there was the 'due process revolution' in which for a decade the Supreme Court tried to impose external control and standardization on police powers (Duffee, Hussey, and Kramer 1978: 56); in Britain under a Labour government there was relaxation of 'morals' legislation and proposals to do so for drugs (Whitaker 1979; Schofield 1971); and in The Netherlands a 'culture of tolerance' ushered in one of the most lenient criminal justice systems in the world (Downes 1982). Yet all three societies saw an increase in crime rates and particularly the rise of predatory street crime and more sophisticated forms of 'organized' crime (Wilson 1975; Rhodes 1977; Schur 1969).

Alongside these issues went a growing critical consciousness of the 'police problem', of resilient and corrosive practices such as brutality, prejudice, and corruption, which were sealed from accountability and redress by defensiveness and secrecy, (cf. for Britain, *New Statesman* 18 January, 1980; *Sunday Times Magazine* 26 September, 1982; and *The Economist* 4 July 1981). To summarize the matter bluntly, the last two decades witnessed a persistent attempt by influential groups to get a firmer grip on the police organization and on its inbred malpractices. One consequence is that the traditional police culture has been challenged externally by scandals, exposure, commissions, the media, legal reform, and academic research and internally, by new styles of reforming management, new technology, and new ways of approaching and structuring work. From all these complex and intertwined developments there has emerged the concept of 'occupational paranoia' whereby policemen feel isolated from the community and deprived of legitimacy (with symptoms of alienation, persecution, and an extreme sensitivity to criticism: Fogelson 1977: 112). Police were only of interest when they were brutal, corrupt, or dead (Cain 1977).

The point here is twofold. First, whether or not the policeman is justified in his paranoia is not as important as the fact that the elements generating it are potentially most dangerous for the integrity of the police because, isolated and aggrieved, they have an excellent practical, and latent ideological, justification for their deviance in terms of a 'soft' but over-regulated society 'forcing' them to break the law in order to enforce it. And, second, some of the old-style, low-level graft at the community level was virtually open, blatant, and even legitimate. Where the policemen belonged in the community, was low-paid and expected to enjoy his perks along with other public servants, and was not rapacious, then paying him was perhaps done as automatically as 'feeding coins in a parking meter' (Bayley 1974: 86). Now the policeman has lost the simple, monopolistic world of cosy arrangements with the community (which, of course, represents only one particular level of 'graft') and faces threats and challenges from new groups ready to compete with him and expose him (social workers, legal aid groups, an investigative media, private security, watchdog agencies, and also internal enforcement entrepreneurs). These changes at the macro-level as to how societies and cities are run and controlled, with new specialized units and complicated, competing jurisdictions, may mean that police deviance has to be more devious and more sophisticated in order to compete and be successful. In brief, societal and institutional change, leading to occupational paranoia, may make straightforward corruption more difficult, as the policeman loses legitimacy in the community, and may inadvertently sponsor the more insidious forms of police deviance. Predatory and combative corruption and perversion of justice may be seen as the only way to get things done and, in addition, be justified with an almost ideological, self-legitimating fervour.

The policeman's jaundiced and pessimistic view of society may be given a measure of credence if we turn to deviance elsewhere in public and political life. For many scholars have maintained that there is some relationship between the moral climate of society and corruption in various areas (Goldstein 1977; Simpson 1977; Wicker 1977; Bell 1953). It is quite clear from many sources, for instance, that crime and deviance have been extensively documented in western societies in business, control agencies, security services, and voluntary organizations and, at times, bizarre links have been glimpsed between these and organized crime (Cressey 1969; Gardiner 1970; Morton 1976; Chambliss 1978; Geis and Stotland 1980; Johnson and Douglas 1978). This raises the issue of hypocrisy and double-standards.

Vice detectives in Chicago had organised stag parties for politicians; the Knapp Commission offered a free lunch to experts to discuss free lunches among policemen: when Harlech Television (Wales) set out to investigate levels of hospitality in local government it put on 'sumptuous hospitality' for contributors to the programme; in Washington DC senators have a rule of thumb that 'if you can eat it, drink it, or smoke it within twenty-four hours then it can't be corruption'; and the huge overseas payments by American corporations in the sixties are said to be dwarfed by domestic bribery (Beigel and Beigel 1977: 76; personal communications Herman Goldstein and Phil Fennell; Reisman 1979: 51). In particular, there are indications of 'massive corruption' in the legal system of certain large American cities (Daley 1979: 27; Dershowitz 1983) and in a recent federal undercover operation, 'Gray Lord' in Chicago, judges, lawyers, and prosecutors were indicted (*De Volkskrant* 16 December, 1983). But lawyers form a powerful profession in the United States, and elsewhere, and, like many professions, can also be highly secretive and solidaristic when challenged by external complaints (Bok 1978). Furthermore, compared to many professionals, and criminals, the police are generally poorly paid and a policeman may come to feel that 'he lives and works in the middle of a corrupt society, that everyone else is getting theirs and why shouldn't he?' (Gardiner and Olson 1974: 365).

It may well be that policemen are simply the most vulnerable to control of all the actors in the criminal justice system and that they serve as scapegoats for its multiple deficiencies. This can be accentuated in periods of moral and political crisis. The early and mid seventies in all three societies saw a backlash, in lesser or greater measure, against permissiveness (Hall *et al.* 1978), economic retrenchment, and a number of highly publicized scandals which were seen as symptomatic of general moral decay and distrust of public life (Reisman 1979: 109; with Watergate in the USA, Poulson and spy scandals in Britain; and Prince Bernhard in Holland; Bernstein and Woodward 1975, Tomkinson and Gillard 1980; Boulton 1978). The New York scandal was held to be symptomatic that the 'city was falling apart 'while the 'public mores' and 'natural cynicism' of New Yorkers were said to have played a crucial role in changing police attitudes to corruption (Sherman 1974: 34; Kennedy School of Government, 1977a: 10); the Met complained long and loud about bent lawyers, fixed juries, and cover-ups in high places at a time when people were 'out to get them' in a 'beat the Met' period (McNee 1983: 121; Will 1980c: 351); and Amsterdam was continually flagellated by the conservative press as the socialist inspired 'Sodom and Gommorah' of Holland where police corruption was a 'sore on a critically sick body' (*De Telegraaf* 16 April, 1977) and where the public image of the city was that of riots, squatters, and 'junkies living among piles of garbage' (*De Volkskrant* 8 June, 1984). In addition, Reisman (1979: 101–06) argues that Americans tend to get more angry about bribery than Europeans because it offends their democratic credo, that they often launch 'crusades' which, indispensably aided by the media with its long muck-raking tradition, provide popular catharsis in 'sound and fury' while the results in terms of genuine reform are minimal. Indeed, corruption is viewed as an enduring problem in American politics and periodic exposure leads to 'shock, disbelief, incredulity, outrage' followed by 'politics as usual' (Gardiner and Olson 1974: ix).

In terms of hypocrisy, double standards, and scapegoating it is worth taking into account the general moral and ethical standards and conduct in public and private life in the three societies, and three cities, for the period under consideration. One principal actor in Amsterdam, for instance, came into the office one day in a rather despondent mood; he began to rail against contemporary society.

'I feel as if my batteries are run down. What does it all mean? The clear-up rate for crimes in the district is 4 per cent. Who cares? I don't care anymore. No one believes that a better performance leads to anything. What's there to motivate us? Nothing's done about the underlying problems. The laws on gambling are hypocritical; licensing of premises is a shambles; the parking problem is horrendous. People just throw the parking tickets away.

What sort of society do we live in? It's full of contradictions. It's a society where less and less people work, where fewer and fewer people are productive, where civil disobedience is increasing, where you're almost sanctioned if you display ambition or industry. Imagine a policeman has to regulate residence permits for foreigners. Maybe he thinks, "If I don't give him one he'll run into a church and get it anyway, so I'll take the money he's offering.' [He is referring to cases where illegal aliens facing deportation took refuge in a church, generated publicity and support, and were eventually permitted to remain in Holland] Why not? You hear nothing else these days except black work, black money, tax avoidance, and everyone's doing well and laughing at the law and at values. Why should the policeman be the exception?'

If we could assemble all the evidence then the police might be seen to have some justification for feeling hard done by and singled out for abuse (Fennell and Thomas 1983; Box and Russell 1975; Bouman 1978). But, then, in all three cities the police departments had already been involved in a long series of controversial disputes and the corruption scandals were perhaps golden opportunities for their opponents to hammer them unmercilessly.

Typically, the scandals in New York and London were ignited by the press, whereas in Amsterdam the police can take some credit for the fact that they themselves initiated the matter. This is indicative of a lack of investigative journalism and a general reluctance to probe sensitive issues by journalists and academics in Holland. In a rapidly changing social and criminal environment the police in Amsterdam began to react with specialization and new enforcement techniques and experienced both symptoms of 'paranoia' and new forms of deviance previously not associated with Dutch policing (Chorus, van Houcke, and Stuart 1981; Bommels 1982). It is difficult to believe in the light of recent revelations that standards of conduct in Dutch business, for example, are any more meritorious or virtuous than those among policemen and yet the latter provided an excellent target for moralizing and for media titillation. But the scandal never generated the public outrage and political determination to reform the police that occurred in New York and London.

An explanation for this is that when deviance is exposed in Dutch society people try to contain it within the appropriate 'pillar' for fear of embarrassing colleagues in other pillars (*verzuiling* or 'pillarization' refers to the vertical blocks that traditionally dominated Dutch social and political life – Lijphart 1968: 66 and 130). In a small society, with a tiny interrelated elite used to secrecy, compromise, negotiation, avoidance of conflict, and accommodation, scandals can quickly threaten others and there is a noticeable tendency not to hound opponents, not to disgrace public figures, and not to hang dirty washing out in public. For the scandal remained an issue for the Amsterdam justice system alone and never became a national or party-political issue seriously threatening the mayor or other public figures. Although it was a prime scandal, kept alive for over four years by the press, there was no popular groundswell demanding change and no appreciable organizational reform. If anything the 'public' was amused and entertained rather than shocked. Moral crusaders are not a noticeable phenomenon of Dutch society where complacency, cover-up, compartmentalization of deviancy, and 'pillarization' tend to defuse and deflate potentially explosive issues. In a low-key, pragmatic, soporific society with highly ambivalent, if not hypocritical, norms about deviance, and where there is a considerable discrepancy between private practice and public virtue, scandal is treated with a display of ritual shame and then the veneer of complacency and moral self-righteousness is briskly replaced.

In this section I wish to make the point that modern society has structured a number of contradictions which create acute dilemmas for a number of institutions in general and for the police in particular (Wilson 1963). Critical groups, and the media, moreover, may be undermining the legitimacy of the police at the very same moment that they demand increased legitimacy for the police in the community, thereby strengthening the cumulative and dangerous symptoms of 'occupational paranoia'. That paranoia may be fuelled by high-level decisions (by parliament, Supreme Court, or even foreign governments with drug enforcement becoming a matter of foreign policy) which percolate down to the man or woman on the street as leaving them with an impossible job and facing demands that are almost inherently contradictory (Goldstein 1977: 9–10). But the central issue of contemporary policing is that society expects the police to tackle the problem of crime while systematically restricting the means to achieve that end (Wilson 1975; Manning 1977). That tends to induce either indifference or else imaginative ways of surmounting the obstacles (Marx 1980a). One path leads to frustration, futility, and ritualism; and the other path leads to corruption.

Policemen in modern society may feel justified, then, in feeling that they serve as 'whipping boys' for society's neurotic attitude towards corruption (Alex 1976: 94) and in turning to deviancy. What makes them different from businessmen and others, however, is precisely the trust invested in officials with considerable legal powers. Police corruption represents a betrayal of public confidence and is frequently accompanied by a sense of outrage. Police corruption represents not just venality, benign or carnivorous, but also injustice and avoidance of accountability. The injustice is no less reprehensible when its victims are criminals (which police rationalize by saying 'People do get fixed up but they are always good villains' – Laurie 1972: 272); but because criminals are of low status and low credibility they make ready victims, with few channels of protest and redress. One reason policemen get away with 'murder', as in sending an innocent criminal to prison on false evidence, is that they prey on the weak and the vulnerable and, while they may feel that there is implicit support for this from 'society', the very vulnerability of the victims makes this reprehensible in terms of morals and the ideals of justice. Depriving someone of his liberty for a number of years is of a quite different order to 'mumping' a free cup of coffee and, when discovered, it can lead to vitriolic condemnation because it is seen by legal and moral spokesmen as fundamentally threatening the administration of justice.

The lesson seems clear. If police genuinely wish to retain public trust then arguments about scapegoating and double standards, however valid, are irrelevant; moral spokesmen for society simply demand higher standards of policemen than of other officials, businessmen, and public figures. In that sense, Black Henkie Boersma was right. When the police are corrupt that tells us something significant about the moral health of the community, for the police are one of those central institutions – such as the law, government, and religion – which symbolize the identity of the society itself. Deviance in them suggests something negative about the entire society (Sherman 1978: 61).

Business as Usual?

'A good police force is one that catches more criminals than it employs.'

(*New Statesman* 18 January, 1980)

There is a general pessimism about changing organizations in general and the police organization in particular (Manning and Van Maanen 1978: 8; Schon 1970: 724). Interactionists are perhaps particularly prone to fatalism because they spotlight the resilient and devious patterns of everyday norm-breaking (with a predeliction for 'dwarfs, stutterers, and thieves' rather than the powerful: Downes and Rock 1982: 158) while the ethnographic 'hero' is a fixer rather than a strategist (Dingwall, Payne and Payne 1980: 16). Yet clearly organizations can be changed; or, to put it differently, for those in charge and faced with acute problems, they have to be considered changeable.

If we view organizations as power structures with their essential dynamic lying in the exercise of, and resistance to, power (Watson, 1980: 194) then all organizations have to cope with problems related to deviance, control, power, and change (Salaman 1979). Public bureaucracies tend to be seen as particularly intractable in terms of resistance to change, the levelling down of performance, and the failure to achieve goals (Wilson 1978; Katz and Danet 1973; Merton *et al.* 1952). For example, one could generalize that the police organization appears to be a semi-military bureaucracy with high levels of command and control but is rather characterized in practice by considerable autonomy for the lower ranks, the alienation of senior staff from street work, training unrelated to practice, considerable rivalry between units, a cynical and secretive occupational culture, and poor performance in terms of cultivating leaders and managers, setting coherent policy, and achieving efficiency and effectiveness (Manning 1977). This appears damning, although it would probably apply also to the organization of social work and education (Lipsky 1980), but it applied patently to the Amsterdam Police. Policemen kept telling me there were no policies, there was no control and leadership, there were no guidelines; and hence there developed informal policies, control, and leadership, and informal guidelines. Or, to put it another way, the Amsterdam Police was a shambles.

Goldstein (1977: 210) remarks that 'corruption thrives best in poorly run organizations where lines of authority are vague and supervision is minimal.' This recognizes that to tackle deviance you also have to turn around the organization. This was the fundamental insight that Murphy and Mark brought to their attempts to tackle corruption in New York and London; that if you did not alter the institutionalized factors leading to the operational code then you were not going to achieve anything. Taking a crowbar to the lockers, an irate chief 'socking corrupt cops on the jaw' (Murphy and Plate 1977: 217), and transferring deviant personnel will clearly not help unless fundamental reforms are undertaken (Beigel and Beigel 1977: 284). McGlennon (1977) indicates also that internal change on its own will not be sufficient, for, on the basis of his study of reform in four police departments in the United States, it was the mayor who was essential in determining the success or failure of the clean-up campaign (Sherman 1977). Both chiefs in New York and London set about their task by decentralizing authority and responsibility, by reducing the autonomy of the detective branch, by new standards of accountability for senior officers, by instigating proactive investigatory procedures for deviance, by altering certain aspects of enforcement, by rotation of personnel, and by emphasizing integrity in training. As Murphy put it, 'power corrupts to the extent that it is unsupervised and not held strictly accountable' (Murphy and Plate 1977: 84); and, while power could be said to reside low down in the organization, responsibility for it was located at the top. In other words strategies for reform have to focus not only downwards but also upwards. And Amsterdam serves as an example of the difficulty in turning the organization around through a small, professional cadre from 'middle management'.

While the consequences of these drastic changes are difficult to evaluate precisely (effects may be ambiguous and be spread over years – Reisman 1979: 110), I believe that both chiefs made it more difficult for policemen to be corrupt and helped to restore confidence in their respective forces. More generally from the literature one can distil a number of key features apparent in successful reform programmes. The personal commitment of the top man is essential (Sherman 1978: 122); the strengthening of front-line supervision is vital; and a programme of 'positive discipline' stressing and rewarding integrity is crucial (Goldstein 1977; Simpson 1977; Ward and McCormack 1979). Under certain circumstances, then, it is possible to take concrete measures to combat corruption with varying measures of success as in the cases of New York and London but also in Oakland, Cincinatti, Los Angeles, and Kansas City.

From the evidence at my disposal there is little confidence that in Amsterdam comparable changes have taken place in terms of decentralization, enforcement patterns, investigation procedures, the power of the investigative branch, and accountability of senior officers (Punch 1981a). The stability and rigidity of Dutch institutions, the hold of a civil service appointment, the minute regulation of rights, obligations, and safeguards, the leniency (ironically) of criminal and disciplinary procedures for officials (Hoetjes 1984), and the unwillingness to let heads roll in cases of bureaucratic incompetence, all conspire to make it extremely difficult to alter radically the structure of public institutions in The Netherlands. The Chief Constable in Amsterdam was once described to me 'as the most powerless man in the whole force' (faced by the stranglehold of lateral entry, civil service tenure, unions, automatic promotions, and appointments by seniority). And as Kanter (1977: 164) astutely notes, 'Powerlessness corrupts. Absolute powerlessness corrupts absolutely.' Murphy and Mark took the power offered to them by circumstances and ruthlessly applied it. For better or worse, ruthlessness is a quality in short supply in Dutch institutional life.

But tackling internal organizational deviance is a profoundly difficult and hazardous process. On the one hand procedures, resources, and experience are often ineffective and inadequate while, on the other hand, investigations can get out of hand once the ball starts rolling, may sponsor resistance, and can blow up in the chief's face. Understandably, it is aggravating for critics of the police to hear that an agency geared specifically to criminal investigation is not particularly capable of conducting investigations within its own walls. For instance, Goldstein (1977: 203 and 215) makes two telling points about the police investigation of deviance. First, the police have all the techniques for investigating serious criminal activity but tend to rely on a reactive strategy; and, second, they argue strongly that if deterrence in regard to criminals is to be meaningful then 'the probability of apprehension and conviction must be high, the certainty of punishment clear, and the process must function without reasonable delay.' Applying these arguments to structures for investigating police deviance – which are primarily reactive, low in resources, and lead to cases where acquittals are high and penalties are low (Turner 1968: 34) – then the deterrent effect can scarcely be considered high. Outsiders might also add that policemen will obviously go easy on their own colleagues and will treat them more leniently than other suspects. Yet some policemen may pursue bent cops as relentlessly, if not more so, as they hunt other criminals (both Mark and Murphy expressly took this position). Indeed, policemen themselves are often convinced that investigations against them are more stringent than against non-police suspects (Reiner 1978: 88) which is ironic in the light of constant outside proposals for a larger external element in the pursuance of police deviance. Frustration and disbelief at police inability to clean out their own stables may also arise because corruption arises in predictable areas of police work, particularly detective work in the 'victimless' crimes area, and there may be readily available evidence of dubious enforcement patterns contained in administrative records (Ward and McCormack 1979: 11).

But we also have to recognize that investigations of police deviance are technically far from easy and that requiring a control agency to reverse its focus on to itself is a laborious and painful business. In general, internal disciplinary procedures are slow, cumbersome, inadequately manned, and hindered by the perceived illegitimacy of a vast array of petty and out-of-date discipline regulations (Cook 1980); investigations of serious deviancy are largely reactive, have problems finding willing and reliable witnesses, have difficulty establishing proof in terms of reciprocation without proactive methods, and face the 'blue curtain' or conspiracy of silence; and external control may not challenge internal deviance effectively because variously outside agencies may lack staff and resources, the judiciary may be amenable to shifts in policy, career patterns may mean a rapid turnover of young prosecutors (in the United States), appeals may drag on interminably, juries may be reluctant to convict, while journalists, federal agents, and prosecutors may go easy on deviance because of their reliance on policemen in their own work (Chibnall 1977: 153; Beigel and Beigel 1977: 259 and 265; Goldstein 1977: 217). The strategies and resources of internal and external control agencies, then, limit the actual and potential effectiveness of investigating deviance in organizations (Ermann and Lundman 1978 and 1982b: 273; Reiss 1983).

This is held to be true particularly of the police organization, where peer-group pressure and the rule of silence protect deviants. However, it is clear that policemen do talk under certain circumstances and will even exert peer control of deviance (Sherman 1978: 216). But because this is palpably in conflict with the occupational culture, and because the reimposition of control may be seen as petty and negative (Will 1980d: 357), this is often not accomplished without considerable conflict and resistance. In Amsterdam, for instance, policemen set out to hunt other policemen and the methods they used were precisely those used against ordinary criminals (secret surveillance with binoculars, interviewing witnesses and pressurizing them with hints of reprisals, attempting to identify suspects with photos, etc.). Yet this process set up extraordinary tensions inside the organization. It seemed to blow policemen's minds that they should be treated as if they were criminals. Ironically, they reacted to investigation not unlike criminals in that they counter-attacked with an assault on the integrity of those assembling the evidence and on the standards of the investigation.

In particular, senior officers tend to dominate formal enquiries and to focus downwards where the lower ranks, feeling that they are being made scapegoats, fight back with resistance and hostility. The lower ranks retaliated with leaks to the press, informal social control against investigating officers, leaking of documents to the media, and collusion with the suspects. There was internal and external lobbying with unlikely coalitions developing that brought about a prolonged institutional crisis. Within the period 1976–80, and even beyond, informal resistance within the Amsterdam Police was powerful enough to deflect investigations and to impede change (Punch 1981b). To a certain extent, then, this book provides a portrait of a police organization incapable of coping with change as illustrated by allegations of corruption and scandal; and also of a traditional, almost archaic, institution with a leadership frustrated and unable to understand and to deal strategically and politically with a changing social and criminal environment. Indeed, the legally oriented police mind tends to ask 'Who is to blame?' rather than 'What went wrong?' Writing of military organizations Nixon (1979: 43) states that it is a sad feature of 'authoritarian' organizations that they often do not learn from experience and are

'past masters at deflecting blame. They do so by denial, by rationalization, by making scapegoats, or by some mixture of the three. However it is achieved, the net result is that no real admission of failure or incompetence is ever made by those who are really responsible: hence nothing can be done about preventing a recurrence.'

The same bleak message exudes time and again from my Amsterdam material.

Furthermore, one of the most significant features of the research recounted in this book is how difficult it is to reimpose control in an organization following a long period of indulgency and how powerful the informal system can be when threatened. Weber (Gerth and Mills 1946: 123), for instance, wrote that 'he who lets himself in for politics, that is for power and force as means, contracts with diabolical powers and for his action it is *not* true that good can only come from good and evil from evil, but that often the opposite is true.' In a sense Mark and Murphy contracted with diabolical powers because they used force and power to change organizations in order to achieve 'good' in situations not only where the cure might have sponsored a fatal mutinous eruption, but also where the cure could have made the illness worse and actually sponsored 'evil'. A crusading campaign against police deviance may prove counter-productive (Anderson 1973) by driving a wedge between grass-eaters and meat-eaters (removing restraining peer control), may confirm some policemen in their secondary deviance, may force 'bent' police to be more devious and sophisticated to be successful, and may simply push up the price of corruption.

Two features may reinforce legitimacy for internal deviance and informal resistance. First, conscious use of the media to sustain a campaign may back-fire with hostile resentment at the public labelling (Alex 1976), and this may be particularly true if the authorities themselves use dubious methods in investigations or in the imposition of discipline. It is yet a further irony that generally policemen feel obliged to bend rules in order to make cases (Wilson 1978) and investigators of corruption, determined not to come up empty-handed, may themselves feel forced to break the rules in order to establish that the suspects broke the rules. Second, how far, and for how long, should the campaign go? The head of 'Countryman' said he could carry on indefinitely investigating allegations against the Met (*New Statesman* 18 January, 1980). But how much investigation can an organization take? And how much energy and resources can an organization allocate to control mechanisms without the exercise becoming self-defeating in terms of an inflated, predatory unit that destroys the social bases of trust and cooperation, however minimal, without which organized social life is impossible? In Amsterdam the lesson for the middle-ranking officers was that the price of relentlessly pushing their enquiries into deviance was to destroy the organization. They unleashed four years of turmoil, bitterness, intrigue, and misery, and the result, in terms of combating deviance and altering the organization, was minimal.

Taking Amsterdam as an example of the unintended consequences of tackling corruption, and of the internal tensions set up by investigations, I would argue that the social processes surrounding the definition of deviance and imposition of control lead to the supposition that the most we can expect is a cycle of deviance, scandal, reform and repression, gradual relaxation and relapse into former patterns of deviance, followed by a new scandal (Sherman 1974: 33). Crusades and campaigns gain their strength by being short-lived and once reforms are institutionalized or investigations are put on a semi-permanent footing then atrophy, manipulation, and cooptation may set in. When the sound and fury die away, it is all too often a case of returning sooner, or later, to business as usual.

It's Just a Job

'You gotta learn two fundamentals on this job. The first law of survival is to bend. Fundamental two of survival: the best way to pass your thirty years on this job is to do nothing. You will change when you get it through your head that this police thing is not real.'

(Advice of experienced patrolman to 'rookie cop' in NYPD;
Sorrentino 1980: 195–96)

A close examination of police organizations following exposure to corruption scandals might lead to the conclusion that those organizations were failing massively in their appointed task and were unwilling, or incapable, of putting their own house in order. From the interactionist perspective it is possible to argue that, to a greater or lesser extent, this is typical of organizational life in general and that control is problematic, order is reconstructed, rules are open to negotiation, and deviance is built in to the on-going, everyday nature of the work situation. Put under the microscope all organizations would reveal discrepancies between actors as means to organizational ends and as creating ends for themselves (Crozier 1973: 69; Mechanic 1962). This implies that the deviance is always open to revelation internally or externally, that subterfuge has to be practised to cloak practices, and that it is not deviance that needs to be explained so much as its *exposure*. We may delight in catching policemen with their trousers down, some of them literally, but who knows what a fundamental scrutiny of the organization in which we work might bring to light (including a penetrating search for academic fraud in universities – Broad and Wade 1983)? For instance, when Manning (1980) analyses drug enforcement as characterized by intractable ambiguity, by the concealing of information, by suspiciousness and distrust, and by a segmented, specialized, covert organizational structure, it is plain that he sees these features as not unique to the police organization. Furthermore, while the tasks performed by policemen may seem to the layperson peculiar and extreme, people experience their work not as bizarre but as ordinary (Ditton 1977: 12). In terms of the experience of, and meaning attached to, their work policemen are not very different from other types of workers and may seek to express themselves beyond the bounds of the formal task structure (Terkel 1975). For, when policemen are accused of deviance, their riposte is frequently in terms of 'We were only doing our job.'

This requires us to look at the nature of police work and at what policemen are asked to do as a routine and accepted part of the job. In Amsterdam, for example, what clearly emerged was the rivalry, competition, hostility, and non-cooperation between units who were jealous of information and territory and who all sought juicy arrests and interesting cases. The ends justified the means and led to paying informants with heroin, 'padding' and 'flaking', and 'fishing with live bait'. Also corruption was fun, exciting, and easy (bringing in predictable arrests – Cox, Shirley, and Short 1977: 217). But, crucially, from the point of view of most policemen you had to cut corners, had to use informants, had to cultivate relationships with criminals, and had to bend rules. It was simply the accepted way to achieve results. This was seen against a background of a lenient penal and judicial system; of structural handicaps in making drug cases; and of the creation of a normative ghetto in the city centre of Amsterdam which created a corruptive environment where laws were suspended and were not meant to be enforced. This sponsored an opportunity structure of selective enforcement condoned by the 'bosses' (senior police officers, politicians, and judicial representatives).

Many of the deviant practices uncovered involved low-level, occupational deviancy such as perks and gifts but also stretched to serious offences. An investigation exposes immediately the 'normal' everyday, informal rewards and behaviour of occupational deviance but often finds it difficult to break through to the more insidious forms of criminal deviance based on conspiratorial relationships with the underworld or between policemen. The bitterness and resentment arises because the lower ranks believe that the former practices are 'harmless', universal and legitimate – in fact you would be deviant *not* to indulge in them – and are perhaps even more pronounced among senior officers. Even the more 'dodgy' practices, such as 'planting', may be considered appropriate as informal punishment in a weak justice system. Above all, the men feel that even some of the more serious practices were either actively condoned or passively accepted by other officers who protected themselves from guilty knowledge. In essence, the policemen in Amsterdam felt that they were being abandoned and condemned for doing precisely what was expected of them.

Indeed, a review of the standard literature on the police and journalistic accounts does reveal graphically and indubitably that practical policing is characterized by deviant behaviour which is built into the routine way work is constructed and which performs important functions in terms of cementing solidarity

(Lundman 1979; Bracey 1976). Lying, perjury, undue violence, planting evidence, 'fitting-up' criminals, verbals, padding, flaking, altering documents, manipulation of suspects and informants, falsifying evidence, intimidation, and a battery of seamy tactics are resorted to by some policemen in some situations as legitimate techniques in getting their work done (Ericson 1981: 94; Skolnick 1975: 138). Of course some policemen may avoid these practices, as Holdaway (1982) consciously did when he worked as a sergeant in the Met, and there are several typifications of styles of policing including the idle, ritualistic policeman who avoids work and trouble (for typifications of policemen see, Chatterton 1975: 361; Manning 1977: 149; Reiner 1978: 228–253). The perusal of the literature does, however, suggest that policemen place considerable emphasis on 'real' police work (with paper work seen as 'shit work': Manning 1980: 320) and on procedural rules as an irksome hindrance to their fighting crime; that they may perceive their work as almost a mission rather than merely as a job (Mills 1973; Reisman 1979: 147; Shover 1980: 15); and that, particularly among detectives, the cosy fraternity and solidaristic camaraderie of the police culture can be laced with rivalry, competition, jealousy and betrayal.

Above all, then, police corruption and deviance needs to be understood in terms of how police work actually gets done and how policemen view their occupational reality with all its perks, rewards, risks, and pitfalls (Manning 1977; Rubinstein 1973; Lundman 1980a). Lies, deception, and falsification may simply become part of the job – and be perceived as normal, legitimate, and even essential – until, that is, the 'shit hits the fan' (Manning 1974). When that happens, the ensuing upheaval leads to a redefinition and renegotiation of reality that may divide the organization and that may lead to complex and protracted patterns of conflict, challenge, and defence based on a perception of betrayal. In essence, a police investigation of corruption involves betrayal at three levels; the 'public' as represented by watchdogs hypocritically imposes standards which it does not itself follow; senior officers abandon the lower ranks and point the enquiry inexorably downwards; and, most crucially, policemen themselves are forced to break the powerful norms of secrecy and solidarity by hunting other policemen and by breaking the rule of silence to save their own necks. All these self-justificatory rationalizations and sour feelings of betrayal were present in Amsterdam, form the core of Leuci's tragic story of betrayal in New York (Daley 1979), and suffuse 'Adam's Tale' of his downfall in the Met Drug Squad (Honeycombe 1974). Perhaps we should approach concepts such as secrecy and solidarity (which are particularly emphasized in American studies of urban policemen who exhibit almost a siege mentality) with more caution and view them as variables rather than givens. Police use suspicion as a weapon against others but when they turn it on themselves it can generate mistrust, divisiveness, and betrayal that corrodes solidarity and secrecy. (Suspicion is referred to as the 'disease' of intelligence officers in the novel *The Human Factor*: 'what a damn silly profession ours is. You can't trust anyone' – Greene 1978: 142).

It is possible, then, to view corruption as part of a spectrum of deviance designed to assist in constructing work. In organizations, generally, success may go to those 'who make things happen by breaking, bending, and twisting rules and cutting through red tape' (Marx 1982: 174); this perspective emerges strongly in a number of studies of work organizations (Dalton 1959; Crozier 1973; Kanter 1977), where power tends to go to those most able to cope with uncertainty and prepared to innovate within the constraints placed upon them (Pfeffer 1981). In this light, the cunning, devious detective may be perceived as the archetypally good policeman, congratulated for cutting corners and admired for sailing close to the wind, until the day he pushes his luck too far or lets his guard drop. One of the sad, even tragic aspects of police corruption is that 'bent' policemen may once have been very good policemen indeed,

> 'Hardly any detective survived SIU with reputation intact. Imagination, fearlessness, a sense of adventure, a disregard for procedure – SIU men had these qualities in abundance. They were great detectives. Of course it was these same qualities that got them into trouble.'
>
> (Daley 1979: 329)

Possibly some people may feel that this is letting deviant policemen off the hook too lightly, in that everything can be excused and rationalized away as being part of the job (à la Eichmann), and that it does not fully explain some of the more serious forms of deviance which in no sense can be considered 'for' the benefit of the organization.

This requires an examination of one vital element of police work that does differentiate policemen substantially from many other workers; namely, the perception of, and the involvement in, 'dirty' work (Hughes 1963; Wollacott 1980). To a certain extent policing is surrounded with the aura of a military ethos, espousing duty, a code of honour, and even chivalry and this imbues the role with elements of the 'sacred' (Manning 1977: 5) which is supported by imagery of dedication, self-sacrifice and heroism. In practice, policemen can arrive at an aggrieved perception of themselves as dirty workers engaged in potentially contaminating relationships with the outcasts and outlaws of society and also as cast in the menial, thankless role of cleaning up the messy by-products fostered by contemporary society (a role that they feel they perform *on our behalf* – Hughes 1963). Westley (1970: 56), for example, wrote of the policeman as pariah and martyr who becomes cynical because 'his is a society emphasizing the crooked, the weak, and the unscrupulous'.

The policeman's predicament, exposed to divergent and even contradictory expectations, can lead him to develop a rather embittered, defensive ideology that can aid in justifying involvement in deviance. Scholars speak of policemen's sense of 'impotence and cynicism', of their 'low morale and disillusion', and that police view themselves collectively as 'failures', 'dirty workers', and as a 'minority without honour' (Preiss and Ehrlich 1966: 22; Cain 1973: 62; Manning 1977: 315). In this light police can be viewed both as repressors *and* as underdogs (Fielding 1982: 92). One way of coping with the stigma that attaches to those involved occupationally with evil, crime, perversity and disorder (Bittner 1975: 39) is to embrace the label and become truly 'dirty'. A number of features of the work and occupational culture may amplify and foster this process. First, for certain styles of detective work Manning (1980: 51) notes that the closer the policeman is to the 'criminal's style of life, argot, and behaviour – the less he is like a cop – the more successful he is'. Second, police and criminals may come to enjoy each other's company (as in the Met: Ball, Chester, and Perrott 1979: 43). Third, especially in 'instigative' detective work requiring infiltration and undercover roles policemen may become absorbed by the 'allure and power' of clandestine activities and find them almost addictive to the point of being unable to readjust to the 'straight' world (Marx, 1982: 166). And, fourth, criminals and deviants can be perceived as displaying courage, daring, playfulness, and a concern for reputation, face, excitement, toughness, and masculinity (Downes and Rock 1982: 68). For the professional bank-robbers described by Ball, Chester, and Perrott (1979: 176) the criminal act was 'central to the concept of their own manhood'. They were elated by the bank raids, and perceived themselves as 'free spirits with the guts to chuck the system'.

Some policemen can come to share precisely these values and this style to the extent that they engage in criminal activity (Bunyan 1977: 79). Policemen may commit robbery, sell drugs, smuggle, deal in weapons, lie and steal for a number of reasons, but an important one may be the development of an identity that actively desires risk, that emphasizes an ethic of masculinity (involving physical and sexual prowess, courage, profanity, and aggression toward authority), that enjoys the attractiveness of clandestine work, and that shares the criminal's conception of self and dichotomous world-view. This enables the dirty workers not only to indulge in dirty work for its own sake but also as a form of revenge against 'the system' (Harris 1973: 58). In the film *Prince of the City*, Ciello (pseudonym for Leuci of the SIU) was 'wired' to record the conversations of his colleagues in order to incriminate them. This involved a considerable risk of discovery and reprisal and demanded skilful bluff and play-acting. Emerging from one meeting 'Ciello' is elated and shouts, 'It's a fucking game. I love it!' Some people might find this a reprehensible and almost perverse way of getting one's kicks.

But it can be taken as symptomatic of an extreme strain in police work whereby the complex of bitterness, cynicism, and defensiveness noted among policemen can be converted into an offensive, adventurous, manipulative style that reverses connotations of respectability, virtue, and honour by embracing the deviant label and living out the deviant identity. The evidence and analysis presented in this book might possibly lead to two negative observations. On the one hand, the interactionist is a pessimist and fatalist accepting the inevitability of deviance so that this approach represents a gospel of despair. And, on the other hand, the policeman is an example of an extreme and unusual occupation that either selectivity recruits deviants or socializes them into deviance. In other words, policemen are bad people and police work is unlike work in most other occupations. First, if one wishes to generate insights that might lead to solutions to the dilemmas of practical policing then it is necessary to break through the 'unwarranted assumptions, and speculative inferences' surrounding policing for 'it is difficult to imagine how criticisms of the police and proposals for reform could be sustained in the absence of detailed systematic knowledge and analysis of the background context out of which the "undesirable" consequences arose' (Chatterton 1975: 2).

This book is an attempt to investigate and make visible the policeman's world-view, his occupational culture, the way he approaches his work, and the manner in which he copes with organizational constraints and opportunities. Comparative and historical evidence does induce a measure of pessimism about the persistence and near universalism of serious police deviance and it may simply be unrealistic to expect to eliminate it entirely (Sherman 1978: 242). At the same time there are some clear guidelines from New York, London, and Amsterdam as to how to tackle, or not to tackle, an anti-corruption campaign. Hopefully, this modest piece of research may assist in attempts to change the 'operational code' of policing, however resilient it seems and however intractable its origins may appear. The point perhaps is to understand the world before trying to change it.

Second, delving into police deviance may seem to dredge up an unpleasant and unwholesome world infused with suspicion, secrecy, lies, manipulation, distrust, and betrayal. One could argue strongly, however, that the police are not at all extraordinary, that most occupations and organizations (including the professions) are characterized by routine and systematic rule-bending (Manning and Redlinger 1977: 298–300; Bryant 1974), but that police are simply more vulnerable to public scrutiny and successful labelling. Indeed, deviousness, concealment, and mis-representation can be held to be true of social interaction in general. Goffman's important opus revolves constantly around these issues and he notes (1969: 81) first that it is mainly 'wanted criminals, spies and secret police' who present false personal or social identities but, then, that this is true of almost everyone at some time which 'renders agents a little like us and all of us a little like agents'. Indeed, Reisman (1979: 119) observes that the 'dilemmas of bribery are not an extraordinary experience. Like adultery and betrayal, they are woven into the fabric of society with potential, if not actual, universal incidence.'

Taking these insights into account I have attempted to capture something of the intricate occupational complexity of the police-man's working world (Lundman 1980a). This is morally ambiv-alent, if not paradoxical, for he is an enforcer of the law and of moral standards who may routinely lie, double-cross, falsify evidence, and break the law. The occupational reality of the policeman flitting between backstage behaviour and formal interaction in public is that of an unconsciously accomplished actor caught up in a schizophrenic, or even dialectical, relation-ship with a system that dictates bureaucratic, universal standards of conduct for him that are deemed situationally inappropriate. In brief, the pivotal concern of the active policeman represents a near universal dilemma: how does he get his hands on the pot of gold without landing himself in the shit?

Finally, the perspective espoused and explored in this study can be summarized by stating that police occupational and organizational deviance is generated and sustained by the nature of the work which may be seen as impossible without short cuts and rule-bending; by an occupational culture that condones illicit practices and that legitimates techniques of subterfuge and deception which undermine control; by an organization that implicitly stimulates deviancy as a solution to getting results while proving incapable of controlling and monitoring behaviour; and by a social environment that demands that police tackle crime, that expresses moral indignation at moments of lapse, but that remains fundamentally ambivalent about the ends and means of law enforcement. This perspective is built upon a conception of organizations as a creation of acting, defining, and working persons dealing with the 'ongoing practical tasks and problems' (Manning 1980: 41) whereby common-sense understandings and recipes for action are developed in the 'here and now' for the 'mastery of routine problems' (Berger and Luckman 1971: 57). An examination of police deviance, with its important implications for accountability and control of the police, must focus on the social processes and the nature of the social order created by the complex interplay of power, authority, control, legitimacy, and human interaction (Lemert 1972) both within the police organization and with external control agencies. I would plead for analysis to begin at the basis, with the tasks people are required to perform (Wilson 1978: 211; Manning 1977: 373; Chatterton 1976: 114).

At a time of scandal policemen themselves aid us in unravelling and decoding the submerged reality of policing. While corruption is frequently surrounded with imagery of temptation, personal failure, and individual pathology (Chibnall 1977: 66), academics and critics of the police maintain that it is an endemic feature of policing. When 'the wheel comes off', the organizational representatives endeavour to bolster the myth system and to defend the institution against outside attack by employing precisely that imagery, of the few 'bad apples', who only need to be purged to reestablish organizational integrity. In defending themselves, the vulnerable lower orders counter-attack by articulating the operational code and by elaborating that the deviance is, in fact, institutionalized and 'organizational' (Sherman 1979 and 1980). In so doing, they indelibly expose how deviant practices are inseparably enmeshed in the routine social construction of police work.

Appendix:
Research Methods

Background and Access

The primary insight that I gained early on when meeting police-men is that there exists a wide disparity between the public presentation of police work – as sober, legal, competent, pro-fessional, and even 'sacred' (Manning 1977: 5) – and the back-stage reality. My first contacts with this largely concealed world were with policemen in Britain where, although I was unable to conduct official field-work, I built up a close relationship with a number of officers who studied at the university where I taught. The standard literature on the police, novels, press accounts, and personal socializing with policemen gradually helped to peel away the layers of myth and imagery that protect the hidden reality of policing from public scrutiny to reveal a profane, bawdy, irreverent, and even devious subculture. Perhaps the central paradox of this world is contained in the remark of one informant who told me, 'One thing you have to understand is that when you join the police you have to learn to break the law.'

My initial views on the police, then, were permeated with per-ceptions of in-built deviant practices which were also strongly conveyed in the standard American works of the time. Then, in the early 1970s, I began to focus increasingly on policing in The Netherlands (where I have lived since 1975) and gained access to the Amsterdam City Police where I was able to conduct three projects between 1974 and 1980.

(a) Project 1: 1974–76. My first piece of research was an observational study of patrol work in the inner-city district of Amsterdam (Punch 1979). Most of my time was spent with patrolmen and I was struck by the *absence* of deviance. In fact it was going on around me, almost literally under my nose, but I did not see it.

(b) Project 2: 1977–78. In the summer of 1976 I was extricating myself from the field when a corruption scandal involving policemen in the research station began to surface. By 1977 the scandal was front-page news and, prompted by a number of colleagues, I decided to see if I could get back in to the department to look at police deviance. Permission was granted and the research was based primarily on interviewing policemen and on gathering documentary evidence.

(c) Project 3: 1979–80. As I was teaching in a business school I decided to study senior police officers in terms of 'managing' a police district and returned to part-time observation in the original research station. This project brought me into closer touch with the world of senior officers, and also of detectives, and proved particularly revealing because I could witness the reverberations of the scandal which continued deeply to affect relationships within the force. I began to perceive more clearly that deviance is endemic to police work and found myself in effect still carrying out Project 2 under the guise of Project 3. Although I had not planned it as such, it was clearly advantageous to have been in the field before, during, and after the scandal.

Gaining entry to the Amsterdam Police was quite easy and all three projects were readily accepted and supported by the Chief Constable. Although some academics have encountered problems with officialdom in attempts to research the police (Reiner 1979; Ericson 1981), I found nothing but open doors in gaining formal access in Amsterdam. This continues to be true for other researchers not only in Amsterdam but elsewhere in The Netherlands, which must have one of the most open criminal justice systems in the world. The key question here is what motivated the Amsterdam Police to allow me in to examine a scandal while the department was still in the throes of an unprecedented criminal investigation into corruption. First, I believe that many senior officers just did not know what had hit them and were clutching at straws. Second, I had shown myself not to be negative towards the department in publications and had built up a relationship of trust with a number of policemen which meant that I was less threatening than a complete outsider. Third, I now had powerful sponsors within the department and the chief of the station which was at the centre of the storm was supporting the project. Fourth, I couched my investigation in palatable terms of analysing 'dilemmas of law-enforcement in the city centre' in order not to frighten off people by blazoning the word 'corruption' all over the proposal. Fifth, as an individual researcher working in his own time I had no need to go through any academic gate-keeping institution with a proposal for funds. But sixth, and perhaps most importantly, the department was petrified of an external commission of enquiry. I could be passed off, if necessary, as an outside academic who was already investigating the issue (there were still hints in the press of an external enquiry as late as 1979). Later, a senior officer in the Warmoesstraat Station confirmed this:

'This is something so serious, and so serious that it's happened to the Amsterdam Police, that we must prevent it happening again. And I suppose there was a degree of pressure in all the publicity that might have led to questions in Parliament. We wanted to prevent people saying that we weren't doing enough and I think that now the Ministry of Justice and the Town Hall are satisfied.'

The Chief Constable agreed to the research in May, 1977, and promised access to senior officers, police suspected of corruption, and to the case dossier.

Having said all this, it did prove more difficult to gain 'secondary' access (Manning and van Maanen 1978: 317). Initially, however, things went well and I began to arrange interviews. Being granted a second bite at the cherry proved fascinating. People seemed to be far more candid about the practical dilemmas in policing and about making mistakes than they had been during my first project, while the word corruption was no longer taboo. I interviewed senior officers at Headquarters and in the Warmoesstraat (the research station), plainclothesmen, detectives, investigating officers from the Misfeance Department and the State Detectives, journalists, and representatives of the legal authorities (over fifty people were interviewed and several key actors were questioned on two or three occasions). Gradually it began to dawn on me that many people were often not talking about 'corruption' at all but that my questions were sparking off heartfelt diatribes about more general defects in the organization and I formed the idea of studying more closely the police *organization* and, more specifically, the work of senior officers. Once more I returned to the Warmoesstraat and, assured of the cooperation of the three senior officers (continuity of personnel in the station increased my chances of acceptance), approached the Chief with yet another research proposal which he accepted, and observations began in December, 1978. I entered this third phase with the second project uncompleted as the repercussions of the corruption cases were still echoing throughout the department. To a certain extent, then, the two projects had an element of overlap which none of us had foreseen.

It was at this stage that I began to encounter resistance and deflection. During the first two projects I was not conscious of doors being closed, and even now no one actually refused to be interviewed, but I was excluded from certain conversations between senior officers in the Warmoesstraat, discovered coolness outside of the Warmoesstraat, was explicitly not welcome at secret meetings of a clique of officers engaged in lobbying within and without the organization for a more stringent investigation, was asked not to interview the police suspects, was refused the case dossier which had been promised, encountered friction in the field situation, and was barred from sensitive confrontations between officers and detectives in the Warmoesstraat. In retrospect, this appears only natural whereas at the time I felt rather disappointed and let down. The resistance was partly due to the fact that in my third project I was getting much closer to powerful interests at the top of the organization and was discovering that my acceptance outside of the Warmoesstraat was tenuous, and partly because I was caught in the continuing backlash of the corruption affair which aggravated inter-rank relationships at the very time when I was observing both senior officers and detectives. To a certain extent access was continually problematic, particularly in the third project, and to some parts of the organization I was a stranger and was treated accordingly. Furthermore, I was gaining different sorts of data at different stages and, although the third project was not ostensibly about corruption, it did open my eyes to the scandal as part of a much wider struggle related both to resilience to change and to hostility to the investigation within the organization.

Evidence

All information is managed to a greater or lesser extent and all observations are subject to interpretation and reinterpretation.

The data for this study, then, have varying levels of validity and the observations, interviews, documents, and journalistic accounts on which I rely are all biased in certain ways. This would be true of any study but it is particularly so of one concerned with deviant behaviour which, by definition, is sensitive and subject to concealment. In this section I wish to deal with the nature of the evidence collected and the extent to which respondents were open and truthful in their accounts.

In the first project, for instance, I had a close relationship with one group of patrolmen and a couple of them functioned as 'informants' whom I thought were reasonably honest with me. Indeed, the person who first seriously broached the subject of corruption to me was Chief Inspector 'Maartens', who in the summer of 1976 told me that he had been confronted with some practices among his plainclothesmen that amounted to corruption. Then, shortly afterwards, my patrol group had been out drinking one evening and we ended up at someone's flat. There the conversation turned to the growing rumours about corruption.

> 'a subterranean police culture which had largely escaped me suddenly emerged. There was talk of policemen sleeping with prostitutes, accepting bribes, keeping an extra round from the range to use in case of a hasty shot which the constable did not want to report, covering up for colleagues in delicate situations, and running messages for members of the Chinese underworld. Hans and Tom explained: "How much do you think you found out when you were with us? You wrote somewhere that you thought we were openhearted. Well, we only let you see what we wanted you to see. You only saw about fifty percent. We showed you only half of the story.'
>
> (Punch 1979: 13)

Clearly, my informants had been less than open and knew a great deal more than they were prepared to tell me. However, the informants became particularly frank after I had completed the first project and after one of them had moved from the station. Two men told me of dubious practices, including fabricating statements, forging signatures on crime reports, and of one case where they 'were one thousand per cent certain' that a suspect was a dealer so they replaced his fake heroin with real heroin in order to get a conviction. One of them explained to me later that it was impossible to trust anyone in that milieu, including your partner, and that you had to learn to keep your mouth shut 'otherwise you are digging your own grave'. He then recounted an incident where he had searched a flat for firearms with 'Ton'. It appears that Ton may have removed a revolver from the flat:

> 'When I heard that story later I felt really pissed off. This has now led me to the practice of never letting a colleague out of my sight when we're engaged in a search. Pulling a stroke like that can land you in sticky situations. Which boss or judge is going to believe your story? "You were with your partner, weren't you?"'

This revealing comment shows not only the *absence* of trust among policemen but also their vulnerability to control when engaged in risky escapades. Some of the patrolmen were clearly locked into intricate and intimate relationships of collusion and cooperation which would be almost impossible for an outsider to prise open.

In the two later projects no one really emerged as a classical informant although one or two senior officers were particularly helpful and a certain marginal figure within the organization approached me at a late stage with a good deal of inside information. I never had the close relationship with people that I enjoyed in the first project and yet people still seemed reasonably, and in some cases remarkably, frank. This was probably because 'the shit had hit the fan', people had taken sides, and I was seen as a chronicler who could represent their particular point of view. However, it proved impossible for some time to get in touch with the policemen under suspicion of corruption. The Chief Constable had suddenly requested that I postpone interviews with the suspects until after the trial. This may have been a seriously missed opportunity in that the suspects were suspended, were sitting at home biting their nails, were deeply frustrated by their treatment, were uncertain of the outcome of their cases, and might have been willing to talk. When I did get to talk to them almost two years had elapsed, their cases had been to court, they had told their stories to journalists, and had doubtless developed a pat version that they had been mulling over for two years and which they could trot out on request. As it was, I only managed to talk to four of the eight men who had been arrested and, significantly, all four were from the Warmoesstraat. My acceptability was plainly much more limited at Headquarters. In addition, the Chief Constable also went back on his promise to provide me with the case dossier which he said was now the responsibility of the Justice Department and, therefore, outside of his authority to give me. Fortunately, however, I managed to

get my hands on a copy of the 350-page dossier, containing tran-
scripts of interrogations of witnesses and suspects up to the trial
in May, 1978, with the help of a journalist to whom it had been
leaked.

To a large extent I never actually witnessed the phenomenon I
was studying – 'corruption' – so that observation (and certainly
participant observation) is something of a misnomer in relation to
an activity that is basically concealed from view. This means that
my major data sources are interviews and documents which are
biased in the sense that the interviews are forms of special pleading and the documents represent official versions of reality.
During the second project it felt as if I was getting through to
levels of information about the department which are not normally accorded to outsiders while I was under the impression
that I was concerned with a number of cases in the *past* but that
those cases revealed considerable current defects within the
department.

During the third phase of my involvement with the Amsterdam
Police, however, I became increasingly aware that the continuous and unforeseen internal rumblings and external criticism
surrounding the corruption issue had began to overshadow the
original intention of studying senior officers as 'managers'. During this stage, moreover, material was gathered incidentally and
partly covertly for the corruption research under the mantle of
the third project and this came from the continued contact with
senior officers who were closely involved in the affair and who
occasionally said things pertaining to the persistence of the
investigations, from interviewing the suspects, from obtaining
the corruption dossier, from keeping in touch with a number of
informants, and from field-work with detectives that largely by
chance led to a glimpse of yet more widespread and ongoing corruption than I had anticipated. In a sense, I had moved into a new
level of information which proved uncomfortable to handle
because it identified highly placed individuals who were difficult
to disguise, because the information itself was either given in
confidence or might reveal my source, and because I had moved
into a circuit of gossip and rumour which by its very nature was
impossible to verify.

All the evidence presented here needs to be treated with more
than the usual dose of caution. The quality of press reporting was
patchy and tended to follow events rather than take an 'investigative' strategy. The case dossier was incomplete and contains
only what witnesses and suspects were prepared to reveal and

what the investigators considered worth writing up (including the occupational filtering and linguistic techniques that detectives employ in report writing, amplified by the 'hidden agenda' of a highly sensitive enquiry). My acceptance within the organization was varied and I received different sorts of information from various parts of the organization. The interviews are smoothed out reconstructions based on extensive notes taken at the time (but not containing the erratic rhythm of actual conversation and also not pretending to be a totally accurate, word-for-word record). Most of the incidents referred to in the investigation occurred *before* my arrival, so that by 1976 when the first internal investigation commenced some people were already running for cover. And, of course, some people were simply keeping quiet, having doubtless sound reasons for saying as little as possible.

Dilemmas of the Research Role

A number of accounts of field-work touch on the stress, the deep personal involvement, the role-conflicts, the physical and mental effort, the discomfort, and the time-consuming nature of observational studies for the researcher (e.g. Whyte 1955; Wax 1971; Clarke 1975; McCall and Simmons 1969). Increasingly I experienced frustration, fatigue, despondency, and ethical qualms as the research developed and these, together with other considerations, made me leave the field prematurely in the middle of my third project.

It became clear, for example, that some people were lying to me, or were spreading misinformation, and I began to have this 'Rashomon' feeling of hearing varying versions from different people. But what finally confirmed my intention to depart was, paradoxically, two moments when the veil was lifted to reveal yet a deeper layer of deviance. Detectives in the station had become involved in a complex case involving several professional criminals. Then one evening a young woman walked in with clean clothes for one of the prisoners concerned in the case. It turned out that she was the daughter of a senior police officer, was living with one of the suspects, and had a child by him. In addition, the suspect's alibi for a particular evening was that he was at the senior policeman's house with the daughter. Now clearly this was a highly delicate issue but one of the policemen, X, wanted to treat the woman as a suspect. The daughter of the senior officer was so incensed at her treatment that she complained to her father. The detectives believed that the senior officer would get his own back on X. Subsequently, X, who could have expected a move to a specialized detective unit, was put back into uniform. The detectives were convinced that X had been 'screwed' and that the daughter had been avenged. The significance of this was that I could glimpse the informal system at work in terms of retaliatory sanctions and the manipulation of a policeman engaged in a criminal case involving the relative of a senior officer. But all my information on this matter came from gossip which was sometimes impossible to verify and too personal to be used without identifying both the people concerned and my sources.

By chance I was also present one evening when the detectives involved in the case came back from interrogating a key suspect. They seemed almost physically disgusted and emotionally they expressed considerable sympathy for the suspect. One said, 'I tell you poor old "Jansen" [the suspect] has been screwed right and proper. If you listen to him then you open up a right old cess-pit and it really turns your stomach. If we told you everything then your hair would stand on end.' Then they went on to detail how 'Jansen' had been conned by detectives elsewhere and was being set up for the shooting of a policeman. Furthermore they claimed that senior officers, public prosecutors, and detectives at Headquarters maintained close contacts with members of the underworld (to the extent that a detective visited an escaped prisoner who was on the run the evening before the fugitive wounded a uniformed policeman during a traffic-control). 'We're telling you that you can't trust anyone, but especially at Headquarters. The Warmoesstraat is clean but other departments are not to be trusted and that includes public prosecutors as well.'

Now this conversation took place in the detective room and the detectives concerned seemed out of their depth and somewhat distraught. They were on to something but it was getting too big for them but also for me. A sergeant advised them to call in X and Y (senior officers) from their homes, put their cards on the table, and take the matter to one of the more trustworthy public prosecutors. X and Y arrived and went straight into a conclave with the detectives. From the detective room we could look across to another part of the building and into X's room. The remaining detectives were now also rather distraught and concerned. One said.

'It's just like three years ago all over again [he is referring to the first corruption investigation]. Then you would watch X and Y pacing around that room and wonder what was going to come next. Now they are going to use those detectives to get at the people they couldn't get three years ago. But those detectives will suffer because they'll become contaminated and they will suffer as a consequence. This district has already been through it once and now once again we'll be contaminated because "Kees" and "Wim" [two detectives on the big case] have started to push a case against powerful people.'

He went on to say that detectives from the Warmoesstraat would find it difficult to get transfers because they would be painted as 'guys who screw their own mates'. The ordinary detective would suffer, and not the officers, 'because you can't take on Headquarters and hope to get away with it. There are senior officers involved and we're convinced that things are just not right with some of them, that they are bent, but you can't expect to take them on and get away with it. They are just too powerful.'

I was on the verge of a breakthrough to an area that promised to expose a network of connections in Amsterdam between policemen and criminals that perhaps also involved senior officers and even public prosecutors. And yet I decided to leave. Why did I get out at this stage? There were a number of pressures outside of my research but the basic reasons were disillusion with the research role and growing scepticism about getting to the mucky area exposed by this big case. I was not Woodward and Bernstein with unlimited time to spend on a case. I was, in effect, a part-time researcher and I baulked at the time and energy that would be required to complete the picture.

But basically I felt that I could not get further within the police organization without betraying my purpose to expose the new vein of corruption and that too many powerful interests were at stake to allow me to do this. It was tantalizing to be part of the gossip circuit, but more concrete evidence was needed if I was to piece together a much deeper investigation. But I just could not see how I would ever get to the level of information needed. It was clearly in no-one's interest to give it to me. Perhaps we have to recognize that, as we move higher up the hierarchy of an organization and as we begin to encounter powerful, entrenched groups and individuals who are identifiable, jealous of their reputations, prepared to fight for their survival, and powerful enough to deflect attention, that we may be attempting to research areas of institutional life which are to all intents and purposes unresearchable, such as unmasking the relationship between police and Free Masonry in Great Britain (cf. Knight 1983). For me, at any rate, the 'breakthrough' had proved to be a dead-end.

Ethical Considerations

Generally discussions of ethics in research centre on informed consent, deception, privacy, identity, confidentiality, and spoiling the field for further research (Bulmer 1982). Applying BSA and ASA Codes of Ethics in field-work seems ludicrously inappropriate here as there was no way I could have employed them without destroying my research. All three projects were formally permitted by the Amsterdam Police and were overt but in the third project I concealed my motives and interests and therefore engaged in a measure of deception. Disguising the name of the town scarcely seemed feasible as it is instantly recognizable to anyone in The Netherlands. Also it is the case that many people mentioned in this book were public figures in the sense that their names, and their photos, were kept in the news over a period of years and that much of what I have to say about them was covered extensively in the press. I promised that all interviews would be confidential in the sense that quotations could not be directly attributable to individuals (and the interviews would not be available to anyone else). In retrospect, my research raised a number of ethical issues with regard to the conduct of field-work and, while I engaged in a measure of deception and misrepresentation, I did endeavour to follow convention as closely as possible in terms of avoiding identification and harm. My general position echoes that of Gans (1962: 46 and cf. Manning and Van Maanan 1978: 334), 'If the researcher is completely honest with people about his activities, they will try to hide actions and attitudes they consider undesirable, and so will be dishonest. Consequently, the researcher must be dishonest to get honest data'.

It is ironic, and even amusing, that academic researchers end up in the same moral predicament as policemen and even employ the same imagery of muddy boots (Fielding 1980: 96) and grubby hands ('in getting at the dirt one may get dirty oneself' – Marx 1980b: 27). When I withdrew from the field I did so with a disappointed feeling that I had failed to investigate corruption satisfactorily. I had began with the cosy, cohesive world of the patrol group but ended up studying the predicament of a large, incoherent organization caught in the intense glare of publicity and ineptly endeavouring to set its house in order. In addition, I was accorded a view of the nasty side of the organization with feuds, victims, taking revenge, pulling strokes, 'screwing' opponents, broken promises, and broken careers. I believe that part of my problem was that I commenced with what might be called a 'supportive' approach (Becker 1970: 124) and became frustrated at my inability to change research paradigms to an 'investigative' or 'conflict methodology' approach (personal communication, M. Clarke). In the last resort I shrank from getting my hands too dirty.

References

Accent (1977) Hoe Fout was Oom Agent in '40–'45?. April 16, 23, 30; May 7, 14, 21.

—— (1977) Politietop ook Zwaar Corrupt: Omkoping Verdoezelt Zware Corruptie in Politietop. May 7.

Alderson, J. C. (1973) The Principles and Practice of the British Police. In J. C. Alderson and P. J. Stead (eds) *The Police We Deserve*. London: Wolfe.

Alex, N. (1976) *New York Cops Talk Back: a Study of a Beleagured Minority*. New York: Wiley.

Algemeen Dagblad (1979) Eis: Cel voor Agenten. June 1.

Altheide, D. L. and J. M. Johnson (1980) *Bureaucratic Propaganda*. Boston: Allyn and Bacon.

Anderson, R. E. (1973) Police Integrity: Accent on the Positive. *Police Chief* **40** (December): 38–40.

Angenent, H. L. W. and H. O. Steensma (1977) *Onveilig Nederland?* Nijkerk: Callenbach.

Annual Crime Statistics (1977). Amsterdam: Amsterdam City Police.

Ascoli, D. (1979) *The Queen's Peace: The Origins and Development of the Metropolitan Police 1829–1979*. London: Hamish Hamilton.

Baena, Duke de (1967) *The Dutch Puzzle*. The Hague: Boucher.

Baldamus, W. (1961) *Efficiency and Effort*. London: Tavistock.

Ball, J., L. Chester, and R. Perrott (1979) *Cops and Robbers*. Harmondsworth: Penguin.

Banton, M. (1964) *The Policeman in the Community*. London: Tavistock.

Barker, T. (1977) Peer Group Support for Police Occupational Deviance. *Criminology* **15** (3): 353–66.

Barker, T. and J. B. Roebuck (1973) *An Empirical Typology of Police Corruption: a Study in Organizational Deviance*. Springfield, Ill.: Thomas.

Bayley, D. H. (1974) Police Corruption in India. In L. W. Sherman (ed.) *Police Corruption*. New York: Anchor Press.

Bayley, D. H. (ed.) (1977) *Police and Society*. Beverly Hills, Calif.: Sage.

Bayley, D. H. (1983) *Knowledge of the Police*. In M. Punch (ed.) *Control in the Police Organization*. Cambridge, Mass.: MIT Press.

Beames, T. (1850) *The Rookeries of London, Past, Present and Prospective*. London: Thomas Bosworth.

Becker, H. S. (1970) *Sociological Work*. London: Allen Lane.

Beigel, H. and A. Beigel (1977) *Beneath the Badge: A Story of Police Corruption*. New York: Harper and Row.

Bell, D. (1953) Crime As An American Way of Life. *Antioch Review* **13**: 131–54.

Berger, P. L. and T. Luckman (1971) *The Social Construction of Reality*. Harmondsworth: Penguin.

Berghuis, A. C., C. H. Brants, and H. M. Willemse (eds.) (1984) *Witteboorden Criminaliteit*. Nijmegen: Aers Aequi Libri.

Bernstein, C. and R. Woodward (1975) *All the President's Men*. New York: Warner Paperback Library.

Bianchi, H. (1975) Social Control and Deviance in The Netherlands. In H. Bianchi, M. Simondi and I. Taylor (eds) *Deviance and Control in Europe*. London: Wiley.

Binnenspiegel (1981) Nota Over een Intern Onderzoek naar Normafwijkend Gedrag en Wat er aan te Doen is. Amsterdam City Police.

Birch, J. W. (1983) Reflections on Police Corruption. *Criminal Justice Ethics*. Summer/Fall: 83–5.

Bittner, E. (1967) The Police on Skid Row. *American Sociological Review* **32** (5): 699–715.

—— (1970) *The Functions of the Police in Modern Society*. Washington, DC: US Government Printing Office.

—— (1975) Police Research and Police Work. In E. Viano (ed.) *Criminal Justice Research*. Farnborough: Heath.

Blanken, M. (1976) *Force of Order and Methods: an American View into the Dutch Directed Society*. The Hague: Martinus Nijhoff.

Blau, P. M. (1955) *The Dynamics of Bureaucracy*. Chicago: Chicago University Press.

Blauw, J. A. (1982) Corruptie-aanpak: Droom van een Biechtvader. *Algemeen Politieblad* 131 (24): 538–42.

Blumer, H. (1969) *Symbolic Interactionism*. New Jersey: Prentice-Hall.

Bok, S. (1978) *Lying*. New York: Pantheon.

Bommels, B. (1982) *Het Blauwe Leger*. Haarlem: De Haan.

Bordua, D. (ed.) (1967) *The Police: Six Sociological Essays*. New York: Wiley.

Boulton, D. (1978) *The Grease Machine*. New York: Harper & Row.

Bouman, H. (1978) *Ambtelijke Willekeur en Corruptie in Nederland*. Baarn: Wereldvenster.

Bowden, T. (1978) *Beyond the Limits of the Law*. Harmondsworth: Penguin.

Bowes, S. (1968) *Police and Civil Liberties*. London: Lawrence & Wishart.

Box, S. and K. Russell (1975) The Politics of Discreditability: Disarming Complaints Against the Police. *Sociological Review* 23: 315–416.

Bracey, D. Heid (1976) *A Functional Approach to Police Corruption*. New York: John Jay College.

Bresler, F. (1981) *De Chinese Mafia*. Amsterdam/Brussel: Elsevier (translation of F. Bresler (1980) *Trial of the Triads*. London: Weidenfeld & Nicolson).

Brittan, A. (1973) *Meanings and Situations*. London: Routledge & Kegan Paul.

Broad, W. and N. Wade (1983) *Betrayers of the Truth: Fraud and Deceit in the Halls of Science*. New York: Simon & Schuster/Touchstone.

Broer, W. and K. van der Vijver (1982) Some Developments in the organization of Police Change in The Netherlands. *Police Science Abstracts* 10 (3): i–v.

Bryant, C. D. (ed.) (1974) *Deviant Behaviour: Occupational and Organizational Bases*. Chicago: Rand McNally.

Bulmer, M. (ed.) (1982) *Social Research Ethics*. London: Macmillan.

Bunyan, T. (1977) *The Political Police in Britain*. London: Quartet.

Burke, K. (1962) *A Grammar of Motives and Rhetoric of Motives*. Cleveland: Meridian Books.

Cain, M. (1973) *Society and the Policeman's Role*. London: Routledge & Kegan Paul.

—— (1977) An Ironical Departure: The Dilemma of Contemporary Policing. In K. Jones (ed.) *Yearbook of Social Policy in Britain 1977*. London: Routledge & Kegan Paul.

—— (1979) Trends in the Sociology of Police Work. *International Journal of the Sociology of Law* 7 (2): 143–67.

—— (1984) Review of PSI Reports on Metropolitan Police and Holdaway's *Inside the British Police*. *The Times Literary Supplement* 4217 (27 January): 89.

Carr, A. Z. (1968) Is Business Bluffing Ethical? *Harvard Business Review* 46 (1): 425–441.

Carson, W. G. (1982) *The Other Price of Britain's Oil*. New Brunswick, NJ: Rutgers University Press.

Chambliss, W. J. (1971) Vice, Corruption, Bureaucracy, and Power. *University of Wisconsin Law Review* 4: 1150–73.

Chambliss, W. J. (1978) *On the Take*. Bloomington: Indiana University Press.

Chatterton, M. R. (1975) *Organizational Relationships and Processes in Police Work: A Case Study of Urban Policing*. Unpub. PhD dissertation: University of Manchester.

Chatterton, M. R. (1976) The Social Contexts of Violence. In M. Borland (ed.) *Violence in the Family*. Manchester: Manchester University Press.

Chatterton, M. R. (1979) The Supervision of Patrol Work Under the Fixed Points System. In S. Holdaway (ed.) *The British Police*. London: Arnold.

Chibnall, S. (1977) *Law and Order News*. London: Tavistock.

Chibnall, S. and P. Saunders (1977) Worlds Apart: Notes on the Social Reality of Corruption. *British Journal of Sociology* **28**: 138–177.

Chorus, B., S. van Houcke, and H. V. Stuart (1981) *De Colonne Eenmaal in Beweging*. Leeuwarden: Pamflet.

Christianson, S. (1973) Albany's Finest Wriggle Free. *The Nation* 3 (December).

Clark, J. P. and R. Sykes (1974) Some Determinants of Police Organization and Practice in a Modern Industrial Democracy. In D. Glaser (ed.) *Handbook of Criminology*. Chicago: Rand McNally.

Clarke, M. (1975) Survival in the Field: Implications of Personal Experience in Field-Work. *Theory and Society* **2** (1): 95–123.

Clarke, M. (ed.) (1983) *Corruption*. London: Frances Pinter.

Clinard, M. B. and P. C. Yeager (1980) *Corporate Crime*. New York: The Free Press.

Cohen, B. (1970) *The Police Internal Administration of Justice in New York City*. New York: Rand.

Cohen, H. (1976) Drugs, Drug-Users and Drug-Scenes. *Sociologica Neerlandica* **12** (1): 3–18.

Command Corruption Profile (1973). Report by Intelligence Section of International Affairs Division. New York: New York Police Department.

Commissie Enschedé (1967) *Rapport van de Commissie van Onderzoek Amsterdam*. Den Haag: Staatsuitgeverij.

Cook, F. J. (1966) *The Secret Rulers: Criminal Syndicates and How They Rule the U.S. Underworld*. New York: Duall, Sloan and Pierce.

Cook, P. (1980) Organizational Control of Police Misconduct. Unpublished paper for seminar on 'Management and Control of the Police Organization'. Nijenrode, Breukelen.

Corruption Case Dossier. Photostat copies of documents (reports, arrest warrants, interrogations, confessions, etc.) related to the Amsterdam corruption investigation and covering primarily the period 1976 up to the trial in 1978.

Cornwell, R. (1983) *God's Banker*. London: Gollancz.

Cox, R. (1983) The Second Death of Peron? Review Article. *The New York Review of Books* **xxx** (19): 18–22.

Cox, B., J. Shirley, and M. Short (1977) *The Fall of Scotland Yard*. Harmondsworth: Penguin.

Cressey, D. R. (1969) *Theft of the Nation*. New York: Harper.

Cressey, D. R. (1972) *Criminal Organization*. London: Heinemann.

Critchley, T. A. (1978) *A History of Police in England and Wales: 900–1966*. Revised edition, London: Constable.

Crozier, M. (1964) *The Bureaucratic Phenomenon*. London: Tavistock.

—— (1973) *The Stalled Society*. New York: Viking.

Daily Mirror (1977) Evil Web of the Yard's Porn Squad. December 22.

—— (1982) 'McNee Out' Call Grows. July 21.

Daley, R. (1971) *Target Blue*. New York: Delacorte Press.

—— (1979) *Prince of the City*. London: Panther.

Dalton M. (1959) *Men Who Manage*. New York: Wiley.

Daniel, W. W. (1973) Understanding Employee Behaviour in Its Context. In J. Child (ed.) *Man and Organization*. London: Allen and Unwin.

Davies, D. and L. Goodstadt (1975) Crawling Out of the Woodwork. *Far Eastern Economic Review* 7 March.

Deeley, P. (1970) *The Manhunters*. London: Hodder and Stoughton.

Dershowitz, A. M. (1983) *The Best Defence*. New York: Vintage Books.

Dingwall, R., G. Payne, and J. Payne (1980) *The Development of Ethnography in Britain*. Oxford: Centre for Socio-Legal Studies.

Ditton, J. (1977) *Part-Time Crime*. London: Macmillan.

Doig, A. (1983) 'You Publish at Your Peril!' – the Restraints on Investigative Journalism. In M. Clarke (ed.) *Corruption*. London: Frances Pinter.

Douglas, J. D. (ed.) (1971) *Understanding Everyday Life*. London: Routledge & Kegan Paul.

Douglas, J. D. and J. M. Johnson (eds) (1977) *Official Deviance*. Philadelphia: Lippincott.

Douglas, M. (1966) *Purity and Danger*. London: Routledge & Kegan Paul.

Downes, D. (1982) The Origins and Consequences of Dutch Penal Policy. *British Journal of Criminology* 22 (4): 325–362.

Downes, D. and P. E. Rock (1982) *Understanding Deviance*. Oxford: Oxford University Press.

Duchaine, N. (1979) *The Literature of Police Corruption: Vol. 2: A Selected, Annotated Bibliography*. New York: John Jay Press.

Duffee, D., F. Hussey, and J. Kramer (1978) *Criminal Justice: Organization, Structure, and Analysis*. Englewood Cliffs, NJ: Prentice-Hall.

Durkheim, E. (1964) *Rules of Sociological Method*. New York: Free Press.

Economist, The (1981) Policing the Police. July 4.

—— (1982) Police Corruption: Copy Honkong, Mr. Whitelaw. August 7.

Ellis, J. (1982) *The Sharp End of War*. London: Corgi.

Elseviers Magazine (1976) Warmoesstraat Rapport: Gevecht Tegen de Misdaad op één Vierkante Kilometer. February 21.

—— (1977) Amsterdam; het Chicago van Europa?. February 19.

—— (1977) Het Amsterdamse Corruptieschandaal: Warme Buurt werd Politie te Heet Onder de Voeten. May 14.

—— (1978) De Lessen van de Amsterdamse 'Politie-Corruptiezaak.' May 27.

—— (1980) De Commissaris Slaat Terug. February 23.

—— (1981) Politiemensen Zien Taak als 'Hopeloos'. July 18.

—— (1982) Amsterdam Begint Dood-Eng te Worden. August 21.

—— (1983) De Korpsleiding is een Middeleeuwse Bloedraad. October 1.

Ericson, R. V. (1981) *Making Crime: A Study of Detective Work*. Toronto and Vancouver: Butterworth.

Erkelens, L. H. and O. J. A. Janssen (1979) Hard Drug Use: Use and Crime. Paper delivered at Research Committee for Sociology of

Deviance and Social Control, International Sociological Association Conference, The Hague.

Ermann, M. D. and R. J. Lundman (eds) (1978) *Corporate and Government Deviance*. New York: Oxford University Press.

—— (1982a) *Corporate and Government Deviance*. 2nd ed. New York: Oxford University Press.

—— (1982b) *Corporate Deviance*. New York: Holt, Rinehart and Winston.

Extra (1978) Exclusief Onderzoek in Corruptie-Schandaal bij Amsterdamse Politie. December 29.

—— (1979) De Heroïne Oorlog. January 12.

—— (1979) Heroïne Wijkt Alleen voor Terreur. January 5.

Fennell, P. and P. A. Thomas (1983) Corruption in Britain: an Historical Analysis. *International Journal of the Sociology of Law* 11: 167–189.

Fielding, N. (1982) Observational Research on the National Front. In M. Bulmer (ed.) *Social Research Ethics*. London: Macmillan.

Fijnaut, C. (1976a) De Opbouw van Het Nederlandse Politiewezen-1. *Nederlands Tijdschrift voor Criminologie* 18 (Juni): 119–30.

—— (1976b) De Opbouw van Het Nederlandse Politiewezen – 2. *Nederlands Tijdschrift voor Criminologie* 18 (Oktober): 248–57.

—— (1979) *Opdat de Macht een Toevlucht Zij?* Antwerpen: Kluwer.

—— (1983) *De Zaak Francois*. Antwerpen-Deurne: Kluwer Rechtswetenschappen.

Fogelson, R. M. (1977) *Big-City Police*. Cambridge, Mass.: Harvard University Press.

Fong, M. L. (1981) *The Sociology of Secret Societies*. Oxford: Oxford University Press.

Foster, G. P. (1966) *Police Administration and the Control of Police Criminality*. Unpub. DPA diss.: Los Angeles: University of Southern California.

Fox, A. (1974) *Beyond Contract: Work, Power and Trust Relations*. London: Faber.

Gans, H. J. (1962) *The Urban Villagers*. New York: Free Press.

Gardiner, J. A. (1970) *The Politics of Corruption: Organized Crime in an American City*. New York: Sage.

Gardiner, J. A. and D. J. Olson (eds) (1974) *Theft of the City*. Bloomington: Indiana University Press.

Geerts, R. W. M. (1982) *En Anders Dien Je Maar Een Klacht In*. Nijmegen: Instituut voor Toegepaste Sociologie.

Geis, G. (1967) White Collar Crime: The Heavy Electrical Equipment Antitrust Cases of 1961. In M. B. Clinard and R. Quinney (eds) *Criminal Behaviour Styles: A Typology*. New York: Holt, Rinehart and Winston.

Geis, G. (ed.) (1968) *White Collar Criminal*. New York: Atherton.

Geis, G. (1982) The Heavy Electrical Equipment Antitrust Cases of 1961. In M. D. Ermann and R. J. Lundman (eds) *Corporate and Government Deviance*. 2nd ed. New York: Oxford University Press.

Geis, G. and R. F. Meier (eds) (1977) *White Collar Crime: Offences in Business, Politics and the Professions*. Revised ed. New York: Free Press.

Geis, G. and E. Stotland (eds) (1980) *White Collar Crime: Theory and Research*. Beverly Hills, California: Sage.

Gerth, H. H. and C. Wright Mills (1946) *From Max Weber: Essays in Sociology*. London: Routledge & Kegan Paul.

Gillers, S. (1977) Four Policemen in London and Amsterdam. In R. Shrank (ed.) *American Workers Abroad*. Cambridge, Mass.: MIT Press.

Goffman, E. (1959) *The Presentation of Self in Everyday Life*. Harmondsworth: Penguin.

Goffman, E. (1961) *Encounters*. Harmondsworth: Penguin.

—— (1969) *Strategic Interaction*. Philadelphia: University of Pennsylvania Press.

—— (1971) *Relations in Public*. Harmondsworth: Penguin.

—— (1972) *Interaction Ritual*. Harmondsworth: Penguin.

Goldstein, H. (1977) *Policing the Free Society*. Cambridge, Mass.: Ballinger.

Goode, W. J. (1967) The Protection of the Inept. *American Sociological Review* 32 (1): 5–19.

Goodendorp (1978) De Jonge Nederlandse Politie-Officier. *Intermediair* 14 (36): 43–53.

Goudsblom, J. (1967) *Dutch Society*. New York: Random House.

Gouldner, A. W. (1954) *Patterns of Industrial Bureaucracy*. New York: Free Press.

—— (1965) *Wildcat Strike*. New York: Free Press.

Greene, G. (1978) *The Human Factor*. New York: Avon.

Greenwood, J. (1876) *Low Life Deeps*. London: Chatto and Windus.

Gross, E. (1980) Organization Structure and Organizational Crime. In G. Geis and E. Stotland (eds) *White Collar Crime*. Beverly Hills, California: Sage.

The Guardian (1974) Police Chief made £400,000 from Hongkong Vice. October 8.

Haagse Post (1973) Een Heroïnedeal, De Politie en een Tipgever. November 16.

—— (1976) Is de Amsterdamse Politie Corrupt? October 9.

—— (1977) Dossier Corruptie – 1: De Zelfkant van de Amstedamse Politie. April 30.

—— (1977) Dossier Corruptie – 2: De Oorzaken van het Bederf. May 14.

—— (1977) Extra. Heroïne. May 14.

—— (1977) Politiecorruptie: Veel Verklaringen, Weinig Getuigen. October 8.

—— (1978) Politie Special. Burgemeester 'Cohen' over de Politie. Hoofdcommissaris 'Adema' over de Politie. May 13.

—— (1978) De Ondergang van de Narcoticabrigade: Is de Amsterdamse Politie nog steeds Dom en Goedkoop? November 4.

—— (1978) Pieter Menten's Staatsgeheim. November 25.

—— (1979) 'Promoties' bij de Amsterdamse Politie: Tom Jones en Loempia op Afscheidtstournee. February 10.

Hain, P., D. Humphry, and B. Rose-Smith (1979) *Policing the Police: Volume 1*. London: Calder.

Hain, P., M. Kettle, D. Campbell, and J. Rollo (1980) *Policing the Police: Volume 2*. London: Calder.

Hall, G. van (1976) *Ervaringen van een Amsterdammer*. Amsterdam: Agon Elsevier.

Hall, S., C. Critcher, A. Jefferson, J. Clarke, and B. Roberts (1978) *Policing the Crisis: Mugging, the State, and Law and Order*. London: Macmillan.

Halperin, M. H. (1977) *The Lawless State*. Harmondsworth: Penguin.

Harris, R. N. (1973) *The Police Academy*. New York: Wiley.

Hawkins, K. (1984) *Environment and Enforcement: The Social Construction of Pollution*. Oxford: Oxford University Press.

Have, P. ten (1972) The Counter Culture on the Move. Unpublished paper, presented at American Sociological Association, Annual Meeting, New York.

Heek, N. V. J. van (1934) *De Chineesche Immigranten in Nederland*. Amsterdam: Emmerings.

Heerikhuizen, B. van (1982) What is Typically Dutch? *The Netherlands Journal of Sociology* 18: 103–25.

Heertje, A. and H. Cohen (1980) *Het Officieuze Circuit*. Utrecht: Spectrum.

Heidenheimer, A. J. (ed.) (1970) *Political Corruption: Readings in Comparative Analysis*. New York: Holt, Rinehart and Winston.

Henry, S. (1978) *The Hidden Economy*. London: Martin Robertson.

Hill, H. (1981) *Competition and Control at Work*. Cambridge, Mass.: MIT Press.

Hoetjes, B. J. S. (1984) Geschenken, Relaties en Corruptie bij de Nederlandse Overheid: een Beschouwing naar Aanleiding van Recente Omkopingszaken. In A. C. Berghuis, C. H. Brants and H. M. Willemse (eds) *Witteboorden Criminaliteit*. Nijmegen: Aers Aequi Libri.

Holdaway, S. (1977) Changes in Urban Policing. *British Journal of Sociology* 28 (2): 119–37.

—— (ed.) (1979) *The British Police*. London: Arnold.

—— (1980) *The Occupational Culture of Urban Policing: An Ethnographic Study*. Unpublished PhD: University of Sheffield.

—— (1981) Telling It Like it is: an Analysis of Police Humour. Unpublished paper: University of Sheffield.

—— (1982) 'An Inside Job': A Case Study of Covert Research on the Police. In M. Bulmer (ed.) *Social Research Ethics*. London: Macmillan.

—— (1983) *Inside the British Police*. London: Basil Blackwell.

Honeycombe, G. (1974) *Adam's Tale*. London: Hutchinson.

Hughes, E. C. (1958) *Men and their Work*. New York: Free Press.

—— (1963) Good People and Dirty Work. In H. S. Becker (ed.) *The Other Side*. Glencoe: Free Press.

Johnson, J. M. (1975) *Doing Field Research*. New York: Free Press.

Johnson, J. M. and J. D. Douglas (eds) (1978) *Crime at the Top: Deviance in Business and the Professions*. Philadelphia: Lippincott.

Judge, A. (1972) *A Man Apart: the British Policeman and his Job*. London: Barker.

Juris, H. A. and P. Feuille (1973) *Police Unionism*. Lexington: Lexington Books.

Kam, F. de and F. van Empel (1983) *De Zaak is uit de Hand Gelopen*. Amsterdam: Bakker.

Kanter, R. M. (1977) *Men and Women of the Corporation*. New York: Basic Books.

—— (1982) Power and Entrepreneurship in Action: Corporate Middle Managers. In P. L. Stewart and M. G. Cantor (eds) *Varieties of Work*. Beverly Hills, California: Sage.

Kanter, R. S. and B. A. Stein (eds) (1979) *Life in Organizations: Workplaces as People Experience Them*. New York: Basic Books.

Katz, J. (1979) Legality and Equality: Plea-Bargaining in the Prosecution of White-Collar and Common Crimes. *Law and Society Review* **13** (Winter): 431–59.

Katz, E. and B. Danet (eds) (1973) *Bureaucracy and the Public*. New York: Basic Books.

Kennedy School of Government (1977a) Note on Police Corruption in New York in 1970. Mimeo. Cambridge, Mass.: Harvard University.

—— (1977b) The Knapp Commission and Patrick Murphy (A). Mimeo. Cambridge, Mass.: Harvard University.

—— (1977c) The Knapp Commission and Patrick Murphy (B). Mimeo. Cambridge, Mass.: Harvard University.

—— (1977d) The Knapp Commission and Patrick Murphy: Sequel. Mimeo. Cambridge, Mass.: Harvard University.

Kicinski, K. (1982) Corruption and Social Structure. Unpublished paper, Conference on Corruption: University of Birmingham.

Knapp, W. (1972) *The Knapp Report on Police Corruption*. New York: Braziller.

Knight, S. (1983) *The Brotherhood*. London: Granada.

Koot, W. (1983) De Segmenten Organisatie. *Management en Onderneming* **5**: 333–54.

Kornblum, A. N. (1976) *The Moral Hazards: Police Strategies for Honesty and Ethical Behaviour*. Lexington, Mass.: Lexington.

Krisberg, B. (1975) *Crime and Privilege: Toward a New Criminology*. Englewood Cliffs, N.J.: Prentice-Hall.

Laere, E. M. P. van and R. W. M. Geerts (1984) *Wetshandhaver of Wetsontduiker?* Den Haag/Nijmegen: Ministerie van Binnenlandse Zaken/A.B.G.V.

Lambert, R. (1969) *The Hothouse Society*. London: Weidenfeld & Nicolson.

Laurie, P. (1972) *Scotland Yard*. Harmondsworth: Penguin.

—— (1973) The Man who Purged Scotland Yard. *Inside London* **1**: 11 October.

Lee, P. N. (1977) The Pattern and Causes of Police Corruption in Hong Kong. Paper delivered at Project on Bureaucratic Behaviour and Development, Singapore.

Lemert, E. (1972) *Human Deviance, Social Problems and Social Control*. Englewood Cliffs, NJ: Prentice-Hall.

Lentink, H. W. (1983) *Corruptie bij de Nederlandse Politie*. Unpublished paper for the course 'Inspecteurs der Rijksrecherche 1982/1983', Den Haag.

'Lexow Commission' (1895) New York (State). Senate Committee Appointed to Investigate the Police Department of the City of New York. *Report and Proceedings*. Albany (NY): J. B. Lyon.

Lijphart, A. (1968) *The Polics of Accommodation*. Berkeley, Calif.: University of California Press.

Lipset, S. M. (1969) The Politics of the Police. *New Society* **13** (336): 355–58.

Lipsky, M. (1980) *Street-Level Bureaucracy*. New York: Russell Sage Foundation.

Lofland, J. (1971) *Analyzing Social Settings*. New York: Wadsworth.

Lundman, R. J. (1979) Police Misconduct as Organizational Deviance. *Law and Policy Quarterly* **1** (1): 81–100.

Lundman, R. J. (1980a) *Police and Policing: A Sociological Introduction*. New York: Holt, Rinehart & Winston.

—— (ed.) (1980b) *Police Behavior: A Sociological Perspective*. New York: Oxford University Press.

Lyman, S. M. (1971) Red Guard on Grant Avenue. Included in H. S. Becker (ed.) *Culture and Civility in San Francisco*. Chicago: Aldine/Transaction Books.

Lyman, S. and M. Scott (1970) *Sociology of the Absurd*. New York: Appleton Century Crofts.

Maas, P. (1974) *Serpico*. London: Fontana.

Manning, P. K. (1973) Review Essay: Deviance. *Contemporary Sociology* **2** (2): 123–128.

—— (1974) Police Lying. *Urban Life and Culture* (3): 283–305.

—— (1977) *Police Work: The Social Organization of Policing*. Cambridge, Mass.: MIT Press.

—— (1978) Rules, Colleagues and Situationally Justified Action. In P. K. Manning and J. van Maanen (eds) *Policing: A View from the Street*. Santa Monica, California: Goodyear Publishing Company.

—— (1979) The Social Control of Police Work: Observations on the Culture of Policing. In S. Holdaway (ed.) *the British Police*. London: Arnold.

—— (1980) *The Narc's Game*. Cambridge, Mass.: MIT Press.

Manning, P. K. and L. S. Redlinger (1977) Invitational Edges of Corruption. In P. E. Rock (ed.) *Drugs and Politics*. New Brunswick, NJ: Transaction Books.

Manning, P. K. and J. van Maanen (ed.) (1978) *Policing: A View from the Street*. Santa Monica, California: Goodyear Publishing Company.

Mark, R. (1977) *Policing a Perplexed Society*. London: Allen & Unwin.

—— (1978) *In the Office of Constable*. London: Collins.

Mars, G. (1982) *Cheats at Work*. London: Allen & Unwin.

Marx, G. T. (1974) Thoughts on a Neglected Category of Social Movement Participant: 'Agents Provocateurs' and Informants. *American Journal of Sociology* **80** (2): 402–40.

Marx, G. T. (1980a) The New Police Undercover Work. *Urban Life and Culture* **8** (January): 399–446.

—— (1980b) Notes on the Discovery, Collection and Assessment of Hidden and Dirty Data. Unpublished paper delivered at Society for Study of Social Problems, Annual Meeting, New York.

—— (1981a) Ironies of Social Control. *Social Problems* **28**: 221–46.

—— (1981b) Types of Undercover Operation and Activity. Paper for Hastings Centre Conference on Undercover Activities, Harvard University.

—— (1982) Who Really Gets Stung? *Crime and Delinquency* **28** (2): 165–92.

Matza, D. (1964) *Delinquency and Drift*. New York: Wiley.

—— (1969) *Becoming Deviant*. Englewood Cliffs, N.J.: Prentice-Hall.

Mauss, M. (1970) *The Gift*. London: Routledge & Kegan Paul.

McCall, G. and J. L. Simmons (eds) (1969) *Issues in Participant Observation*. Reading, Mass.: Addison-Wesley.

McClure, J. (1980) *Spike Island: Portrait of a Police Division*. London: Macmillan.

McGlennon, J. J. (1977) *Bureaucratic Crisis and Executive Leadership: Corruption in Police Departments*. Unpublished PhD dissertation, Johns Hopkins University.

McIntosh, M. (1975) *The Organization of Crime*. London: Macmillan.

McMullan, M. (1961) A Theory of Corruption. *Sociological Review* **9**: 181–201.

McNee, D. (1980) Keeping the Queen's Peace. *Police Review*, 25 January.

—— (1983) *McNee's Law*. London: Collins.

Mechanic, D. (1962) Sources of Power of Lower Participants in Complex Organizations. *Administrative Science Quarterly* **7**: 349–64.

Meltzer, B. N., J. W. Petras, and L. T. Reynolds (1975) *Symbolic Interactionism*. London: Routledge & Kegan Paul.

Merton, R. K., A. P. Gray, B. Hockey, and H. C. Selvin (eds) (1952) *Reader in Bureaucracy*. New York: Free Press.

Meyer, J. C. Jr. (1976) *The Nature and Investigation of Police Offences in the New York City Police Department*. Unpublished PhD dissertation. State University of New York, Albany.

Middendorp, C. P. (1978) *Progressiveness and Conservatism*. The Hague: Mouton.

Miller, W. R. (1977) *Cops and Bobbies: Police Authority in New York and London, 1830–70*. Chicago: University of Chicago Press.

Mills, C. Wright (1940) Situated Actions and Vocabularies of Motive. *American Sociological Review* **5**: 904–913.

Mills, J. (1973) The Detective. In T. Wolfe (ed.) *The New Journalism*. New York: Harper and Row.

Moore, M. (1977) *Buy and Bust*. Lexington, Ma.: Lexington Books.

Morgan, W. P. (1960) *The Triad Societies in Hong Kong*. Hong Kong: Government Press.

Morton, H. (1976) *The Lawless State: The Crime of the US Intelligence Agencies*. Harmondsworth: Penguin.

Muir, W. K. (1977) *Police: Streetcorner Politicians.* Chicago: University of Chicago Press.

Murphy, D. (1983) The Journalistic Investigation of Corruption. In M. Clarke (ed.) *Corruption.* London: Frances Pinter.

Murphy. P. V. and T. Plate (1977) *Commissioner.* New York: Simon and Schuster.

Newman, G. F. (1978a) *Sir, You Bastard.* London: Sphere.

—— (1978b) *You Flash Bastard.* London: Sphere.

—— (1978c) *You Nice Bastard.* London: Sphere.

New Statesman (1977) Williamson's Law. May 20.

—— (1980) The Story of Operation Countryman. January 18.

Newsweek (1984) A Rogue Cop Finally Gets What He Was After. February 27.

New York Times (1977) Bernhard, A Year After Disgrace over Lockheed, Shows No Scars. July 5.

—— (1982) Decade After Knapp Inquiry, a Sense of 'Revolution' Pervades Police Dept. November 29.

New York Times Magazine (1976) The Lockheed Affair. September 26.

Niederhoffer, A. (1969) *Behind the Shield.* New York: Doubleday Anchor.

—— (1975) *The Police Family.* Farnborough: Saxon House.

Niederhoffer, A. and A. S. Blumberg (1970) *The Ambivalent Force.* Boston: Ginn/Blaisdell.

Nieuwe Revue (1977) Politie Bezwijkt voor Geld. January 28.

—— (1978) De Corruptie Zaak. June 7.

Nixon, N. F. (1979) *On the Psychology of Military Incompetence.* London: Futura.

Observer, The (1982) Obstruction in Countryman Enquiry. April 4.

Palmier, L. (1983) Bureaucratic Corruption and Its Remedies. In M. Clarke (ed.) *Corruption.* London. Frances Pinter.

Panorama (1979) Dossier Amsterdamse Politie: Tipgever als Wegwerpartikel. January 26.

—— (1979) Dossier Amsterdamse Politie: 'Supersmeris "Litjens"'. February 2.

—— (1979) Dossier Amsterdamse Politie: Zijn de Amsterdamse Bonze Amerikaanse Marionetten? February 9.

Parker, R. (1981) *Rough Justice.* London: Fontana.

Parool, het (1978) Van Corruptie Verdachte Amsterdamse Politiemannen: 'Geld niet Beschouwd als Omkoping'. May 18

Parool, het (1979) Series: Het Doodzieke Corps van Amsterdam. January 12, 16, 23, 31; February 5, 9, 18, 19, 23, 27; March 11, 21.

—— (1979) Opnieuw Agenten Betrokken bij Corruptiezaak. January 17.

—— (1979) 'Litjens' ziet in Overplaatsing geen Degradatie. January 30.

Pearce, F. (1976) *Crimes of the Powerful.* London: Pluto Press.

Pennsylvania Crime Commission (1974) *Report on Police Corruption and Quality of Law Enforcement in Philadelphia.* St. Davids, Pa.

Perrick, F. (1982) *Politie in Nederland.* Zwolle: Tjeenk Willink.

Pfeffer, J. (1981) *Power in Organizations.* Boston: Pitman.

POS (Projectgroep Organisatie Structuur) (1977) *Politie in Verandering*. Den Haag: Staatsdrukkerij.

Preiss, J. J. and H. J. Ehrlich (1966) *An Examination of Role Theory: the Case of the State Police*. Lincoln: University of Nebraska Press.

President's Crime Commission (1967) *The Challenge of Crime in A Free Society*. Washington, DC: US Government Printing Office.

Punch, M. (1976) *Fout is Fout: Gesprekken met de Politie in de Binnenstad van Amsterdam*. Meppel: Boom.

—— (1979) *Policing the Inner City*. London: Macmillan.

—— (1981a) *Management and Control of Organizations*. Leiden/Antwerp: Stenfert Kroese.

—— (1981b) *Organizational Change and Police Deviance*. Paper delivered at American Sociological Association, Annual Meeting, Toronto.

—— (1982) Developing Scandal. *Urban Life* 11 (2): 209–30.

—— (ed.) (1983a) *Control in the Police Organization*. Cambridge, Mass.: MIT Press.

—— (1983b) Officers and Men: Occupational Culture, Inter-Rank Antagonism, and the Investigation of Corruption. In M. Punch (ed.) *Control in the Police Organization*. Cambridge, Mass.: MIT Press.

—— (1983c) *De Warmoesstraat*. Deventer: Van Loghum Slaterus.

Read, P. P. (1979) *The Train Robbers*. London: Coronet.

Reiner, R. (1978) *The Blue-coated Worker: A Sociological Study of Police Unionism*. Cambridge: Cambridge University Press.

—— (1979) Assisting with Enquiries: Problems of Research on the Police. Paper presented to British Sociological Association, Survey Research Group Colloquium on 'Survey Research and the Law', Warwick University.

Reisman, M. (1979) *Folded Lies* New York: Free Press.

Reiss, A. J. Jr. (1966) The Study of Deviant Behavior: Where the Action Is. *Ohio Valley Sociologist* 32: 60–66.

—— (1971) *The Police and the Public*. New Haven: Yale University Press.

—— (1977) Foreword. In A. E. Simpson, *The Literature of Police Corruption*. New York: John Jay Press.

—— (1978) Foreword. In L. W. Sherman, *Scandal and Reform*. Berkeley: University of California Press.

—— (1983) The Policing of Organizational Life. In M. Punch (ed.) *Control in the Police Organization*. Cambridge, Mass.: MIT Press.

Reiss, A. J. Jr. and D. J. Bordua (1967) Environment and Organization: a Perspective on the Police. In D. J. Bordua (ed.) *The Police: Six Sociological Essays*. New York: Wiley.

Report of the Commissioner of Police of the Metropolis for the year 1975 (1976) Cmnd. 6496. London: HMSO.

Reuss-Ianni, E. (1983) *Two Cultures of Policing*. New Brunswick: Transaction Books.

Rhodes, R. P. (1977) *The Insoluble Problems of Crime*. New York: Wiley.

Richardson, J. F. (1974) *Urban Police in the United States*. Port Washington, NY: Kennikat.

Rock, P. E. (ed.) (1977) *Drugs and Politics*. Rutgers, NJ: Dutton/Society Books.

—— (1979) *The Making of Symbolic Interaction*. London: Macmillan.

Rokyo, M. (1971) *Boss: Richard J. Daley of Chicago*. New York: Ditton.

Rookhuyzen, B. (1978) *Corruptie bij de Politie*. Apeldoorn: Nederlandse Politie Academie.

Rose-Ackerman, S. (1978) *Corruption: A Study in Political Economy*. New York: Academy Press.

Roy, D. F. (1955) Efficiency and the 'Fix': Informal Intergroup Relations in a Piece-Work Machine Shop. *American Journal of Sociology* **60**: 255–266.

—— (1960) Banana Time: Job Satisfaction and Informal Interaction. *Human Organization* **18**: 156–168.

Royal Commission on the Police (1962) Cmnd. 1728: London: HMSO.

Royal Commission on the Police (1981) *Report* Cmnd. 8092. London: HMSO.

Rubin, J. (1974) Police Identity and the Police Role. In R. F. Steedman (ed.) *The Police and the Community*. London: Johns Hopkins University Press.

Rubinstein, J. (1973) *City Police*. New York: Ballantine.

Salaman, G. (1979) *Work Organizations: Resistance and Control*. London: Longman.

Salaman, G. and K. Thompson (eds) (1973) *People and Organizations*. London: Longman.

—— (eds) (1980) *Control and Ideology in Organizations*. Milton Keynes: The Open University.

Sanders, W. B. (1977) *Detective Work: A Study of Criminal Investigations*. New York: The Free Press.

Sayre, W. S. and H. Kaufman (1960) *Governing New York City: Politics in the Metropolis*. New York: Russell Sage Foundation.

Schoeman, F. (1981) Privacy and Police Undercover Work. Unpublished paper, presented at conference, Morals in Policing, Boston University.

Schofield, M. (1971) *The Strange Case of Pot*. Harmondsworth: Penguin.

Schon, D. (1970) Beyond the Stable State: Reith Lectures. *The Listener* **84** (2174): 724–28.

Schur, E. M. (1969) *Our Criminal Society*. Englewood Cliffs, NJ: Prentice Hall.

Schutz, A. (1967) *The Phenomenology of the Social World*. Translated by G. Walsh and F. Lehnert. Evanston: North Western University Press.

Scott, J. (1972) *Comparative Political Corruption*. Englewood Cliffs, NJ: Prentice Hall.

Scott, M. and S. Lyman (1968) Accounts. *American Sociological Review* **33**: 46–62.

Shearing, C. D. (ed.) (1981) *Organizational Police Deviance: Its Structure and Control*. Toronto/Vancouver: Butterworth.

Shecter, L. and W. Phillips (1974) *On the Pad*. New York: Putnam.
Sherman, L. W. (ed.) (1974) *Police Corruption*. New York: Anchor.
—— (1977) *City Politics, Police Administrators, and Corruption Control*. New York: John Jay Press.
—— (1978) *Scandal and Reform: Controlling Police Corruption*. Los Angeles and Berkeley: University of California Press.
—— (1979) Organizational Deviance: Concepts, Scope, and Theory. Mimeo: State University of New York at Albany.
—— (1980) Three Models of Organizational Corruption in Agencies of Social Control. *Social Problems* **27**: 478–91.
Shover, N. (1980) The Criminalization of Corporate Behaviour: Federal Surface Coal Mining. In G. Geis and E. Stotland (eds) *White Collar Crime*. Beverley Hills, Calif.: Sage.
Silverman, D. (1970) *The Theory of Organizations*. London: Heinemann.
Simpson, A. E. (1977) *The Literature of Police Corruption Vol. 1: A Guide to Bibliography and Theory*. New York: John Jay Press.
Skolnick, J. H. (1975) *Justice Without Trial*. 2nd edn New York: Wiley.
—— (1981) Deception and Detecting. Unpublished paper, presented at conference, Morals in Policing, Boston University.
Small, S. (1983) *Police and People in London, Vol. 2: A Group of Young Black People*. London: Policy Studies Institute.
Smart, N. (1983) Classes, Clients and Corruption in Sicily. In M. Clarke (ed.) *Corruption*. London: Frances Pinter.
Smith, D. J. (1983a) *Police and People in London Vol. 1: A Survey of Londoners*. London: Policy Studies Institute.
—— (1983b) *Police and People in London, Vol. 3: A Survey of Police Officers*. London: Policy Studies Institute.
Smith, D. J. and J. Gray (1983) *Police and People in London, Vol. 4: The Police in Action*. London: Policy Studies Institute.
Smith, R. L. (1965) *The Tarnished Badge*. New York: Crowell.
Smith, W. H. T. (1973) Deceit in Uniform. *Police Chief* **40** (September): 20–21.
Sorrentino, J. (1980) *The Gold Shield*. New York: Dell.
Stead, P. J. (1975) Some Notes on Police Corruption: The English Experience. *Police Journal* **48** (January): 24–29.
Steffens, J. L. (1957) *The Shame of the Cities*. New York: Hill & Wang, (originally published 1903).
Stewart, P. L. and M. G. Cantor (eds) (1982) *Varieties of Work*. Beverly Hills, California: Sage.
Stoddard, E. R. (1968) The Informal Code of Police Deviancy: A Group Approach To Blue Coat Crime. *Journal of Criminal Law, Criminology and Police Science* **59** (2): 201–13.
Stone, C. D. (1975) *Where the Law Ends: The Social Control of Corporate Behaviour*. New York: Harper.
Straten, J. van (1976) De Triades. *Het Tijdschrift van de Politie* **38** (6): 225–229.

Straten, J. van (1977) De Gouden Driehoek. *Het Tijdschrift van de Politie* **39** (2): 49–52.

Sunday Times (1976) My Anguish – by a Porn Squad detective. November 26.

—— (1977) Porn Trial. March 6.

—— (1977) Mason Moody Partners, corruption a speciality. May 15.

—— (1979) 'Swedey' Probe into Police is in Danger. September 16.

—— (1977) Nobblers fail to stop big probe into police. December 2.

Sunday Times Magazine (1977) Top of the Cops. November 3.

—— (1982) Special Issue: How Should Britain be Policed? September 26.

Sutherland, E. H. (1982) White Collar Crime is Organized Crime. In M. D. Ermann and R. L. Lundman (eds) *Corporate and Government Deviance*. 2nd ed. New York: Oxford University Press.

Sykes, G. (1958) *Society of Captives*. Princeton, NJ: Princeton University Press.

Sykes, G. and D. Matza (1957) Techniques of Neutralization. *American Sociological Review* **22**: 664–670.

Telegraaf, de (1974) In Amsterdam Woedt Strijd tegen Wreedste Drug: Heroïne. August 17.

—— (1975) Chinezen Rouwden om Vermoorde 'Peetvader'. March 8.

—— (1976) Politie Verliest Greep op Heroïne-Smokkel. May 1.

—— (1976) Heroïne-Hoofdstad Amsterdam: Slagveld der Triades. May 1.

—— (1976) Heroïnestrijd nergens zo Genadeloos als in Amsterdam. November 6.

—— (1977) Maar één op de 200 Heroïne-Koeriers wordt Gepakt. January 21.

—— (1977) Amsterdamse Politiemannen voor de Rechter: 'Agenten Bezweken bij zien van Geld.' February 25.

—— (1977) Amsterdamse Politieman in de Cel. April 13.

—— (1977) Twee Agenten Verdacht van Corruptie. April 14.

—— (1977) Agent had Soft-Drugs en Illegale Vuurwapens. April 15.

—— (1977) De Warme Buurt, één Vierkante Kilometer Ellende. April 16.

—— (1977) Onthullende Feiten in Corruptie-Schandaal: Hoofdagenten bij Chinezen op 'Loonlijst'. April 27.

—— (1977) Schandaal bij Amsterdamse Politie Groeit. Grootse Chinezen-Experts in Arrest. April 26.

—— (1977) Geheimzinnigheid Schaadt Beeld Amsterdamse Politie. April 29.

—— (1977) Agenten door Tegenstanders Uigeschakeld. April 30.

—— (1977) Massaal Politie-Protest in de RAI. May 13.

—— (1977) Chinees Gokgeld Bracht de Politie geen Geluk. October 1.

—— (1978) Hoofdinspecteur Getuigd in Corruptieproces: Nog Steeds Gevaar voor Omkopingen. May 18.

—— (1978) Officier Eist Cel tegen 'Corrupte' Politiemannen. June 1.

—— (1978) Geen Pardon 'Corrupte' Politieman. June 1.

—— (1978) 1978: Het Jaar van de Corruptie. December 23.

Telegraaf, de (1979) Narcotica-Expert op Zijspoor. January 29.
—— (1979) Procureur-Generaal Accoord met Overplaatsing van 'Litjens'. January 30.
—— (1979) Politiechef 'Otten' Overleden. February 13.
—— (1979) Positie Amsterdamse Hoofdcommissaris 'Adema' in Geding: Vertrouwenscrisis Rond Politiechef. March 8.
—— (1979) Vragen over Onrust bij de Politie. March 9.
—— (1979) Under-Cover Agent Dringt door in Onderwereld: Het Levensgevaarlijke Spel van Die Man die niet Bestaat. March 17.
—— (1980) Justitie Stuurde Twee Criminelen op Pad. January 11.
—— (1980) Nieuwe Beschuldigingen tegen 'Litjens'. February 15.
—— (1980) Joop T: 'Litjens' Gaf Tip Over Miljoenen van Cocaïnehandelaar. February 16.
—— (1980) 'Litjens' Mag Visie Geven op Corruptie Affaire. February 18.
—— (1984) De Zwakke Plekken van de Sterke Arm, deel 2. February 28.
—— (1984) De Zwakke Plekken van de Sterke Arm, deel 3. February 29.
Terry, W. C. III (1980) Police Stress. Paper delivered at American Society of Criminology, San Francisco.
Terkel, S. (1975) *Working*. New York: Avon.
Tifft, L. L. (1970) *Comparative Police Supervision Systems: An Organizational Analysis*. Unpublished PhD dissertation: University of Illinois at Champaign – Urbana.
Tifft, L. L. (1974) The Cop Personality Revisited. *Journal of Police Science and Administration* 2: 266–78.
Time Magazine (1976) The Lockheed Mystery. September 13.
—— (1976) Heroin Rides on Orient Express. November 29.
—— (1979) Cops on Trial: Law and Disorder in Philadelphia. August 27.
Tobias, J. J. (ed.) (1972) *Nineteenth Century Crime, Prevention and Punishment*. Newton Abbot, Devon: David and Charles.
Tomkinson, M. and M. Gillard (1980) *Nothing to Declare: The Political Corruption of John Poulson*. London: John Calder.
Turner, W. W. (1968) *The Police Establishment*. New York: Putnams.
Vandivier, K. (1982) Why Should My Conscience Bother Me? In M. E. Ermann and R. L. Lundman (eds) *Corporate and Government Deviance*. 2nd ed. New York: Oxford University Press.
Van Maanen, J. (1973) Observations on the Making of Policemen. *Human Organization* 32 (Winter): 407–418.
—— (1978) On Watching the Watchers. In P. K. Manning and J. Van Maanen (eds) *Policing: A View from the Street*. Santa Monica, California: Goodyear Publishing Company.
—— (1980) Beyond Account. *The Annals of the American Academy of Political and Social Sciences* 425 (November): 145–156.
—— (1983) The Boss: First-line Supervision in an American Police Agency. In M. Punch (ed.) *Control in the Police Organization*. Cambridge, Mass.: MIT Press.
Vaughan, D. (1983) *Controlling Unlawful Organizational Behaviour*. Chicago: Chicago University Press.

238 *Conduct Unbecoming*

Vellinga, M. L. and W. G. Wolters (1971) *De Chinezen van Amsterdam*. Anthropologisch Sociologisch Centrum: Universiteit van Amsterdam.

Verwey, D. (1983), Chinezen in Nederland. *Intermediair* 16 December.

Volkskrant, de (1974) De Lange Kille Zomer van de Horse. August 3.

—— (1977) Raadslid Vraagt Corruptie-Debat. May 4.

—— (1977) Manifestatie in Amsterdam: Getergde Politie Hekelt Aanvallen. May 18.

—— (1977) Amsterdam: Die Verziekte Stad – 1. June 9.

—— (1977) Amsterdam: Die Verziekte Stad – 2. June 16.

—— (1977) Politie-Agenten Geschorst na Klacht Vrouw. July 26.

—— (1977) Beelden van Politiebureau. October 3.

—— (1977) Overplaatsing Agente: Rechter Verklaart Zich Onbevoegd. October 26.

—— (1977) Eis Drie Weken voor Politieman wegens Diefstal. November 26.

—— (1977) Verdachten Eisen Opening van Zaken. December 3.

—— (1978) Op Verdenking van Corruptie: Agenten in Maart voor de Rechter. January 25.

—— (1978) Lubbers als Minister in Zaken. March 8.

—— (1978) Agent hoort Zes Weken Eisen na Gezagsmisbruik. May 10.

—— (1978) Van Corruptie Verdachte Agenten: 'Weigeren van Bedragen Nadelig voor Contacten'. May 18.

—— (1978) Agent Veroordeelt tot Zes Weken Cel. May 24.

—— (1978) Politieman Verdacht van Verduistering Auto. May 27.

—— (1978) Politieambtenares Krijgt Baan Terug. May 30.

—— (1978) Omkoping door Onderwereld: Celstraffen Geeist tegen Zes Agenten. June 1.

—— (1978) Officier Hekelt Berichtgeving. June 1.

—— (1978) Andere Onbestraft: Drie Agenten Beboet voor Aannemen Giften. June 15.

—— (1978) Vootzitter Vakbond: Personeelsbeleid Politie Verhard. June 20.

—— (1978) Nu Boetes Verlangd van Hoofdagenten. August 31.

—— (1978) Beschuldiging tegen Politie in Onderzoek. October 9.

—— (1978) De Undercover-Agent Rukt op naar Nederland. November 4.

—— (1978) Over Corruptiezaak: Uitspraken Politie Nader Onderzocht. November 4.

—— (1979) Rechercheurs Voorgedragen voor Ontslag. January 19.

—— (1979) Verdachte Beschuldigt: 'Politie Betrokken bij Heroïneschandaal'. January 24.

—— (1979) Corruptie-zaak: Rechercheurs Horen weer Boete Eisen. January 25.

—— (1979) Greep Raad op Politie Minimaal. January 25.

—— (1979) Na Corruptie-onderzoek: Chef van Politie Overgeplaatst. January 20.

—— (1979) Undercover-Agent Scherp Controleren. February 3.

Volkskrant, de (1979) Bij Opsporing Narcotica: Hof Acht Gebruik Infiltranten Legaal. February 3.

—— (1979) Twee Agenten Veroordeeld voor Corruptie. February 8.

—— (1979) Heroïne-handelaar weer Vrijgelaten. February 22.

—— (1979) Schorsing Twee Rechercheurs Opgegeven. March 5.

—— (1979) Agenten weer aan de Slag: 'Chinezen Experts' Overgeplaatst. March 7.

—— (1979) Beroep op Rechter: Chinezen-Expert Eist Baan Terug. April 12.

—— (1980) Uitlokking Inbraken: Celstraffen Geëist tegen Agenten. January 22.

—— (1980) Politiechef Reed Onder Invloed. February 9.

—— (1980) Politiechef Overtrad Korps-Voorschriften. February 19.

—— (1980) 'Litjens' Vrijuit na Studie Minister. February 29.

—— (1980) Fiscale Fraude naar f. 4 Miljard. May 20.

—— (1982) Heroïne Onderdeel Cultuur Geworden. April 23.

—— (1982) Werkgroep Gevormd voor Reorganisatie Politie Amsterdam. August 12.

—— (1983) Chinezen in Nederland. February 26.

—— (1983) 'Litjens' Ontslagen Wegens Contacten met Drugshandel. September 23.

—— (1983) Aantal Amerikaanse Juristen in Opspraak na Corruptie. December 16.

—— (1984) Verandering en Integriteit bij de Amsterdamse Politie. January 3.

—— (1984) Slechte Imago Amsterdam. June 8.

——(1984) Commissaris met Vervroegd Pensioen. June 18.

Vrij Nederland (1977) Wat Gebeurde er Echt in de Warmoesstraat?: De Keiharde Handel tussen Politie en Chinezen. December 3.

—— (1977) Retour Keulen: Waarom de Nederlandse Politie een Hasjsmokkelaar even liet Glippen. February 3.

—— (1978) De Chinezen-Experts van de Warmoesstraat en Lisette Scholten kunnen nog lang Wachten. May 13.

—— (1981) Koos Zwart over zijn Beursberichten, de Politie, de Horse, en het Kruisinga-effect. January 10.

—— (1984) De Politie van New York. January 21.

—— (1984) Afscheid: Een Amsterdamse Commissaris en zijn 'Minder Gewenste Contacten in de Wereld van de Drugshandel'. July 14.

Ward, R. H. (1975) An Analysis of Police Corruption Investigations in New York City: 1894–1972. Paper presented at American Society of Criminology, Toronto.

Ward, R. H. and R. McCormack (1979) *An Anti-Corruption Manual for Administrators in Law Enforcement.* New York: John Jay Press.

Watson, T. J. (1980) *Sociology, Work and Industry.* London: Routledge & Kegan Paul.

Wax, R. H. (1971) *Doing Fieldwork.* Chicago: University of Chicago Press.

Weber, M. (1947) *The Theory of Social and Economic Organization.* New York: Oxford University Press.

Westley, W. A. (1970) *Violence and the Police*. Cambridge, Mass.: MIT Press.

Whitaker, B. (1964) *The Police*. Harmondsworth: Penguin.

—— (1979) *The Police in Society*. London: Eyre Methuen.

Whitehead, L. (1983) On Presidential Graft. In M. Clarke (ed.) *Corruption*. London: Frances Pinter.

Whyte, W. F. (1955) *Street Corner Society*. 2nd edn. Chicago: University of Chicago Press.

Wicker, T. (1977) The Climate of Corruption. In M. Neary (ed.) *Corruption and its Management*. New York: American Academy for Professional Law Enforcement.

Will, I. (1980a) Inside the Yard –1: Management. *Police Review* 8 February: 254–59.

—— (1980b) Inside the Yard –2: The CID Before Mark. *Police Review* 15 February: 302–305.

—— (1980c) Inside the Yard –3: Process of Destruction. *Police Review* 22 February: 350–80.

—— (1980d) Inside the Yard –4: Investigation and Integration. *Police Review* 29 February: 402–403.

Wilson, J. Q. (1963) The Police and their Problems: A Theory. *Public Policy* **12**: 189–216.

—— (1968) *Varieties of Police Behaviour*. Cambridge, Mass.: Harvard University Press.

—— (1975) *Thinking About Crime*. New York: Basic Books.

—— (1978) *The Investigators: Managing F.B.I. and Narcotics Agents*. New York: Basic Books.

Wise, D. (1976) *The American Police State*. New York: Random House.

Wolfe, T. (1980) *The Right Stuff*. New York: Bantam.

Wolff, K. H. (ed.) (1950) *The Sociology of George Simmel*. New York: Free Press.

Wolk, E. van der (ed.) (1977) *De Bedreigde Burger*. Antwerpen/Utrecht: Intermediair/Het Spectrum.

Wollacott, J. (1980) Dirty and Deviant Work. In G. Esland and G. Salaman (eds) *The Politics of Work and Occupations*. Milton Keynes: Open University Press.

Wycoff, M. A. (1981) Detectives: Current Perspectives. Unpublished paper, Washington, DC: Police Foundation.

Wycoff, M. A. and Kelling, G. L. (1978) *The Dallas Experience: Organizational Reform*. Washington, DC: Police Foundation.

Name Index

Subject Index

Note: Sub-entries are in alphabetical order, except where chronological order is significant.